# hard rain

## a dylan commentary

## tim riley

### updated edition

DA CAPO PRESS • NEW YORK

Library of Congress Cataloging-in-Publication Data

Riley, Tim.
   Hard rain: a Dylan commentary / Tim Riley.—Updated ed., 1st Da
Capo Press ed.
    p.   cm.
   Discography: p. ••••
   Includes bibliographical references (p. ••••) and index.
   ISBN 0-306-80907-9 (alk. paper)
   1. Dylan, Bob, 1941– . 2. Dylan, Bob, 1941– —Discography. I.
Title.
ML420.D98R54  1999
782.42164′092—dc21                           98-54777
                                           CIP
                                         MN

Owing to limitations of space, acknowledgments for permission to reprint previously published material may be found following the Index.

First Da Capo Press edition 1999

This Da Capo Press paperback edition of *Hard Rain* is an unabridged republication of the edition first published in New York in 1992, with the addition of a new epilogue and updated discography by the author. It is reprinted by arrangement with Alfred A. Knopf, Inc.

Published by Da Capo Press, Inc.
A Member of Perseus Books Group
233 Spring Street, New York, N.Y. 10013

**For Mark Moses**

# contents

# contents

# hard rain

# introduction

Not all great poets—like Wallace Stevens—are great singers. But a great singer—like Billie Holiday—is always a great poet.

**—Bob Dylan**,

*In His Own Words,* 1968

**Bob Dylan's voice** can crook emotion the way a prism refracts light. His coyote yowl and scurry-to-catch-up phrasing scatter furious accusation, self-mocking glee, postromantic loathing, self-directed bile, lost chances, fleeting regrets, earned cynicism, false cynicism, and contempt for falsity with biting, unsentimental candor. The way he lobs lines of titanic illogic ("The geometry of innocence / flesh on the bone") can con you into thinking not just that fate turns on his singing, but that his rash fits of imagery make internal sense.

As a pop songwriter, Dylan perfects the come-on taunt, but inside all his derision lies an identification with his subject that's impossible to discount. In "Like a Rolling Stone," he works both sides of the aisle, identifies perhaps too strongly with the sins of privilege he throws up to his victim. In a tirade like "Positively 4th Street," lines of utter derision come tumbling out with such caustic dander they beg the question of motives. With insights darting around all the convex emotions, Dylan is savvy enough to know that cutting his ex-lover down so publicly, so viciously, amounts to a projection of insecurity. Even when the listener gets caught in the crossfire, Dylan's delivery has the power to turn that insecurity into a kind of power, a weapon of innuendo against the lover he's rebuking. He convinces you that he knows her thoughts better than she does: "I used to be among the crowd you're in with. . . ." The fringe meanings he drops along the way are cocked triggers of invective that fix your ears, and keep you guessing about the riot act that's suddenly lunging from the radio: "When I was down / You just stood there *grinning* . . ." Who's grinning now?

## introduction

Those who dismiss Dylan's voice because of its nasal timbre don't listen far past the surface of his songs, and are probably missing the point, since many of his narrative angles cast darts at this preoccupation with surface orientation (something for which his European audience reveres him). The "Dylan can't sing" crowd often agrees that he's the best interpreter of his own material, which only means that his emotional purview lives up to his voice. This argument falls apart when he takes on his contemporaries' songs (Paul Simon's "The Boxer," which Dylan turns into an apologetic whine), where he rarely matches what he invests in his own material; his emotional purview is essentially a private matter. He reinvigorates older material ("Take Me as I Am," "Copper Kettle") better than he renders songs by colleagues (Gordon Lightfoot's "Early Morning Rain" or John Hiatt's "The Usual").

When he takes on his predecessors, Dylan can reveal even more than he intends. Dipping into his sources summons even greater wonder from his voice, and more voltage. His version of "Pretty Boy Floyd," Woody Guthrie's parable of Oklahoma's dust-bowl Robin Hood, which Dylan recorded on *Folkways: A Vision Shared* in 1987, maps how Dylan can imbue the most familiar tale with nuances of character and motivation. His held notes trip shifting emotional colors from single syllables ("Others tell you of a stranger who come to beg a meal / And underneath their napkin . . . left a thousand dollar bill_____"), pull layers of sarcasm from Floyd's grocery note ("You say that I'm an outlaw, you say that I'm a thief / Well here's a Christmas dinner . . . for the families on relief_____"), and he takes a knowing pause in the last line ("Some will rob you with a six-gun . . . and some with a fountain pen_____"). Dylan characteristically throws lines away for emphasis via understatement (the myth of Floyd's popularity that seeps through "Oklahoma knew him well," and the scapegoating that doesn't need any more spelling out in "Every crime in Oklahoma was added to his name"), and as he jiggles established rhythms, he fields hidden patterns of meaning. When he bends the opening words of verse eight, Dylan punctuates how after roaming as far as Canada, Floyd returns to leave the authorities a message smack in the state's capital: " 'Twas in Oklaho_____ma City, 'twas on a Christmas day / There come a whole carload of groceries . . . ." Dylan's performance not only rises to Guthrie's modestly indomitable prototype, it makes you aware of how persistently contemporary these ideas are, and how adaptable Guthrie's plain-stroke writing style is to Dylan's interior dramatization.

With his wise-guy exaggeration of all that conventional pop vocalism smooths over—the odd crack, the missed high notes, the late entry, the quick-fix line scrunchings—Dylan towers over pop as a deity of crudities. His riveting peculiarities are analogous to what James Dean's eyes expressed as looming humiliation, what Marlon Brando's facial twitches portrayed as subliminal commentary. Very few singers match or better Dylan at his own interpretations, and the best of these (Jimi Hendrix, Van Morrison, Rod Stewart, Sandy Denny, Jason and the Scorchers) are reworkings of attitudes that Dylan hints at in his own versions. The compassion that Morrison and Hendrix hone from his songs is the subtext to what Dylan sets up as a lover's recrimination in "It's All Over Now, Baby Blue," a rock star's spitting in the hand that feeds him in "All Along the Watchtower," or a prima donna's class comeuppance in "Like a Rolling Stone." It's cliché to say Dylan brought a psychological complexity to popular song, but it's naive to claim that you can separate that aspect of his work from his voice.

And aside from all the expressive arrows, Dylan's voice registers the duplicities rooted in the sixties mindset he helped to shape: arrogance and insecurity; acute class consciousness and free-spirited utopianism; generational resentment and communal solidarity; personal odysseys that were traced inside political vistas. He accomplishes this not only because he becomes so adept at writing about such polarities—the cunning self-references of "Mr. Tambourine Man," which both trace a pied-

## introduction

piper sensibility and expose its transparencies—but because he catches these contradictions in his voice. Cornered by crackpot-brilliant ideas, Dylan's songs helped him transcend the sexual mystique Americans demanded from pop singers like no other figure since Frank Sinatra. Sinatra used his unremarkable, scrawny New Jersey frame to titillate screaming girls by hanging on to his microphone stand as if he might otherwise wither. Fred Astaire let his legs do the flirting; Bing Crosby, smaller and skinnier still, escaped the sexual trap with a golfer's smugness. Dylan certainly wasn't the first to ignore his audience's demand for erotic titillation, but his idea-driven persona is all the more impressive when you consider the rock 'n' roll presence Elvis Presley established. For the Presley audience, sexual charisma was everything, even though the race mixing that charged his voice was inseparable from the erotic danger he flirted with. It was Presley's range of sexual energy—from tenderness to animalism—that opened the flood gates for Jerry Lee Lewis's leers, Little Richard's hoots, and Chuck Berry's capers. Dylan would ultimately compete with the sexual euphoria of the Beatles and the menace of the Rolling Stones to realize fantasies that his audience hadn't bothered to seek out—beyond the sexual, be-yond the dance floor. His verbal tenacity lifted his folkie guise above cut-and-dry crank, and his rock rhythms were downright awkward: dancing was not a means to making sense out of "Sub-terranean Homesick Blues." Dylan is the most important Amer-ican rock' n' roller since Presley, and the only one to stake his reputation on rock 'n' roll verities that don't truck in sex or dancing.

Imposing himself so severely on his songs, and with such different emphases during different performances at different points in his career, Dylan carried his own renditions of his songs to a level that demanded intrinsic association with their material. To hear him sing "Don't Think Twice, It's All Right" is at once to be stung by the harshness to which the relationship's closing scene has driven the singer and at the same time to respond to the ruefulness couched in the guitar figures, which reassemble all the hurt into an undertow of forgiveness, regret, and remembrance. When Peter, Paul and Mary sing it, with their stern, prudish togetherness, the song itself survives, but they lose layers of feeling in their earnest attacks—each verse seems to hit the same preformulated ebbs and swells.

His wide swings of emotion suit the varying points of view Dylan songs demand of their singers. A Dylan story is often the act of a narrator turning over an idea, or trying out varying points of view on a character, a theme, or a situation ("It's All Over Now, Baby Blue," "Lay Down Your Weary Tune," "You're a Big Girl Now"). Later, the narrative viewpoint shifts dramatically between verses, to the point where the linear direction of action is completely discarded in favor of an impressionistic blurring of characters and setting: how many lovers pass through the temporal corridors of "Tangled Up in Blue"? How many characters inhabit "Visions of Johanna"? Another Dylan tactic is to situate a simulated narrative outside time altogether: "Stuck Inside of Mobile with the Memphis Blues Again," "Ballad of a Thin Man," "It's Alright, Ma (I'm Only Bleeding)." And song titles are often gleefully unhinged and deliberately misleading arrows to lyrical content ("Rainy Day Women #12 & 35," "Temporary Like Achilles," "Positively 4th Street"). Dylan isn't as interested in being understood as he is in being felt.

**The misconception surrounding** the significance of Dylan's voice isn't the only fallacy of his career; it's just the most central. Dylan's approach to song is as circuitous as his approach to pop. He's always been as much of a hillbilly-folkie as a rockabilly clown, a rock 'n' roll junkie, a country-and-western fatalist, a gospel convert, an Appalachian reveler, an aging formalist—he just took his time unpeeling these layers of his musical personality. For a folkie who had received the blessing of his Newport crowd and the open jealousy of the Greenwich Village scene where he learned the ropes, Dylan's 1965 assault on rock (and therefore pop) was a coup of the highest order, transforming himself from a musical editorialist ("Only a Pawn in Their Game") into a snide commercial double-agent. It was as though the folkies saw themselves as chaste and pure as the gospel crowd—watching one of their biggest talents go pop was like watching him sign a deal with the devil. They didn't seem to get the joke: after getting his audience to take him seriously, he back-pedaled into a sequence of hilarious yarns about the rush of young American life (and the farce of success), by way of saying "Don't take me—or any of this rock 'n' roll stuff—so seriously!" ("I Shall Be Free No. 10" "Bob Dylan's 115th Dream" ). To rock fans, Dylan's move was oddly logical, a peculiar take on a style he understood on a different plane than his peers—and it put his folkie fans in their place even better than his veiled song-swipes ("All I Really Want to Do," "It Ain't Me, Babe," and "It's All Over Now, Baby Blue").

Sexy he was not, but Dylan did make certain that his folk guise carried erotic overtones—the lean, hungry, lovable waif on *Freewheelin'* was a clear homage to James Dean. He became a pop icon the hard way: without looks in his corner, women were drawn to his image because he was a man of ideas; and the way he wooed women ("Girl from the North Country," "Love Minus Zero / No Limit," "To Ramona") could be as seductive as his curtain closers were decisive. His romances could be strident and taxing ("Ballad in Plain D"), but when he let women in, love was rarely a simple matter ("One Too Many Mornings," "Spanish Harlem Incident"). It's been suggested that Dylan's lack of sex appeal was a limitation on his songwriting: in the midst of all his deal cutting, recrimination, ardent idealization, and Monday-morning quarterbacking, he never sounded like he was having any fun with the opposite sex. But even this is an oversimplification: "Can You Please Crawl Out Your Window" remains a free-for-all elopement gambol, and "If You Gotta Go, Go Now" is so over-the-top you can't imagine his date not staying the night.

9

## hard rain

Dylan's career has the same cut-glass contours as much of his singing. He began as a young man fascinated by death, and the songs he attempted on his debut showed how a young white might begin to translate an elder black's concerns and culture. As he probed such loaded subjects as the politics of romance and the war zone of failed love, the odd illusion of romantic politics, Dylan's achievement was to demonstrate how these common plaints could turn into possibilities. What could a person fashion for a hipster identity after all the angry-young-man imagery had been used up? What lay beyond the ardent assumptions we all carried into our love affairs, our politics, our jobs, our sense of individuality—and how could the media which shaped these assumptions be employed to subvert them? If he wasn't always in control of where his material pointed, the implications that spun off his imagery, he made it seem like it hardly mattered. When he sang those emblematic questions all through "Like a Rolling Stone" ("How does it feel?"), you got the feeling that the answer to his queries lay in the asking. The arrows were provocative enough.

After the folk-blues Dylan used as an opening led him to the frayed-wire rock 'n' roll he made on his best records (1965's *Bringing It All Back Home* and *Highway 61 Revisited* and 1966's *Blonde on Blonde*), his creative fuse began to burn rapidly, and he triumphed off-record with his 1966 tour with the Band. After a near-fatal motorcycle accident in the summer of 1966, he dropped out of sight for eighteen months and didn't reappear until a Woody Guthrie memorial concert at Carnegie Hall, where he sang three Guthrie songs with the Band. By this time Dylan had taped scads of songs with the Band in retreat on a home recorder, which began showing up on other people's records. These sessions were finally published in 1975 as *The Basement Tapes*, and they showed Dylan to be as artful and guileless in seclusion as he was in public. From there, his career began a zigzag that made his early period look like a pearl of logic: *John Wesley Harding* (1968), an abstract western, was followed by a

## introduction

straight-faced country record, *Nashville Skyline* (1969), which made him a determined outcast to the counterculture that was blooming in his backyard of Woodstock, New York.

With *Self-Portrait* (1970), Dylan began expressing the quirks and delusions of the counterculture in decline at least as well as he had chronicled its heyday of civil rights with his protest songs. Through *New Morning* (1970), a quietly commanding appearance at George Harrison's Concert for Bangla Desh, and a reunion with the Band on the frumpy *Planet Waves* (1973), he charted the uncertainties of the postsixties period, the lingering futility of the antiwar coalition in the face of Nixon's re-election, Watergate, and a tide of dispiritedness that crept into the popular will like a hangover. With *Before the Flood*, the heraldic live set from his 1974 tour with the Band, Dylan refurbished his mid-sixties classics; and immediately afterwards, with *Blood on the Tracks* in 1975, he gave voice to the tragic fallout of sixties ideals the Nixon years had sown. Along with parts of *Desire* (1976), and many of the Rolling Thunder Revue shows that made their way onto bootlegs, this is the arc on which Dylan's legend is based. From the Guthrie mantle of New York's folk scene to the voice of sixties political consciousness, its tributaries and twilight, Dylan wound up being as central to the disintegration of these values as he was to their inception.

If the sixties—or, say, the period 1962-75—found Dylan in his element, the late seventies were up for grabs. Beginning with *Street Legal* (1978), Dylan's voice began to falter, his songwriting waned, and he never wrote to his potential as much as kept his listeners lying in wait for a sudden resurgence of the vitality he once commanded. Three "sacred" albums (1979's *Slow Train Coming*, 1980's *Saved*, and 1981's *Shot of Love*) reflected an obsession with an Old Testament God who was as wrathful as the New Testament "born again" Jesus was fashionable. After touring with a gospel troupe, shouting down secular hecklers and pledging "never to go back," Dylan's tide of born-again fervor washed away with the same mysterious ambivalence with which it appeared, and the eighties found his talent confronting a pop scene he seemed deliberately estranged from. *Infidels* (1983), *Real Live* (1985), *Empire Burlesque* (1985), *Knocked Out Loaded* (1986), *Down in the Groove* (1988), *Oh Mercy* (1989), *Dylan and the Dead* (1989), and *Under the Red Sky* (1990) ranged from indifferent to awful, even though the best songs on any of these records made it impossible to write Dylan off as a potential force ("I and I," the single "Band of the Hand"). Devotees stayed in touch through cultish fanzines, and traded tapes and stories about particularly good performances and his telling choices of cover songs in concert. But the mainstream audience, seeing him sleepwalk through numbers—as part of a closing act with Ron Wood and Keith Richards at the Live Aid show in 1985, in front of Tom Petty and the Heartbreakers in the *Hard to Handle* video from Australia in 1986, with longtime Dylanologists the Grateful Dead on *Dylan and the Dead*, or the 1991 Grammy Awards show—had trouble relating to Dylan as anything but an aging oddity.

Only with the re-emergence of his humor on *Traveling Wilburys, Volume One* (1989) and *Volume Three* (1990) did Dylan seem to regain his stride: "Tweeter and the Monkey Man," a swipe at Springsteen, only made his once-cutting wit more sorely missed. And "Congratulations" made you aware of how few good disdainful good-byes had been written since "Idiot Wind."

This history may seem too generalized to diehard fans who hang on every word, every performance, and every song, but in casting a critical eye over his entire career, the long view clarifies where his strengths lie and how the rock audience has been segregated and compromised over his thirty-year odyssey.

**Because his singing** conveys so much beyond the words themselves, Dylan's writing accrues depth with repeated listenings.

## introduction

Aside from assuming different personas, voicing first-person characters in song, and risking dramatic incoherence with sly inside jokes, Dylan is constantly singing about more than what a casual listen will reveal. At any moment in his career, during any song, he's likely to be making subtle references to his status as a rock icon, his relationship to his audience, scuffles with critics and interviewers, his interplay with his backup players, and ultimately his relationship with himself—the acute, albeit off-kilter, inner radar that fields all these other references and interactions. This becomes apparent early on when he starts writing songs about his status in the folk community ("My Back Pages" and "All I Really Want to Do"), which work as extensions of romantic metaphors (his favorite kind) and stand up very well on their own terms, without all the popstar baggage. But these overtones run throughout his work, as though he's constantly juggling who he is and where he is in relation to his audience, his critics, his players, and his songs, in ways that baffle even him. This is a self-conscious process that only snowballs as he gets older, and it's his return to earlier classics as a middle-aged man that wrings the most out of this central theme in his work. As a returning hero on the 1974 tour with the Band, he unearths "It Ain't Me, Babe," and the invective toward his audience is unmistakable. Written as a breakup song about the confounding traps of overpossessiveness, an outburst that doubled as a jag to his folk circle that dared to proscribe him song subjects, this song roared back in 1974 as a rock diatribe against all preconceptions from an audience that was older and more loyal than any rock performer had ever toured to, and which received more than it could ever have hoped for. That he triggered this reinterpretation of a song that already enjoyed several layers of meaning when it first appeared was, for Dylan, de rigueur—he still had "Ballad of a Thin Man" and "Highway 61 Revisited" in his hip pocket.

Being rock's most self-conscious performer in a category that includes Mick Jagger and John Lennon is saying something, but while others only visited themselves in song from time to time, Dylan made his persona a subject of his songs from the start. As rock's Zelig, Dylan became obsessed with his pop persona, something he would have to live down or be overtaken by; and in some ways, the fact that he's still playing with these ideas ("Tweeter and the Monkey Man" on *Traveling Wilburys, Volume One*) is enough to make the case that he still enjoys flummoxing critics who are all too ready to write him off. His preoccupation with his public image is all the more ironic because Dylan doesn't embrace his audience in the traditional sense, never apologizes for flops, and rarely caters to the press as a way of maintaining his connection with his listeners. He believes in his songs enough to let them speak for him, and since his songs usually address these concerns, his persona flourishes. Even so, Dylan has relatively few songs about what it feels like to be a rock star (Jagger has several, including "Star, Star," "Monkey Man," "Sympathy for the Devil," and "Start Me Up"), and not a single one that clues you into what kind of life it is writing and singing. Some of the Basement Tapes comes closest: "You Ain't Goin' Nowhere," which is about knocking off work, and "When I Paint My Masterpiece," from the same period, which is about the constant (and comic) struggle to live up to one's muse. "Ballad of a Thin Man" is not so much the rock star staring down a retarded press corps as it is a generational anthem about the establishment's rigid close-mindedness. "Up to Me," an outtake from *Blood on the Tracks* that winds up on *Biograph*, is so self-consciously about the effect of fame on a songwriter that it almost sounds like it's about someone else.

**Dylan bears the burdensome** label of "poet," but it doesn't take a critic to note that a lot of his talent for words stems from an affection for run-on non sequiturs that would embarrass anyone who practices pruning words to heighten their effect. Few of his

## introduction

verses scan better without their music, and many seem written to fill space and provide an atmosphere of largess as much as anything. What distinguishes Dylan from those he's influenced (including all the idiosyncratic wordsmiths, like Randy Newman, Leonard Cohen, Bruce Springsteen, and John Hiatt) are the verbal rhythms he picks up from Woody Guthrie's *Bound for Glory* and from beat poets like Allen Ginsberg. There's more than a hint of Chuck Berry's verses to "Maybelline" in songs like "Subterranean Homesick Blues," and Dylan has the same flair for street language that heightens both character and dramatic tension. Because half of what Dylan is already up to is subverting expectations about pop singers, it's easy not to notice that much of the time he's smearing both his meters and his melodies by singing right through his bar lines. When you hear someone else sing one of his songs, you realize that they've often had to re-shape his melodies out of their own impressions from his recordings—his publishers have a difficult time coming up with just where his words land on the scale.

The Byrds' cover versions pickle Dylan songs with such vocal invention they seem like crystals of harmonic invention. Listening closely to Roger McGuinn's arrangement of "Mr. Tambourine Man" (on *The Byrds*) you hear an exquisitely spaced vocal duet rather than a group refrain. But Dylan's singing usually makes you forget about melody altogether: when he sings "Chimes of Freedom," among his best tunes (and a terrific Byrds cover), Dylan's stark, inelegant approach upstages the way the melody is winning you over with each verse. He gets away with it because his words are cast with such rhythmic élan that they dance all over his stiff meters—they make their impact without relying on melody at all. That's why the 1986 rap version of "Subterranean Homesick Blues" by Wack Attack is as much an update as a convincing rhythmic deconstruction: these words dance on their own, without any pretense at hooking them up to a lyrical line.

# hard rain

. . .

**If Dylan's singing** is about the situation of his career at the moment of his performance at any given juncture, his writing is often about the distance between the traditional and the contemporary, measured in such gaps as that between the traditional-sounding melody and setting of "A Hard Rain's A-Gonna Fall" and its choppy, protomodern words. His recordings make the same leap between modernity of statement and crudity of technique. A media magician who fashions his own mass-outsider cult, Dylan often turns his medium into his subject. The country station that plays soft in "Visions of Johanna" is a loaded symbol that tells not only what kind of music the characters do all their obsessing to but what kind of obsessing they do, and how pop songs color situations—relationships, phases of growth, emotional seasons—indiscriminately.

Pop has never been comfortable with Dylan's sprawling talent and disregard for boundaries. His contempt for limits first registered as unruly folk subversiveness bucking for a role that better suited his manic talent. As rock's least likely longest-running act, Dylan fulfills an impressive array of fantasies of the inimitable American pop icon—folkie troubadour, rock subversive, country crooner, Las Vegas showman—without submitting his image to the inundating sameness that afflicts most careerists.

But then pop has never been comfortable with its own boundaries, and originals never paid any attention to them. In Bill Flanagan's *Written in My Soul*, Dylan talks about visiting jazz clubs during his early Greenwich Village days—unusual for a folkie—and he was always emphasizing his fondness for black music, be it dreaming about hooking up with Little Richard in high school, or latching onto the blues as a way of making sense out of his self-willed identity as a young man.

The folk-blues that was popular in the early sixties was an authentic subgenre of the Chicago electric scene that centered around Muddy Waters. With his acoustic guitar and his harmon-

ica partner, Blind Sonny Terry, Brownie McGhee was a throwback who represented a more rural outlook, which these young
city scribes identified with almost desperately. It was more than
a stand against urban commercialism; it was a symbol of ties with
a preindustrial ideal, a community of agrarian dreamers and drifters who had come before, that made the ethic of self-sufficiency
so romantic to the post-Weavers crowd. Besides, McGhee was
easier to cover than Robert Johnson, whose 1936–37 recordings
were first released on LP around the time Dylan came to New
York City in 1961. With his bracing guitar lines fencing with his
wounded vocals, Johnson set off an instant buzz among blues fans
who had only heard of his legend—it didn't seem possible that
one person could make such an indomitable sound in the first
place, let alone that anyone could imitate it. And alongside all
the stylistic attraction of the folk blues was its racial harmony:
Woody Guthrie had spent the better part of his traveling life
with Huddie "Leadbelly" Ledbetter, composer of "Goodnight
Irene," an enormous black man with a mighty spirit that came
bolting from his operatic voice. The boundaries between folk,
blues, and jazz were often played with and subverted by the
models Dylan looked to for inspiration: Louis Armstrong sitting
in on sessions with Jimmie Rodgers, or Rufe Payne ("Tee-Tot")
teaching Hank Williams how to play the guitar. Dylan came by
his jump-track style twists honestly.

**Long before singer-songwriters** had to carry the cross of "the new
Dylan," people were calling Dylan "the new Guthrie," and it
was Woody Guthrie whom Dylan emulated above all his other
heroes (Hank Williams, Chicago's Big Joe Williams, Buddy
Holly, Johnny Cash, Smokey Robinson). Reading Guthrie's
*Bound for Glory* in Minneapolis in 1960, where he was busy
avoiding classes at the University of Minnesota, Dylan was smitten by more than just this diminutive Okie's wild-eyed prose and
epic plain-stroke songwriting. Like a lot of other people, Dylan

was taken by Guthrie's vision of America and his life as a troubadour for a culture in search of a voice to talk back to the
government, the police, and the landowners who exploited the
peoples' labor. It's hard to figure what Dylan identified with
most: that Guthrie's audience, the hordes of displaced dust-bowl
Okies who descended on California for work, was anything but a
minority; that Guthrie's messianic political ideas withstood his
comic digressions into meandering details; or that Guthrie created a myth for himself that enveloped his vast coast-to-coast
existence, an appetite for constant traveling, bumming, and singing that didn't begin to exhaust what the country had to show
him.

Dylan liked to call Guthrie his "last hero," meaning the last
obsession he carried for another performer on his way to creating
his own mystique. One day in 1961, he hit the road from Minneapolis to Morris Plains, New Jersey, to pay Woody a visit at
the Greystone Park State Hospital, where Guthrie was slowly
dying of Huntington's disease. Within a matter of weeks they
were on friendly terms. "I know Woody," Dylan wrote home,
"Woody likes me—he tells me to sing for him—he's the greatest
holiest godliest one in the world." During Sunday afternoons at
the home of folk-loving family Bob and Sidsel Gleason in East
Orange, New Jersey, Dylan exchanged songs with all the New
York folkies, including Ramblin' Jack Elliott, Pete Seeger, and
young Arlo Guthrie. As Joe Klein writes in his superb biography
of Guthrie (*Woody Guthrie: A Life*): "Over the course of several
months, a real rapport seemed to develop between Woody and
Dylan, with Woody often asking the Gleasons if 'the boy' was
going to be there on Sunday. 'That boy's got a voice,' he told
them. 'Maybe he won't make it with his writing, but he can sing
it. He can really sing it.' And when it came time for Dylan to
make his New York debut at Gerdes' Folk City, Sid Gleason gave
him one of Woody's suits to wear for the occasion. It was an
investiture whose symbolism was lost on no one."

Guthrie's influence on Dylan can't be overstated, but none

# introduction

of Dylan's biographers have troubled to detail the musical connections adequately. Guthrie was prolific: he wrote at least a thousand songs, which librarians are still cataloguing. Much of his recording work is repackaged on Rounder Records' ambitious reissues of the Folkways-label titles Guthrie made for Moe Asch, which are a map of folk in the pre-Weavers era. When Guthrie sat down with Alan Lomax at the Department of Interior for the Library of Congress archives in March of 1940 to tell the story of his life in word and song, he came off somewhat shy, but impatient; a straight-faced ham. Guthrie recounted the con jobs he and his fellow travelers would get suckered into by landowners who knew they had too many hard-luck workers on their hands; the death by fire of his fourteen-year-old sister, Clara, in May 1919; his mother's slow descent into madness (before Huntington's disease was diagnosed); his friendships, his art, his travels. Paradoxically, he spilled his life into Lomax's tape recorder the way he never would in song.

One of the key misunderstandings about what Guthrie passes on to Dylan is that it has more to do with myth than with music. From Guthrie, Dylan learns how an overlapping persona can develop between a song and the way a person delivers it; between the message and the messenger. Guthrie's songs hide their psychological features behind his plain-talk cheer, which is meant to disarm listeners and butter them up for his political message; Dylan uses humor mainly as a satirical device. Guthrie's songs are as point-blank as his vocal delivery: irony and self-mockery are tools, not ends in themselves. Dylan's songs and deliveries are as point-blank as a chess match: masked strategies, hidden consequences, reckless sacrifices, offenses posing as defenses, cunning cloaked in ritual, and intellectual muscle draped in flirtatious gamesmanship.

Guthrie was as much of a song collector as he was a songwriter. Before the phonograph was a staple of the American home, Guthrie was a radio troubadour in the true sense of the term: a roving human channel of an ongoing oral culture. In the late 1930s, with his singing partner, Lefty Lou (Maxine Crissman), Guthrie held forth nightly with his "Cornpone Philosophy" on a two-hour radio broadcast on the Los Angeles station KFVD. The show's signal reached as far as Pampa, Texas, where Guthrie's left-behind wife, Mary, would tune in; and listeners sent in a thousand fan letters a month.

Guthrie knew more than a little about how to get along: folks couldn't go home and put on his records after he sang for them, so he needed to make as simple and direct an impression as he could. Until he became a radio phenomenon in California, a lot of his fellow travelers would hear him once and then never again. His on-the-air musical personality fused familiar melodies and stories, and connected them up to social patterns in novel ways. His songs are repetitious as a matter of strategy: hear them once and they're lodged in your mind forever.

Some twenty years later, most of the personalities on live radio were spinning vinyl. Up in Hibbing, Minnesota, Dylan would tune in his family's Zenith to scratchy faraway signals like KTHS in Little Rock, Arkansas, a clear thousand-watter that broadcast "The Johnny Cash Show" and (picked up from Shreveport, Louisiana) Frank "Gatemouth" Page's "No-Name Jive." Like a lot of other radio converts, Dylan began to understand how repeated listenings to the right kind of lyric could give up different moods, different meanings, and different perceptions of a song. Weaned on early rock's sense of experimentation and complete disregard for civility, Dylan's developing taste in music centered on songs that pivoted off suggestion in ways that Guthrie couldn't afford. Although he was a solid country-and-western fan from early on, Dylan's infatuation with rock 'n' roll radio must have persuaded him that being simple and direct could, in some ways, work against what a songwriter was trying to put across. In what becomes a theme of circular miscommunication, Dylan actually worked to undermine his mass audience's tendency to twist simplicity and directness to their own fancies, be it through abstraction or out-and-out illogic. Long before he went electric,

## introduction

Dylan pulled the rug from the language of his songs—"My Back Pages" is as much antiliteralism as it is antiprotest.

**Along with "Pretty Boy Floyd,"** the Guthrie songs Dylan chose for his appearance with the Band at the Guthrie memorial concert at Carnegie Hall on January 20, 1968—his first appearance since his 1966 motorcycle accident—were emblematic of his connections with Guthrie. "I Ain't Got No Home" epitomized the outsider ethos that fueled Dylan's rock stature; "The Grand Coulee Dam" was an example of the list song Dylan updated with streaks of absurdity. The only component missing from this set was political protest: as roundly stirring as "Dear Mrs. Roosevelt" remained, it's one of the few Guthrie numbers that tacitly absolved Roosevelt of his capitalist war crimes.

The Old Left's relationship with Roosevelt was checkered. In the 1930s, Roosevelt had been a hero of the labor movement, by supporting legislation and voicing moral support for the unions that began forming everywhere. "The New Deal was seen as the ultimate Popular Front coalition—and the President responded with a degree of quiet tolerance," writes Klein. But when World War II broke out, Roosevelt lost his cachet among socialists by taking sides in a capitalist affair with the British imperialists. The Hitler-Stalin pact was a crowbar issue for stateside Communists, who lost many antifascist members over the alliance of their supposed hero Stalin with everybody's archdevil, Hitler.

Guthrie didn't let this theoretical thorn bother him. The Communists were still the only people interested in protecting workers' rights in the San Joaquin Valley. Guthrie painted a message on his guitar—"This machine kills fascists"—and he nicknamed John Steinbeck's novel "The Rapes of Graft." He was passionate to the point of neuroticism about communism (he once argued to his wife that in Russia "the state does the baby-sitting"); and in early 1940 he wrote "Why Do You Stand

## hard rain

There in the Rain?" about an American Youth Congress convention in Washington. Delegates had stood outside the White House in bad weather to protest war loans to Finland and to request more public works jobs, only to get a scolding from Roosevelt. Guthrie's song mocked the President as out-of-touch royalty:

**Now the guns of Europe roar**
**As they have so oft before**
**And the warlords play their same old game again.**
**While they butcher and they kill**
**Uncle Sammy foots the bill,**
**With his own dear children standing in the rain.**

Guthrie was a sometime partner in a cooperative musical troupe modeled after the Group Theatre called the Almanac Singers, which formed around Pete Seeger and Lee Hays (soon to be Weavers), Leadbelly, Burl Ives, Sonny Terry, Richard Dyer-Bennett, and others. In 1940 Pete Seeger began hanging out with Lee Hays and Millard Lampell in a midtown Manhattan loft, an early version of the fifties' beat and the sixties' bohemian scenes, and a rough model for Dylan's Rolling Thunder tour in 1975–76. Woody Guthrie visited an afternoon songwriting session one day with his family, and Lampell fell under the spell of his naturalistic songwriting gift. The first piece Lampell wrote in imitation of Guthrie was an anti-Roosevelt tune called "The Ballad of October 16," which attacked the President and Congress for passing the peacetime military draft bill. These Communist attitudes were way outside the mainstream war fervor, but the song was among the first in a new tradition of folk peace songs— "Blowin' in the Wind" and "Hard Rain" would be descendants. When Hays, Lampell, and Seeger (who was just twenty-one) traveled to Washington to perform for the American Youth Congress, the response to songs ridiculing the President was enthusiastically "explosive," reports Klein.

## introduction

The Almanacs' first record, *Songs for John Doe* (1940), was put out by Eric Bernay, the man who had financed John Hammond's landmark interracial concert, "From Spirituals to Swing," at Carnegie Hall in 1938. Smitten with populist poetics, their second record (*Talking Union*) was titled after a Guthrie-styled blues that detailed how to start up a proper organization, and so incensed President Roosevelt that he reportedly contemplated having the singers arrested (as J. Edgar Hoover and Nixon would sabotage the careers of peacenik singers like John Lennon in the sixties).

Guthrie was in Los Angeles when the Almanacs formed, and traveled to Portland ostensibly to work on a film, where he got work from the Bonneville Power Administration director Dr. Paul J. Raver. For $266.66 per month, Guthrie sat down and wrote some of the greatest tributes to the natural flow of water ever penned, including "Roll On, Columbia" (a sped-up rewrite of his friend Leadbelly's "Goodnight Irene") and "The Grand Coulee Dam" (to the tune of "Wabash Cannonball"). The latter included the kind of inebriated flow of detail that Dylan would later contort into free-form absurdities:

**In the misty crystal glitter of that wild and windward spray,**
**Men have fought the pounding waters and met a watery grave.**
**Well, she tore their boats to splinters, but she gave men dreams to dream**
**Of the day the Coulee Dam would cross that wild and wasted stream.**

Details like this—the names of tributaries, the localities, the personification of natural phenomena—helped draw listeners in, and Guthrie wrote to the Almanacs that the way to reach workers through song was to highlight "the wheels, whistles, steam boilers, shafts, cranks, operators, tuggers, pulleys, engines and all of the well known gadgets that make up a modern factory" (Klein, p. 195). (The "Grand Coulee Dam" image will pop up in Dylan's "Idiot Wind.")

The Works Progress Administration fostered plenty of "subversive" art from painters like Jackson Pollock. The irony in Guthrie's case was more acute: though he was employed by his government to write patriotic songs about the grand achievements of Roosevelt's New Deal, Guthrie's Communist allegiances made him a member of the opposition to Roosevelt's war cause. Still, in Guthrie's songs, the government works project held at least the hope of what an American socialism might mean if it could put its people to work harnessing nature's magnificence. In this period, Guthrie also wrote "Jackhammer John," "Dirty Overalls," "Hard Traveling," and one of his best-known titles, "Pastures of Plenty" ("We come with the dust and we go with the wind . . ."), as well as "Great Historical Bum" or "Biggest Thing That Man Has Ever Done" which Dylan would evoke in "Bob Dylan's 115th Dream" (Klein, pp. 194–95). Guthrie joined the Almanacs for a tour that summer of 1940, singing the union and antiadministration songs with charming aplomb, and then returned to his independent rambling.

Later, when Roosevelt was running for his fourth term, with stateside communism at an all-time low, Guthrie reformed a few of the Almanacs for a "Roosevelt Bandwagon," which toured the Northeast during the 1944 campaign. Guthrie sang "The Girl with the Roosevelt Button," and along with Cisco Houston, actor Will Geer, and some jazz players and dancers, the show won wild applause in Chicago Stadium, where Woody signed copies of his book, *Bound for Glory*.

Despite Guthrie's previous flare-ups, Roosevelt's death jiggled a stirring patriotic hymn out of him. He seems to have concluded (at least temporarily) that Roosevelt's good outweighed his bad, and that his myth was something that inspired even those who disagreed with his foreign policies. His tribute, "Dear Mrs. Roosevelt," does something more than memorialize

## introduction

the grand wizard of the New Deal as it poses as a comfort to his widow, Eleanor. In its frank Guthrie simplicity, where inviolable truth poses as understatement, the song celebrates the Roosevelt mythos and catches the outpouring grief that followed his sudden heart attack.

> He took his office on a crippled leg
> He said to one and all:
> "You money changin' racket boys
> Have sure 'nuff got to fall"
> This world was lucky to see him born . . .
>
> He helped to build my union hall,
> He learned me how to talk
> I could see he was a cripple
> But he learned my soul to walk
> This world was lucky to see him born . . . .

Those words shoot through Guthrie's childlike awe that the man ruled from a wheelchair. They reach towards the widespread identification with Roosevelt's tenacity from all kinds of like-minded small-town folk who had weathered a depression and a dust bowl and found a great deal more strength and endurance than they thought themselves capable of.

That Dylan picks this song to sing in 1968—with his hidden *Basement Tapes* agenda of "Tears of Rage," "Too Much of Nothing," and "Nothing Was Delivered" written and recorded but not released—makes for a strange (for Dylan) sentimental sense of bygone heroes: even giants like Roosevelt have their intimate enemies in Davids like Guthrie. When Dylan sings the swelling refrain, "This world was lucky to see him born," he's doing more than singing about Roosevelt, or even commenting by insidious contrast on the cynical politics of Lyndon Johnson, or the forces that would lead to the first Madison Avenue presidential campaign and Richard Nixon's election that same fall. He's singing about how lucky everybody was—Roosevelt, Dylan, folk music itself—to see Woody Guthrie born.

**"I Ain't Got No Home"** was another of Woody Guthrie's answer songs. Guthrie discovered the upbeat Baptist hymn "This World Is Not My Home," popularized by the Carter Family, at a migrant workers' camp in the late 1930s. It was the beginning of Guthrie's identification with the Communist party, which was organizing laborers in California, and the Carter Family's song failed to scratch an itch that Guthrie felt when he looked around him at the abused workers and the heedless farm owners. Like a lot of songs drawn from the well of pious spiritualism of country and western, the tune directed listeners' attention to an afterlife's rewards for earthly trials. Guthrie was losing patience with such hard-luck reassurance—it didn't justify the trials his boxcar friends had endured. (Guthrie even wrote a song after John Steinbeck's Tom Joad character in *Grapes of Wrath,* and named one of his kids Joady.) If anything, these people deserved dignity in *this* life, not the next; anything less rang hollow to Guthrie. "I Ain't Got No Home" came rolling out with the anger that such realizations spawned in him, and recast flack from policemen, rich landowners, and death itself into a way of giving fate some lip. "I Ain't Got No Home" became a way of saying "My home is my song, wherever I am," and the refrain (although stated in the negative) rang affirmative.

With the Band, Dylan cranks out the song as though Guthrie had sparked the beginnings of rock—which, in its negative-affirmative construction, he had (think of Presley's "Hound Dog," the putdown as hip flattery). They hug the refrain like a barreling freight takes a curve in the tracks, and the song summons the outsider lore that Dylan explores on his next record, *John Wesley Harding.* "The gambling man is rich / The working man is poor" might just sum up all the philosophical inequities that preoccupy the characters in "All Along the Watchtower." To

## introduction

the folk community, which had midwifed his difficult birth to the performing world, and to the rock community, where he faces a comeback that seems almost as daunting as the one Elvis Presley would make on television in December 1968, Dylan sings Guthrie's entreaty as if it might help explain a few things about his pop sabbatical that he could never articulate through his own material.

**talking new york**

"Bob freed your mind the way Elvis freed your body."

**—Bruce Springsteen**,

Rock and Roll Hall of Fame Induction dinner,
January 20, 1988

**At the close of the** 1963 Newport Folk Festival, everybody joined together onstage to sing Woody Guthrie's "This Land Is Your Land." This sing-along gathered folk's elite—Pete Seeger, Joan Baez, Theodore Bikel, Peter, Paul and Mary, and the Freedom Singers—for a harmonious picture of how this performing community saw itself. These singers shared the social conscience of an emerging youth culture, with active ties to the civil rights movement (another show-closer was "We Shall Overcome"). As self-congratulatory sentimentalists, they saw themselves as inheritors of the English and Scottish song-stories and sought solidarity and renewal in the traditional group sing.

Following the populist values championed by Pete Seeger's parent group, the Weavers, in the 1950s, and the heritage of troubadours like Guthrie, this Newport fraternity felt itself on the verge of a commercial awakening: another generation was embracing folk music with new fervor. White-bread acts like the Chad Mitchell Trio and the Kingston Trio were campus favorites, and Peter, Paul and Mary's varsity-cheer recording of Dylan's "Blowin' in the Wind" had just reached number two on the Billboard pop charts the month of the festival (July). "Don't Think Twice, It's All Right" would reach number nine that coming fall.

At age twenty-two, Bob Dylan was being touted as the folk scene's most promising talent. During a mobbed topical-song workshop hosted by Pete Seeger, Dylan sang "Playboys and Playgirls," released only on *Newport Broadside* (*Topical Songs*) ("You insane tongues of war talk / Ain't a-gonna guide my road . . ."). Dylan's solo set at Newport featured "With God on Our Side," "Talkin' John Birch Paranoid Blues," and "A Hard

Rain's A-Gonna Fall." He repeated "With God on Our Side" with Joan Baez, after she had sung his "Don't Think Twice, It's All Right" during her solo set. This pairing led Albert Grossman, Dylan's shrewd manager, to arrange a lucrative deal on Baez's next Northeast tour, where Dylan closed her sets with her and commanded the higher fee.

But if the festival's closing "This Land Is Your Land" group sing counted among folk's finest hours, uniting the generations in the Old Left's godfather, Seeger, and youth's queen, Baez, it was also one of folk's last hurrahs as an undivided community. Although "Blowin' in the Wind" was received as an anthem that ranked with Guthrie's "This Land Is Your Land," nearly everyone on that stage—especially Seeger—seemed to overlook Dylan's concern with crossover styles, or at least view the blues, gospel, and country roots he had staked for himself on his first album somewhat selectively. *Bob Dylan* was an erratic but gallant exploration of black styles: chiefly blues, but with a sprinkling of gospel antics ("Gospel Plow"), Roy Acuff country jollity ("Freight Train Blues"), and a subdued sentimentality that made hero worship sound reasonable ("Song to Woody"). This was American music swallowed whole, refracted through a new voice as strange and arresting as those of backwoods white blues prototypes Dock Boggs and Roscoe Holcomb. Boggs was a former coal miner from Norton, Virginia, who sang the classic church song "Oh Death," on the Old Time bill at Newport in 1963 at age sixty-six (see *Old Time Music at Newport*). Holcomb, an Appalachian warbler, had a voice that hung in the air like ashes (see his album *Close to Home*). Dylan's scrawny frame seemed to house such a voice, a barbed yawp that made him sound like he was born an old-timer. And his choice of material was as close to an ambition without boundaries as was possible for an upstart who came out of nowhere—Hibbing, Minnesota. The stylistic extremes Dylan traversed in saying hello to the world were broader than any of his Newport peers.

For along with the Guthrian social ideals which these per-

formers shared, Bob Dylan, folk's great white hope at the Newport Festivals of both 1963 and 1964, was steeped in the
traditions of the blues and folk-blues. Although folklike in that
both styles were oral traditions performed acoustically, these
other roots of Dylan's featured themes that made the brother-
hood of folkies sound comparatively safe, and certainly elitist,
even if they did affect "common man" personas. The blues material that Dylan took on revolved around the individual voice,
the idea that a person's unique experience governs the music's
personality, no matter who wrote the song. Dylan's singing style,
after all, was inspired more by the manic, operatic flights of
Leadbelly and Robert Johnson than by the homespun pretensions that made Pete Seeger such an affable crowd-pleaser.

The blues greats Dylan revered asserted their identities in
a world that made no place for them; all the great bluffing and
boasting that finds its modern counterpart in rap (and reggae)
was a way of announcing a presence that would otherwise go
unheard, never mind unappreciated. (Group sings are still staples at folk gatherings; sing-alongs are beside the point at blues
concert jams.) The blues themes Dylan embraced grapple with
the certainty of death and seek comfort and release in its expression; confront a weariness with life plagued by sexual misfortune
and redemption; and acknowledge the certainty of evil while
fearing a vengeful God. And the masters he admired deflated all
this philosophical lassitude with skeptical comic relief.

Dylan tackled these black characteristics on his debut, and
they gave his two subsequent folk albums (1963's *The Freewheelin' Bob Dylan* and 1964's *The Times They Are A-Changin'*)
their anchor, lifted them from the more narrowly defined records
made by his Newport colleagues and Greenwich Village peers
like Dave Van Ronk and Phil Ochs. Imagine any of Dylan's
contemporaries howling to the hefty splatter of "Mixed Up Confusion" (1961) as their first single (it finally showed up on *Biograph* in 1985), and you get an altogether different snapshot of
the way Dylan intended to integrate his fanatical Guthrie iden-

tification. For as much as Dylan touted Guthrie and Hank Williams as key figures in his pantheon of influences, his debut album was indebted to white sources only in the larger context of blues and gospel music, and posited where these styles might intersect. The way Blind Lemon Jefferson turned the act of singing into an irrefutable demand ("See That My Grave Is Kept Clean") and Bukka White made the acceptance of death sound anything but cowardly ("Fixin' to Die") are at least as important to Dylan's vocal style as folk music. These were performers Dylan identified with as an outsider, a Jewish cowboy from Minnesota and, more tellingly, as a kind of itinerant musical misfit. Only so much of Dylan's far-flung sensibility meshed with the stylistic dogma of the Newport folkies, just as their music was only a minority faction of what we now know as "folk."

**Dylan's first album** is a spotty outburst of an original talent with a formidable ear for unoriginal material. It serves as a cross-section of influences, both real and fantasized, between the young Dylan and the heritage he taps. His second record, *Freewheelin'*, unleashes a burgeoning songwriting gift that overtakes even his uncombed vocal personality. *The Times They Are A-Changin'* drifts into stiff polemics and muted romantic hopes but doesn't stretch his craft beyond the futuristic language of "A Hard Rain's A-Gonna Fall." It isn't until *Another Side of Bob Dylan* that Dylan makes the connection between his subdued personal laments and the outside political world. With "Blowin' in the Wind" and "Don't Think Twice, It's All Right," *Freewheelin'* marks Dylan as a folk original. *Another Side* is the blueprint for how such a brash young contender can write message songs that transcend their message.

Dylan's most enduring work has a sense of humor. In some ways, *Freewheelin'* is his most free-spirited record until 1965's *Bringing It All Back Home*: "Talkin' World War III Blues" (on *Freewheelin'*) makes the talking blues on *Another Side of Bob*

## hard rain

*Dylan* ("I Shall Be Free No. 10") sound comparatively flat— Dylan even cracks up and points out how clichéd the guitar break is by closing with: "What's this . . . It's nothing—it's something I picked up over in England." The dark strokes on *Freewheelin'* ("Masters of War," sections of "A Hard Rain's A-Gonna Fall") seem supplemental. By contrast, the lack of charm on *The Times They Are A-Changin'* makes it sound self-serious (especially on the heels of *Freewheelin'*). Except for the high spirits of the title song and "When the Ship Comes In," his third record is one long moral and romantic reproach.

These first three records trace Dylan's trademark restlessness, and set an ominous pattern: from aspiring blues acolyte to creative iconoclast to facile cynic who casts issues in black-and-white terms. The trumpet call of "The Times They Are A-Changin' " is equal parts idealism and realism, attitudes Dylan will stretch out into unforgiving attacks like "Ballad of a Thin Man" (1965) and, later, "Idiot Wind" (1974) and "The Groom's Still Waiting at the Altar" (1981), as well as ebullient romps like "I Want You" (1966), "Million Dollar Bash" (1967), and "On a Night Like This" (1973). As song poetry, "The Times They Are A-Changin' " is the rainbow after the surrealistic downpour of "A Hard Rain's A-Gonna Fall." Where the first album is ambitiously tempered folk blues from a voice that makes its mark on the listener long before the spotty selection of covers and the lesser original ("Talkin' New York"), the third album aims at the same core of generational resentment and societal hypocrisy in less inspiring terms, and his singing is less flexible. Between these two, *Freewheelin'* moves fluidly: even when the lyrics are strident, the music assuages. The graceful lilt of the guitar casts a hopeful light across the racial murders in "Oxford Town"; a faded romance gets buoyed by seductive melody in "Girl from the North Country"; and varied emotional colors drape the too-late farewell of "Bob Dylan's Dream." "Masters of War" is a Calvinist sermon next to a bromide like "Blowin' in the Wind." By comparison, the overall tone of *Times* is dour.

## talking new york

As forceful as these first three records are in their own way (especially the second two), the strides that follow are only faintly audible beneath the autodidactic spirit they capture. That first record is a wild pitch, but *Blonde on Blonde* wouldn't make as much musical sense if Dylan hadn't traced his roots back to Bukka White. As a prelude to Dylan's mercurial career, these records hold up extremely well, much better than any of his colleagues' would, and they supply him with a repertoire that he will perform onstage well into the eighties, most notably "With God on Our Side," "One Too Many Mornings," "Don't Think Twice, It's All Right," "A Hard Rain's A-Gonna Fall," "Girl from the North Country" (which he revives with Johnny Cash on *Nashville Skyline*), "Only a Pawn in Their Game," and "Boots of Spanish Leather." "Baby, Let Me Follow You Down," becomes a staple onstage with the Band in 1966, and serves as his hello and good-bye for his set closing the Band's farewell concert.

### Bob Dylan
Released: March 1962

No, I don't like the first album. You know, though, I've done some stuff on that first record that still stands up. Like my harmonica playing. Like in "Man of Constant Sorrow," the arrangement of that I like. "In My Time of Dyin' " still stands up. But as a whole, it's not consistent.

#### —Dylan in 1976
(in Robert Shelton, *No Direction Home*)

**Dylan made certain** that his early pose as a scrawny, bursting-with-talent Greenwich Village bohemian would fit in with the folk scene, which was then the "hip" alternative to the sagging cleverness of post–rock 'n' roll pop. But instead of blending in with his chosen professional crowd, Dylan amplified the very idea of "folk" in his debut and dramatized how his roots lay as much with the blues as with any other music. *Bob Dylan* was the sound of a young man trying to make sense of a black man's heritage, which made it a rock 'n' roll effort in the tradition of Dylan's idol Elvis Presley, even though Dylan didn't presume to inhabit this music with the same authority. Dylan understood the acoustic parallel to the Chicago electric blues, that you didn't need an amplifier to pry out a song's guts; and he admired the acoustic performers like Brownie McGhee, who pulled the equivalent scorched truths and depth of feeling from his solo performances as electric blues figures like B. B. King, Muddy Waters, and T-Bone Walker did fronting amps and drums.

Unwittingly, Dylan outfitted these songs with the same self-consciousness that a lot of other young white singers brought to them, redressed their rural trials with a new urban identification and relevance. As an alternative to the pop puffery of Bobby Vee and Connie Francis, this earthbound music had immediate credibility among listeners who had no patience for the glossy insipidness then popular. Just as Presley had opened up the netherworld of black blues to whites, Dylan brought his Greenwich Village audiences wry backwoods humor and plaintalk leftism. His maps included the three-volume Folkways album *Anthology of American Music*, the Henry Smith collection he had been listening to since his college coffeehouse days in Minneapolis. The Smith anthology is quite a resource: Dylan probably first heard Dock Boggs and Roscoe Holcomb here, along with blues legends like Blind Willie Johnson, Blind Lemon Jefferson, and many others that never made the airwaves north of the Mississippi, if at all.

Assimilating this material involves some nervy imaginative leaps. The cheek it takes to will rural folk into hip urban jargon is part of the fun Dylan has when he sings "Keep your eye on the plow, hold on . . ." in "Gospel Plow"—he's not so much mastering this style as he is winking to both himself and his listeners, having a stab at something he knows full well is larger than he is. By contrast, Dylan's cohort Dave Van Ronk makes the same music sound something like a homework assignment, and he doesn't find anything funny about his detached gentility as he manicures his renditions of "Fixin' to Die" and an early Dylan song, "He Was a Friend of Mine." Dylan apes his sources, to be sure, but what holds you is how closely he captures the sense of adventure in this music—the expectancy he stretches out in "Freight Train Blues," the menace in "See That My Grave Is Kept Clean"—even when his readings betray his age. The "Gospel Plow" becomes a symbol for the stylistic reach Dylan has risked, but he sounds like he's tickled just for the chance to try. This attitude chortles at the self-serious air of his Village circle. It's unruly, caricature music that parades more antsy talent than artistry. What could be more audacious, more weirdly out of the modest midwestern character, than to brave the tightrope of imitating the elusive gospel ideal and then chuckle at yourself as you measure the distance you're reaching across ("Keep your eye on the plow—hold on!")?

Of course, blacks weren't the only folks who didn't fit into the sterilized suburban middle-class mold of the 1950s. As a Jewish kid from Hibbing, Dylan is understandably estranged from the hollow myth of American integration. The mine pits that scarred Hibbing life so embarrass him that he keeps silent about his background, or invents yarns about his upbringing, until professional journalists start digging. With the Rosenberg trial and Hollywood blacklisting, anti-Semitism was as ingrained as any racism, only more covert, more "civilized," and it led directly to early cooperation between Jews and blacks in the civil rights movement. Dylan's appearance at the March on Washington in August of 1963 became a vivid symbol of this tie; his identification with black music has as much to do with shared values as it does with an idealized musical aesthetic. It links up vocal ambition with a will to expose the falsity of the white hegemony and phony integration, and the variety of musics that lie outside mainstream cultural "acceptability."

So calling Dylan a disciple of Guthrie grossly oversimplifies his extraordinary appetite for the full gamut of America's folk styles. His debut travels from the overlooked songwriting model of Jesse Fuller ("You're No Good") to out-of-the-way blues singers like Bukka White ("Fixin' to Die"); from blues spirituals ("In My Time of Dyin' ") to Southern mountain songs ("Man of Constant Sorrow") to traditional Scottish yips ("Pretty Peggy-O") to out-and-out cops from colleagues like Eric Von Schmidt ("Baby, Let Me Follow You Down") and fellow interpreter Dave Van Ronk, a competitor he leaves unmentioned ("House of the Risin' Sun"); from rowdy country hams like Roy Acuff ("Freight Train Blues") to blues heavyweights like Blind Lemon Jefferson ("See That My Grave Is Kept Clean"). Dylan has his way with material like "In My Time of Dyin' " long before it forges through his generation of British blues hounds, and his acoustic version (based on Dock Reed's version) holds up better than Led Zeppelin's metal histrionics on *Physical Graffiti* (1975). By then such false blues prophets have turned it into sacred mush, and Zep stretches the song out into jaded, slide-guitar onanism.

In retrospect, it's curious that more white styles aren't represented on Dylan's debut. In D. A. Pennebaker's 1967 documentary *Don't Look Back*, he plays wistful, abbreviated versions of Hank Williams's "I'm So Lonesome I Could Cry" and Leon Payne's "Lost Highway." And his country sources are clear from his songwriting (the smooth transitions, the gentle reassurances of his softer passages).

These debut songs are essayed with differing degrees of conviction (the way he apes an old man's voice on "See That My Grave Is Kept Clean" is ambition lapsing into comedy) and kept afloat largely by the determination of Dylan's approach. Even when his reach exceeds his grasp, he never sounds like he knows he's in over his head, or gushily patronizing.

## talking new york

Like Elvis Presley, what Dylan can sing, he quickly masters; what he can't, he twists to his own devices. And as with the Presley Sun sessions, the voice that leaps from Dylan's first album is its most striking feature, a determined, iconoclastic baying that chews up influences, and spits out the odd mixed signal without half trying: "House of the Risin' Sun" doesn't sound so much like a young man's fearful trip to the whorehouse as like a young man's fear in the face of a song.

Dylan didn't arrive a fully formed blues artist, but he went on to prove that he didn't need to. The nerve it took to show his sword on these bluesmen's terms is what counted, and what continues to sustain interest is Dylan's song choices. A lot of this first-album material was repertoire Dylan shared with his colleagues: Bukka White's "Fixin' to Die" was done by Dave Van Ronk, as were "See That My Grave Is Kept Clean," "House of the Risin' Sun" and "Cocaine Blues," the traditional drug plaint which Dylan had recorded at a session at his friend Dave Whitaker's house in Minnesota in December of 1961. "Baby, Let Me Follow You Down" came from Eric Von Schmidt ("I met him one day in the green pastures of Harvard University . . ."). Dylan refers to it as a Reverend Gary Davis song, one which Davis used to sing as "Baby Let Me Lay It On You," along with "Twelve Gates to the City," and "Yonder at the Cross." Dylan noticed how Davis felt perfectly at home swerving from religious to bawdy. (This song is an outtake from Dylan's sessions for his debut album on November 20 and 22, 1961, his first solo recording dates.)

But his peers tended to approach some of this same material with varying degrees of detachment, as though there were a certain appropriate way to perform a number. They present the folk style as something more cultivated, a music that relied more on a finely honed tradition of gestures and symbols—the brooding sensitive as archetype, the social conscience as genius. Ironically, because of their reverence for European models (the song of reckoning for folk singers was the Old English "Barbara

Allen"), the Greenwich Village folkie ethic tended to be more culturally removed from the way people thought and acted than the blues realisms that Dylan set in motion. On Joan Baez's 1965 *Farewell Angelina* record, which included four Dylan songs (the title song, a quasi-surreal good-bye waltz; "Daddy, You've Been on My Mind"; "It's All Over Now, Baby Blue"; and "A Hard Rain's A-Gonna Fall"), she went so far as to sing a German translation of "Where Have All the Flowers Gone," as if it were a proper Deutsche Lied.

Dylan's wildcat vocals squashed conventional sophistication (even though, on his own terms, his deliveries became highly sophisticated). His flailing harmonica circled his singing like an itinerant parrot, squawking frantically between lines, chasing his words. When his voice fell short, as it did in "Pretty Peggy-O," his harmonica soared through to make the unstated connections. It's as though he willed that harp he blew to be a lead guitar. In fact, Dylan's earliest recording work was as a harmonica player. In June 1961, he appeared on the title song for Harry Belafonte's *Midnight Special* album and took a credible solo. In October 1961, Dylan played harp and sang on tracks with Big Joe Williams, Lonnie Johnson, and Victoria Spivey for a record called *Three Kings and a Queen*—a picture of the waif-like Dylan with Spivey at the piano later appeared on the back of *New Morning*.

**Given that Dylan** had the chutzpah to ask for an electric backup band for his first single—the hilariously bedraggled "Mixed Up Confusion"—his solo debut represents a crucial daring on Dylan's part, as if he meant to take on the whole notion of a folk artist's prescribed limits. By taking the risk of holding his mettle with the likes of Blind Lemon Jefferson (not to mention Guthrie), his ambition sometimes gets the best of him. What his ambition can't conquer is rescued by his spontaneity. His folk listeners didn't realize that this belligerent attitude towards self-determination had nothing to do with acoustic or electric or folk or even rock or gospel. It had more to do with his abject determination to write and perform as his ear alone dictated. Labels, Dylan insisted, are to be manipulated, not capitulated to.

Dylan's debut is a telling assay, a pretentious stab at folk blues that yields some remarkably scattershot singing but winds up overstating the blues' fatalism—he grasps at the music's signifiers instead of allowing them to carry him. The record is redeemed by its two originals, which, as good as they are, barely hint at the future. The performances show off a talent who knows how to exploit his instruments (voice, guitar, harp) to the fullest effect, and pull more from a song than could ever be notated. His singing alone—anxious yet impertinent—carries the traditional mountain song "Man of Constant Sorrow." When he holds the first note of each verse, teasing the length each time out, making you guess when he'll trip into the verse, he achieves a focused, steady sense of assuredness—he gets a grip on those notes and doesn't let go until he's convinced you of their strength and the tension he can squeeze out of them.

When his voice isn't yanking at expectations, Dylan's squirrellike harmonica work is. In "Pretty Peggy-O," the harp has legs of its own, and Dylan has to scramble just to keep up ("whoohoo!"). It's the story of a soldier who sojourns down in Texas for the rodeo, dies in the next verse, and is buried "somewhere in Louisiana." In "Man of Constant Sorrow," he holds a note out on his harmonica until it floods into a chord and drops down into the lope of his guitar picking. In the final moments, that held harmonica note begins to suggest a landscape, a distant train.

The Guthrie influence in "Talkin' New York" is overt: Dylan assumes the same ambling format as Guthrie's conversational "Washington Talkin' Blues" (available on the *Columbia River Collection*) and "Talking Dust Bowl" (on *Dust Bowl Ballads*), where the banks and the government seem even more stingy than the hard-luck drought ("Mighty thin stew . . . you could read a magazine right through it / If it had been just a little bit thinner, some of these here politicians could have seen through it . . ."). Playing singer as village chronicler, voice of the people, Dylan turns his salad days into a farce about the business of modern-day troubadours, recounting the tin-eared employers he ran into as an upstart on the folkie circuit: "You sound like a hillbilly; / We want folk singers here."

The coffeehouse manager in the song is half right: Dylan's unusual vocal whine is all backwoods nasality. What amuses Dylan is the assumption behind the stereotype: that hillbillies aren't folksingers, and that Dylan's hillbilly yelp is less striking than Phil Ochs's cardboard monotone. (What once sounded strange in Dylan has come to sound downright authentic.) Working his way up through the folk scene to sing in better venues, he joins the musicians' union out of necessity. And he drops his first reference to Guthrie's "Pretty Boy Floyd" when he sings about people who rob with their fountain pens.

Matching Woody at his own game is clearly the intent here; and that the success of the song operates as a comic turn, the kind of on-the-spot shaggy-dog tale he was perfecting in clubs, is an index of Dylan's performing reflexes. His talking blues recounts different sorts of hard times than Guthrie's, but he plays them up for comic effect.

Still, Guthrie is not the only white ghost haunting these songs. Even as he's footnoting Roy Acuff, soaring up into a yodel falsetto, "Freight Train Blues" shows how much Dylan has listened to Jimmie Rodgers—he has no trouble evoking him within his own self-mocking context. When Dylan holds the word "blues" beyond the breaking point until it dissolves into a giggle, he recaptures Rodgers's unfailingly cheery approach, and it leads directly to a more original mixture of sincerity and mock exasperation in "All I Really Want to Do." It's also an example of Dylan's early, Chaplinesque stage demeanor: teasing his listeners, holding forth with his cockeyed wit and screwball timing, stringing non sequiturs together in bloated verses burst by deflating punch lines—just to see if anybody out there was listening. In Anthony Scaduto's *Dylan*, Eric Von Schmidt described Dylan performing in England in 1963:

> There was a little stool almost on the very apron of the stage, and Bob would be playing with his guitar and talking dope remarks, and then he'd collapse right on the stool. Just like Chaplin. And somehow I started getting a connection between the ballet and Dylan. First it horrified me and then I realized this is one of the greatest things I've ever seen in my life. He was doing it. He had all these people buffaloed, doing this great thing, and if they hadn't been so confused they would have seen this was Chaplin reincarnated. He would get up and play a little bit—he did start to play and sing some standards and some of his own things— and then he'd fall and land right on the stool. He never missed that stool. (pp. 154–55)

**If Dylan's singing** is unconventional, something between Dock Boggs's endearing vibrato-less drawl and the midwestern heartland ideal, his recitation of "Last Thoughts on Woody Guthrie" from his Town Hall concert in 1963 is something beyond a reading—the words seem to bolt out of his breathless enthusiasm for his subject. (The prose-poem appears on the multivolume 1985 bootleg *Ten of Swords* and *The Bootleg Series Volume I.*) The onslaught of left-out, identity-corroded, and restlessness-of-youth imagery and the litany of numbingly conforming effects of Madison Avenue's mass-scale salesmanship aren't as effective as poetry on the page (he hits this theme better in "It's Alright, Ma (I'm Only Bleeding)"). "Last Thoughts on Woody Guthrie" is a song without music, and Dylan doesn't merely recite it; he talks the words into singing.

Dylan's earlier tribute, "Song to Woody," sentimentalizes Guthrie without simplifying him as the author of "This Land Is Your Land" or "So Long, It's Been Good to Know You." Instead of canonizing the man, Dylan sings about the themes of the dust-bowl migrants whom Guthrie ennobled through song. For a record that seeks out extremes of experience, the worldview is touching in the most naive manner: "Seems sick an' it's hungry, it's tired an' it's torn, / It looks like it's a-dyin' an' it's hardly been born."

Robert Shelton notes that "Song to Woody" is derived melodically from Guthrie's "1913 Massacre," which Guthrie most likely refashioned from an even earlier melody. Guthrie used folk tunes like templates. Adapting a familiar melody to a topical message was less a crutch than a tool—his listeners responded to the words quicker if they already knew the tune. The same thing is done today with rock songs when chord patterns are recycled beneath new melodies or bits of Led Zeppelin are "sampled" and injected into the Beastie Boys' rants (the copyright lawyers are always playing catch-up).

Sid Gleason, hostess to the Sunday-afternoon folk circles where Guthrie would listen to Dylan sing, said to Scaduto: "Woody had told him, 'Just write. Don't worry where the tune comes from. I just pick up tunes I heard before and change them around and make them mine. Put in a couple of fast notes for one slow one, sing a harmony note 'stead of melody, or a low note for a high one, or juggle the rests and pauses—and you got a melody of your own. I do it all the time' " (p. 80).

Dylan's use of a Guthrie tune reinforces the theme of heroic identification. Guthrie's song is a typical example of how his most sing-songy arrangements could seduce listeners into the darkest stories. "1913 Massacre" is about "copper-boss thug men" and scabs who yell "Fire!" to sabotage a crowded copper miners' union fund-raiser Christmas party in Calumet, Michigan. Seventy-three children die in the crush to get out against doors held by the thugs. The first part of the song reads like a festive scene from *It's a Wonderful Life*: a young girl sits down to play carols at the piano; in the last verse, the piano plays a funeral tune. "See what your greed for money has done," the copper miners moan.

## talking new york

The musical reference in "Song to Woody" imbues Dylan's sentiment with a dark undercurrent that is kept close to the vest. You have to know Guthrie's myth—his "Woody Sez" column for the California Communist newspaper the *People's World*, his merchant marine service in the Second World War—to grasp the full import of how much Dylan is leaving out. What's also left unsaid in the song's echoing stillness is Guthrie's failing physical condition when Dylan first traveled from Minneapolis to visit him in Greystone Park State Hospital. Guthrie's descent into the agonizing decay of Huntington's disease in the late 1950s and early 1960s occurred just as his legend became popularized, sanitizing his union songs and love of country until his music became manipulated by the very forces Guthrie meant to tear down. Instead of exposing the inhumane hardships suffered by the dust-bowl migrants, Guthrie's ironically titled *Bound for Glory* passed into legend as the syrupy emblem of poor folks who strove for better and managed to find happiness in dirt. It's the fate of many songwriters that they're often remembered for the wrong reasons—people join in on Leadbelly's "Goodnight, Irene," but not because it's a suicide note; likewise Bruce Springsteen's "Born in the U.S.A." But Guthrie's overt politicism made his subsequently tame image come close to a betrayal of all he stood for. (With "Blowin' in the Wind," Dylan would soon face a similar fate.) "This Land Is Your Land" was written as a vigilant response to the hollow loftiness of Irving Berlin's "God Bless America"—"it was just another of those songs that told people not to worry, that God was in the driver's seat," writes Joe Klein, paraphrasing Guthrie's contempt for Berlin's puffery (p. 136). Dylan understood how Guthrie was far more than the cheery morale-booster the dust-bowl migrants needed, which is why "Song to Woody" rings sad rather than awestruck.

Dylan doesn't return to "Song to Woody" until his 1974 tour with the Band, not even when he's called upon to perform at the memorial concerts after Guthrie's death. But Dylan's reserve and understatement—what remains untold or underemphasized—are key expressive devices in his work, whether it be withheld intensity (in songs like "Sad-Eyed Lady of the Lowlands") or wry irony (as when he underplays the philosophical sand traps on *John Wesley Harding*).

**Most distinctive about** Dylan's debut is the way his voice mixes mischief with a depth of feeling well beyond his twenty years. His intrepid, hard-luck rasp grapples with stylistic tensions and worldly ambitions that betray his boyish demeanor. Dylan's voice recalls Guthrie's in that it is the sound of a rambling, hobo spirit with a streetwise mind; but in 1962 it was also distinctive in ways that Guthrie's voice was not. Guthrie had a sweetness of character; he played the intuitive average Joe who had an inspired grasp of his fellow travelers' mood and character, not simply because he was one of them but because he could mirror their plight in song—his own personality didn't enter the discussion. Dylan's voice is ripe with empathy for his subject and the situations of his characters; but beyond that, there is an iconoclasm that has as much to do with self-revelation as with fidelity to style. Dylan himself is central to the way we hear these songs; it's his odd sense of phrasing and quirky timings that keep this music alive and make its best moments rise above imitation ("Fixin' to Die," "Man of Constant Sorrow").

Dylan's outsider personality is squirming its way out of this music in ways that Guthrie would have never revealed. Riding the boxcars and hitching rides on the backs of folks' wagons, Guthrie needed to maintain a front; spilling your guts was stupid—akin to opening up your wallet to show others how much money you had inside. To Guthrie, individualism was dwarfed by the necessities of communalism. By the time Dylan reached Greenwich Village, though, revealing something distinctive about yourself was a part of selling yourself, as essential to making it as the blues dictum was to upping the ante on other sensitive-stricken folkies.

●　　●　　●

**The recording sessions** for *Bob Dylan* included four songs not
released on the album: the traditional "House Carpenter"; Dylan's own "He Was a Friend of Mine," which was covered by
Dave Van Ronk and later released by the Byrds with additional
lyrics by Roger McGuinn to make it a sappy tribute to John F.
Kennedy; Woody Guthrie's "Ramblin' Blues" (which is as close
as Dylan ever comes to impersonating Guthrie); and Dylan's
"Man on the Street," which again traced Guthrie's self-
deprecating voice ("I'll sing you a song, ain't very long / 'Bout an
old man who never done wrong"), a song-sketch resembling
Dylan's "Only a Hobo" about a man found dead on the street
who gets jabbed by a cop with his billy club.

Dylan's first album got good reviews from *The Village
Voice, Sing Out!*, and *Little Sandy Review* but sold less than five
thousand copies, which made Columbia skittish about its widely
publicized find. Dylan's producer and discoverer, John Hammond, a Columbia-label kingpin who had Billie Holiday and
Benny Goodman to his credit, found his new signing labeled
"Hammond's folly."

*Lyrics 1962–1985* assigns the lyrics of the following songs to
the *Bob Dylan* period, even though some belong to the sessions
for *Freewheelin'* and other albums. "Hard Times in New York
Town," adapted from the traditional "Hard Times in the Country
Working on Ketty's Farm," is a sprightly parody on the spoils of
Manhattan ("Mister Rockefeller sets up as high as a bird / Old
Mister Empire never says a word") that only bolsters the young
singer's hard-won determination.

"Talking Bear Mountain Picnic Massacre Blues" is one of
the great early Dylan set pieces, a song-gag that finally sees the
light on *The Bootleg Series*. It's an early version of the mockingly
grandiose tall tale Dylan would perfect with "Stuck Inside of
Mobile with the Memphis Blues Again," about a Noah's-ark picnic gone awry, complete with dogs, cats, women, fists, babies,

and cops. Dylan turns a ridiculous yarn into an impish metaphor for political confusion and anarchic release—and it's the first indication that he can master Guthrie's tomfoolery without sounding derivative. In lyrics that are hysterical on the surface with sharp satire swimming just beneath, Dylan twists absurdities into sly symbolic codes (his way of not letting on that he has no intention of letting on). The last verse of the song has an atypical Dylan retribution moral about greed, and what to do with overzealous hucksters: "I think we oughta take some o' these people / And put 'em on a boat, send 'em up to Bear Mountain . . . for a picnic."

In a similar vein, "Talkin' John Birch Paranoid Blues" is the song CBS censors blocked from Dylan's appearance on "The Ed Sullivan Show" in late 1962. Because the song equates anti-commie fervor with Hitler, CBS feared libel suits from members of the John Birch Society. Dylan refused to appear on the Sullivan show unless they let him perform the song he had auditioned with. The corporate blacklist mentality couldn't make head or tail of the lyrics' exaggerations. What does it matter that Hitler killed six million Jews, Dylan asks: "At least you can't say he was a Communist! / That's to say like if you got a cold you take a shot of malaria." After searching everywhere for "them Reds," he "looked deep down inside my toilet bowl. / They got away . . . ." Blacklisting was too recent a blight for such sarcasm to be allowed on the air; and too many folkies, like Seeger and the Weavers, were still trying to shake the stigma of their Communist labels. Dylan's attitude laughs at his elders' paranoia paranoia: ". . . discovered they wus red stripes on the American flag! / That ol' Betsy Ross . . ."

"Rambling, Gambling Willie" refashions Guthrie's "Pretty Boy Floyd" as an ace poker hustler with indiscriminate aims. Will O'Conley "wore no rings or fancy things, like other gamblers wore / He spread his money far and wide, to help the sick and the poor." Naturally, Willie won a little too much one night, pulled some unlucky cards, and got shot through the head.

## talking new york

"Baby, I'm in the Mood for You," in the mold of "Honey, Just Allow Me One More Chance," echoes Jesse Fuller's style, which Dylan later acknowledged in his *Biograph* liner notes. Dylan was still paying respects to Jesse Fuller as late as December 1988, when he performed "San Francisco Bay Blues" at Neil Young's Bridge Benefit concert at Oakland Coliseum, on the heels of Guthrie's "Pretty Boy Floyd," which had come out on the all-star Guthrie-Leadbelly tribute LP, *A Vision Shared.*

**Other songs Dylan records** in this period don't want for ideas— some get reworked, others fall away. "Standing on the Highway" is a frantically syncopated blues with a card-game verse. "Poor Boy Blues" sounds like a sped-up draft of "Dink's Song," a gently chuckling blues that seems to run in place with itself (Van Ronk covered this one, too). "Ballad for a Friend" is a major-keyed blues with civil rights overtones, somewhat similar to "Oxford Town" in melody, about the loss of a friend (a theme Dylan perfects with "Percy's Song").

"The Death of Emmett Till," which borrows a melody from "House of the Rising Sun," tells the story of a Chicago youth beaten and killed by Mississippians, "just for the fun of killin' him and to watch him slowly die." In what will become a tired angle in his broadsides against injustice, Dylan points his finger not only at the thoughtless cruelty of the death but at the "mockery" of a trial, the brothers smiling as they walk from the courthouse, and the silent approval the guilty members of the jury give their crime. There is, however, this morbid snatch of originality amid the generalizations: "While Emmett's body bloats the foam of a Jim Crow southern sea." The song wilts, however, into a forced patriotic ending ("We could make this great land of ours a greater place to live").

•　　•　　•

## hard rain

**The sarcasm is** hard to miss, but stripped of Dylan's caustic delivery "Long Ago, Far Away" would have made the perfect campaign jingle for Ronald Reagan, who throughout his presidency was always romanticizing the past, whitewashing the present, and fantasizing better things for the future. The verses recount the persistence of historical denial from slavery through war with the incessant rejoinder "Long ago, far away / Things like that don't happen no more, nowadays," "Ain't Gonna Grieve" is a slight cheerleading bromide that evades theatrics; "Walkin' Down the Line" is another indistinctive rambling blues.

"Gypsy Lou" is a slight, near-raucous fantasy about an elusive woman who leaves men in her trail: "She left one too many a boy behind / He committed suicide. / Hey, you can't win. . . ." "Long Time Gone" (not to be confused with David Crosby's Robert Kennedy song of the same title) voices a lot of the themes of death that the first album circles around.

"Quit Your Low Down Ways" is a pinched-nerve blues with a yelping yodel that turns the Jimmie Rodgers model into a giddy sarcastic squeal ("Well, if you can't quit your sinnin' / Please quit your low down ways"). "I'd Hate to Be You on That Dreadful Day" anticipates "When the Ship Comes In": it's not as spirited, but it has the same judgment-day comeuppance that makes for a prankish punishment ("You're gonna have to walk naked, / Can't ride in no car"). "That's my calypso tap number," Dylan tells the engineer after the take.

"Hero Blues" gets big laughs at his Town Hall concert in 1963 ("You need a different kind of man, babe / You need Napoleon Boneeparte . . .)—like "It Ain't Me, Babe," it's a howl in the face of overpossessiveness. "Bob Dylan's New Orleans Rag" is a piano stomper in the style of his later "Denise" and "Black Crow Blues": a nervous whorehouse episode where a man stumbles out of his room with a "frightened / Look in his eyes, / Like he just fought a bear, / He was ready to die."

The take of "Tomorrow Is a Long Time" that turned up on *Ten of Swords* (from the M. Witmark and Sons Publishing demo sessions) illustrates why fanatics go to illegal lengths to keep such material available. The song surpasses any of the romances Dylan had yet released, with a leap to impressionist imagery that presages much of his mature work ("I can't see my reflection in the waters, / I can't speak the sounds that show no pain.)" (It finally appeared commercially in 1971, in a live version on *Greatest Hits, Volume 2*.) "Tomorrow Is a Long Time" ennobled itself by being one of two Dylan songs Elvis Presley would record (it's on the *Spinout* soundtrack from 1966). "Are there any particular artists that you like to see do your songs?" *Rolling Stone* asked Dylan in 1969. "Yeah, Elvis Presley," Dylan answered. "He recorded a song of mine. That's the one recording I treasure the most" (*The Rolling Stone Interviews, Volume 1*, p. 317). And on his 1971 masterpiece, *Every Picture Tells a Story*, Rod Stewart turns the song into a model of quiet tension, desire ridden with pools of self-doubt.

**"Let's put this** one down for kicks," Dylan says to the engineer before lighting into "All Over You," a cockeyed devotion in the same scatterbrained camp as "Honey, Just Allow Me One More Chance": "Then you pushed my heart through my backbone, / Then you knocked off my head from my neck."

"John Brown" is an old-style protest song that links the antiwar mentality with the generation gap—it's more about the mother's ignorant pride than about her soldier son's loss of innocence (it appears on the Gaslight club set on *Ten of Swords*). After months of bragging to her neighbors, Mrs. Brown goes to the train station to pick up her boy, only to find "his face was all shot up and his hand was all blow off." Mrs. Brown listens in shock as her son tells her how he realized "That I was just a puppet in a play"; and to seal his bitterness, he drops his medals into her hand. "John Brown" predates a little-known outtake from the Basement Tapes, "Stones That You Throw," which is also about the cost of humility. The last song listed in *Lyrics*

## hard rain

*1962–1985* before *Freewheelin'* is "Farewell," the slow, regretful postscript to "Don't Think Twice," a second-thought contrition from a lover after the argument.

## The Freewheelin' Bob Dylan
### Released: May 1963

**Freewheelin' unveils a** new Dylan in the first of many reincarnations—it's the arrival of an assurance and range his debut keeps under wraps. All original material except for "Corrina, Corrina" (a slowed adaptation of Joe Turner's stomper which Dylan had heard on the radio), it expands folk's naturalism as it tinkers with the language of surrealism. Where "Blowin' in the Wind" remains among the most unforced songs Dylan would ever write, a contemporary map of a nation's wilting but still restless idealism, "A Hard Rain's A-Gonna Fall" is a verbal binge that gets him labeled a rock poet. "Hard Rain" is a tour-de-force modernist refurbishment of traditional ballad form, infused with surrealist imagery that wouldn't sound out of place on *Bringing It All Back Home*, Dylan's first foray into electric rock some two years later. (In *Voice Without Restraint*, English critic John Herdman cites as the song's model "Lord Randal" with its question-and-answer motif: "O where hae ye been, Lord Randal, my son? / Where hae ye been, my handsome young man?")

But even more striking is the way Dylan reinvents himself as something more than a white blues aspirant: his singing and playing on *Freewheelin'* integrate the direct passion and emotional range of the blues with a soft-pedaled irony that conjures a new tension within the folk traditions he evokes. In the first of a string of burnout good-byes, "Don't Think Twice, It's All Right" would be overbearing if it weren't for the guitar's forgiving overtones; like "Oxford Town," it's bitterness cut with compassion.

*Freewheelin'* balances social attitudes against humor both improvisatory and mischievous. The jagged edge of "Masters of War" gets the rug pulled out from under it by the Lone Ranger and Tonto's antics in "Bob Dylan's Blues": ("Fixin' ev'rybody's troubles / Ev'rybody's 'cept mine"). To clue us in that this new Dylan is more than a Guthrie clone, he puts "Blowin' in the Wind" at the top of the song list instead of saving it as the surefire sentimental finale to the hardship and disillusion touched on in the serious songs. "It looks like it's a-dyin' an' it's hardly been born" is the way he described the world he saw in "Song to Woody." On *Freewheelin'* the world that erupts through Dylan's throat is threatening, alienating, and prone towards evil. If Dylan's debut was the sound of a young man possessed by the blues and the myth of independence he could fashion through their pain and comic release, *Freewheelin'* is the young hero's full-gainer dive into self-expression, jammed with promise both in the range it exploits from the same resources (one man and his guitar) and in its futuristic language.

If Dylan's voice rang cocky on his first album, *Freewheelin'* hitches to it a songwriting gift so assured it overshadows everything original about his debut. *Freewheelin'* is the record that cued the Beatles' ears to Dylan's sure command of words via his quixotic singing—the songs are so startling they compete with the confident, layered deliveries he gives them. His voice apes his harmonica in flights that shift between a thin, sandpapery baritone and a goosed falsetto, so that even on his static held notes his songs sound as if the meanings they toss off are in constant flux. Between the turbulent jabs of guitar and harp in "Walking Down the Highway" and "Talking World War III Blues," he howls as if fronting a band in full title; then, just as confidently, he quiets down for the hush of "Bob Dylan's Dream."

## hard rain

Never a crooner, and still roundly misunderstood for the way he mangles vowels, the 1963 Dylan begins to show a vocal presence at once charged and strangely aloof, and his singing brings this material a dynamic of multiple intentions. Amid cocky digressions and no-more-heroes-for-me iconoclasm, he strikes a vocal pose that makes the baldest pronouncements sound double-edged. When he sings "She once was a true love of mine" in "Girl from the North Country," you can almost hear him doubting what he sings as fact (what George Melly described as "his regretful acknowledgment of his failure to accept the chains which tempted him," in *Revolt into Style* [p. 96]). Even "Blowin' in the Wind" has it both ways: believe this song and buy into the worst folk generalizations.

Dylan suddenly seems to know his audience better than they know themselves, and he overturns their expectations of the folksinger as social oracle. As he summons the ghosts of folk's naturalist past, Dylan brings "Blowin' in the Wind" a gnawing awareness that this torch song of dashed hopes is nothing if not a contradiction in terms. With his poker-faced recitations full of as much description as contempt for inhumanity ("How many times can a man turn his head / And pretend that he just doesn't see?"), he dares his listeners to fill in the gaps. Dylan's voice always seems to be harboring secret messages; you never know whether to take him at his word. This goes double when he essays the psychosurreal imagery of "Hard Rain" with nonplussed aplomb.

With the topicality of "Masters of War," the unmentioned-but-pervasive presence of the University of Mississippi's first black student, James Meredith, in "Oxford Town," and the nuclear consciousness of "Hard Rain," *Freewheelin'* is misunderstood as the epitome of Dylan's political poetic, a blueprint for a career his folk admirers would have preferred he stick to. But the record is larger than that: it combines his first record's blues themes ("Down the Highway") and his gift for anthems ("Blowin' in the Wind") with his swing to free-style imagery ("A Hard

Rain's A-Gonna Fall," "I Shall Be Free") and left-field comic yarns ("Bob Dylan's Blues," "Talking World War III Blues"). *Freewheelin'* is a new breed: a drumless rock album with lead guitar impersonating a harmonica, brash attitudes confounding stock assumptions, vision in every common touch. (It's an irony of Dylan's career that when he pares his music down to three-chord electric rock, his language inflates to capricious, inscrutable word-fancies.)

Critics have noted the religious imagery as prophetic to Dylan's late-seventies born-again-Christian phase, even though it isn't until "The Times They Are A-Changin' " that he assumes the messianic voice. ("Blowin' in the Wind" seems to promise retribution if the questions it poses aren't answered, but its poetry lies in how it simply lets all the inhumanity dangle.) He works both Judas and Jesus into "Masters of War," and Adam and Eve into "Bob Dylan's Dream"; and "A Hard Rain's A-Gonna Fall" is an apocalyptic vision of biblical proportions. But add comic turns like "I Shall Be Free" (adapted from Woody Guthrie's song of the same name) and "Honey, Just Allow Me One More Chance," and the larger impression is of a folkie who understands the limits of his genre, deliberately dabbles with its boundaries, and keeps a certain distance from self-seriousness (and cues his audience to do the same) as he lobs his first original "folk" record onto an unsuspecting public.

**"Blowin' in the Wind"** is the number that single-handedly sparks Dylan's career, and puts *Freewheelin'* on most listeners' turntables. With Peter, Paul and Mary's number-two hit in July of 1963 (it followed their March outing, "Puff the Magic Dragon"), Dylan's stock as a songwriter bolts, even though Peter, Paul and Mary do to "Blowin' in the Wind" what Pat Boone does to Little Richard's "Tutti Frutti." They not only sanitize it, they gloss over its dust-bowl echoes, the tired-but-wise understatement in Dylan's delivery. Not that they rob the song of its pungency—there

isn't much to rob, but they do fashion it into a collegiate bromide, give it a tenor of poetic respectability that Dylan underplays. With the overripe sincerity of Peter, Paul and Mary in
your head, it's easy to forget how persuasively the song sidesteps
its own questions.

Dylan sings the song knowingly—he means these questions
to be larger than any answers. In challenging listeners to hear
past the song's inadequacies, his version may be the best example of why he's his own best interpreter. Dylan's poker-faced
delivery gives some of the overblown imagery the necessary
balance—the first verse alone pits a white dove against flying
cannonballs. Its plucked-from-the-air naturalism has turned
"Blowin' in the Wind" into the kind of generic weeper that the
Beatles' "Yesterday" became: taken out of context, these two
songs send off incomplete signals about what these writers have
to say to the world. As Dylan said in 1966:

> I was actually most afraid of death in those first years around
> New York. When I started writing all those songs and every-
> one started calling me a genius—genius this and genius
> that. I knew it was bull, because I still hadn't written what
> I wanted to. I had written "Blowin' in the Wind," but I
> wasn't satisfied with that. I was never satisfied with "Blow-
> in' in the Wind." I wrote that in ten minutes. "Blowin' in
> the Wind" was a lucky classic song. No more, no less than
> "Your Cheatin' Heart." But it was one-dimensional. (Shel-
> ton, p. 60)

Dylan's own estimation of the song doesn't change over the
years, even though the fact that such a social-minded piece could
reach the top of the pop charts was something Guthrie lived to
see someone else accomplish. Even though it never mentions
freedom rides, lunch counters, or bus strikes, "Blowin' in the
Wind" becomes even more identified with Martin Luther King's
nonviolent movement than Dylan's more explicit civil rights

songs (like "Only a Pawn in Their Game," "The Lonesome Death of Hattie Carroll," and "The Death of Emmett Till"). Compact, elegiac, and as terse melodically as anything by Guthrie, "Blowin' in the Wind" is a modest offering of intuitive hymnody, the most adaptable of his early songs, the most widely covered: Stevie Wonder's rendition in 1966 extends the link between folk and soul message songs that Sam Cooke had initiated with "A Change Is Gonna Come" a year earlier. But at the time, seasoned folkies saw right through the song's naiveté. In Bob Spitz's *Dylan*, Dave Van Ronk remembered reacting to it with a mixture of incredulity and jealousy:

> "Jesus, Bobby—what an incredibly dumb song! I mean, what the hell is 'blowing in the wind?' " . . . I figured Bobby could grind out a tune like that on the worst day he ever had in his life. . . . [But a few weeks later] I was walking through Washington Square Park and heard a kid singing: "How much wood could a woodchuck chuck if a woodchuck could chuck wood / The answer, my friend, is blowin' in the wind." At that point, I knew Bobby had a smash on his hands! (p. 193)

When Dylan returns to the song at the Bangla Desh concert in 1971, it's the only number in his set of mid-sixties chestnuts that veers into nostalgia. By then, "Blowin' in the Wind" is so much a piece of sixties oral mythology that it seems as if it's been floating in the air his audience breathed for at least a generation. It serves as the emotionally nostalgic tour-closing with the Band in San Francisco in 1974, an electrified throwback on *Before the Flood*, also with the Band. (Like the rest of the early songs he returns to on *Bob Dylan at Budokan* in 1978, the cheesy "Blowin' in the Wind" makeover is unflattering.)

•　　•　　•

## hard rain

**When it comes** to personal affairs, folk stances are generally conciliatory, rock poses confrontational. The two original love songs
on *Freewheelin'* jumble these attitudes: confrontation is undercut with self-doubt, sour grapes softened by affection. "Don't
Think Twice, It's All Right" is the last word in a long, embittered
argument, a paper-thin consolation (it's all right) sung with spite
(Michael Gray, in *Song and Dance Man: The Art of Bob Dylan*,
points out how the tune is based on Johnny Cash's "Understand
Your Man" [pp. 28–29]). "We never did too much talkin' anyway" is the kind of thorny throwaway Dylan excels at: the singer
hasn't wanted to talk much, either, until now, and the implication is that talking all along wouldn't have led to any different
conclusion. "You just kinda wasted my precious time" implies
that the singer's time is anything but precious: wasting it is no
federal crime.

The way the song's combative words angle off the more
conciliating guitar and melody lines points up the way Dylan has
suddenly transformed the stock folk formula into something more
complex. Like a number of his romantic broadsides ("Like a
Rolling Stone," "Positively 4th Street"), the song begs the question: if the singer is so pissed off, why does he vent his anger so
poetically? The care and compassion beneath the surface of the
song assuage the anger in the narrative voice. Herdman points
out how effectively the shift in narrative point of view is used:
"The effort to sympathize with the girl's point of view is not easy,
and in the lines in which he tries hardest to do so—recognizing
that this woman is emotionally a child—he switches, in order to
make objectivity easier, from addressing her as 'you' to referring
to her in the third person" (pp. 18–19). This is an effect Dylan
will retool to great effect in songs like "I Don't Believe You (She
Acts Like We Never Have Met)" and "Just Like a Woman" and
expand with later journeys like "Tangled Up in Blue." (When he
returns to the song on *Before the Flood*, he burrows into its
resentment, as though the wound had festered for over ten
years.)

Of the other romances, "Corrina, Corrina," the Joe Turner cover, is slowed for intimacy; "Honey, Just Allow Me One More Chance" is comic relief that eases the album out into the free-fall humor of "I Shall Be Free."

"Girl from the North Country" is an absence-makes-the-heart-grow-confused song, but it's suffused with a rueful itch, as though Dylan is singing about someone he may never see again—this isn't the same woman to whom he sings "Don't Think Twice, It's All Right." Unlike Simon and Garfunkel, who polished their old-world pretensions, Dylan worked against folk expectations as part of his strategy: he borrows a line from the traditional folk song "Scarborough Fair" ("Remember me to one who lives there / She once was a true love of mine"). The song would work on its own, but the vocal inflections Dylan brings to it make its self-pity palatable, its lost-love clichés less pat. In the first half of each verse, the melody soars, only to be tempered by the answer in the lower register, where declamations soften and turn inward ("In the darkness of my night, / In the brightness of my day"). Whereas Dylan rings out the first half of these quatrains, he swallows the final couplets, framing frustration with insecurity. The reach to rope someone else into the affair is an insecure move as well—his addressing his lover through someone else ("Remember me to one who lives there") magnifies our perception of the distance he feels from her.

**"A Hard Rain's A-Gonna Fall"** unloads a string of answers—contradictory, erratic, mercurial—to the questions "Blowin' in the Wind" is built around, and it makes a fiercer antiwar statement than "Masters of War." It transforms the naturalist imagery of "Blowin' in the Wind" into flashes of horror (sad forests, dead oceans), the nuclear fallout glimpsed on a ticker tape.

Because of the tight skin he fashions for this kitchen-sink disaster song, Dylan gets away with poets dying in the gutter and clowns crying in the alley. Analogies are incomplete, comparisons out-of-focus, and some of the lines don't seem to have any relation to one another—the sequence tumbles out at random ("I saw a highway of diamonds with nobody on it"). This is expressively untamed writing.

The numbers in the first verse (twelve, six, seven, a dozen, ten thousand) don't rise or work off each other; the number ten thousand crops up in the first three verses but isn't used to escalate tension. The second verse touches more on how it feels to grow up absurd in the modern age and quickly escalates to the emotional burden of physical labor.

The fourth verse is more "structured": "I met a young woman whose body was burning, / I met a young girl, she gave me a rainbow" comes in front of "I met one man who was wounded in love, / I met another man who was wounded with hatred." Dylan manipulates visual images to reflect emotional states so well that he gets away with a mess of easy comparisons— analogizing love's wounds with hatred's, for example. A young woman's burning body is set against the young girl's rainbow, which extends to love and hatred in the next couplet. Amid the scattered impressions that dart out from the rest of the song, it's a moment of poetic clarity.

The climactic fifth verse lengthens this formula and intensifies the song's brutality—it closes with a determinism that evades forced optimism ("And I'll know my song well before I start singin' . . ."). The song's shape expands and contracts: stanzas go from three and a half couplets to four and a half (verses two and three), and then back down to four (in verse four), then, in the last verse, four couplets with two additional couplets that amount to a closing pledge of allegiance: to bear witness to these truths and not shy away from them.

In anybody else's hands, this kind of writing might be dismissed as uncontrolled, an anxious hash of frets about the bomb. But Dylan's poetic havoc taps fears that were conditioned in his baby-boom audience by air-raid drills, in classrooms where flags stood beside triangular yellow-and-black Fallout Shelter signs. Imagine a neat, organized depiction of these ideas and something less jarring springs to mind—and something less original. Against what can be termed an early call to modern-era ecological awareness, much of the imagery is darkly visionary: he pictures weapons held by children, which summons the spectre of adolescent warriors in Ireland, Central America, and the Middle East three decades on; it's a startlingly accurate hallucination of how bad modern warfare will get.

"A Hard Rain's A-Gonna Fall" sets a visionary standard for all the fallout songs yet to come; and it's telling that for all its excess, it never sounds pushed or forced—a lesser mind might wrap these images of disaster in fey sentimentalism. Dylan can imbue a torrent of imagery like this with deadpan calm, as though he's reading a newspaper out loud as his thoughts wander, and still make the words ring prophetic. It's the opposite effect of the laissez-faire surrealism he pulls from his better comedies ("I Shall Be Free"), where cockeyed situations are reported with a stoicism worthy of Buster Keaton. Part of the song's success is its closing pledge of faith in a higher collective truth that depends on individual responsibility and doesn't take on more than what's plausible. Stirring in the centered cynicism behind this laundry list of frights, there's an awareness that only so much can be done, given the enormity of the military complex and the Cold War propaganda that keeps it afloat.

Compared with "Masters of War," "Hard Rain" isn't a protest so much as an apparition (over time, it suggests acid rain). With its grim, pointed guitar riff, "Masters of War" is acerbic to the point of absurdity, the reductive inverse of the imaginative sparks in "Hard Rain." Marked by the knife of bitterness and simplification that better Dylan songs steer clear of, it's basically a list that compounds sins from the first verse's guns, death planes, big bombs, and the evil undertow of bureaucratic respectability on through to the "young people's blood" that gets

## hard rain

shed in the name of some higher corporate God. It's the protest song as indefinite ballast, the one he disclaims in "My Back Pages."

"That's pretty self explanatory, that song," Dylan says in the *Biograph* liner notes. "But I never felt it was goodbye, or hello [to protest]. Not protest for protest sake but always in the struggle for people's freedom, individual or otherwise. I hate oppression, especially on children." Dylan's thought process, like his songwriting, isn't linear—it's associative.

If "Blowin' in the Wind" was something people could identify with, "Hard Rain" causes something of a disquieting murmur in folk circles—even its articulateness voices fears that most prefer to leave safely unspoken. Pete Seeger adds "Hard Rain" to his set; and at the Carnegie Hall concert on June 8, 1963 (now available in complete form on the CD *We Shall Overcome*), he sings each verse as if it constitutes a new scripture of commitment to change, and he doesn't sound at all sheepish about it—but the song's proportions seem to startle him, and he doesn't seem to have a sense of how Dylan's word rhythms can work in his favor. Joan Baez tries to add intensity to the ends of verses by emphasizing the buildup into each refrain (on *Farewell, Angelina*, 1965); but by stressing what doesn't need any more emphasis, she worries her lines, and the song finally cows her. It takes a refined British lounge lizard, Bryan Ferry, to summon up a new kind of modernist ambivalence, upholstered by synthesized anxiety, when he covers the song on *These Foolish Things* in 1973. When Dylan himself returns to the number at the 1971 Bangla Desh concert, he gives it a country twang that manages to transcend cornball. "Hard Rain" remains surprisingly contemporary.

**The waking nightmare** of walking around after the nuclear holocaust is among the more chilling images to go about satirizing in song. But if you're going to have two bomb songs on one record, you'd better subvert the prickly edges of "Hard Rain" with some laughs ("Talking World War III Blues"). Declared insane, Dylan tells his vision of postapocalypse America to a shrink, and the plot is rife with the kind of serendipity and bureaucratic obsolescence that bedevils the characters in "Bob Dylan's 115th Dream": down by the hot-dog stand, Dylan scares away a man who mistakes him for a Communist; a girl he flirts with brushes off his "Adam and Eve" line by saying, "You see what happened last time they started?"; a mechanized telephone operator blurts a static time message into phones.

Of course the irony of "Talking World War III Blues" goes beyond the idea that anybody could survive a nuclear rain. Dylan has his psychiatrist interrupt his session to confess that he's been having the same dreams as his patient—only the psychiatrist doesn't see his patient walking around in *his* dreams.

This isn't just a poke at psychiatric paranoia; it's a compression of the horror Dylan intuits in his listeners. The ghoulishness comes from a shared dream where everybody walks around with nobody else.

Communal estrangement—distance from one another, distance from one's self—is the heart of the matter, the underbelly of sixties solidarity that few seemed hip to until Altamont. This is the sixties youth culture grasped in a single image more potent than the nostalgic regret in "Bob Dylan's Dream," and one that is almost impossible to nail with a straight face. Dylan punctures the mood with a warning for the counterculture not to take itself too seriously: "I'll let you be in my dream if I can be in yours."

This is the closest Dylan comes to speaking directly to his audience's dreams and fears; and he expresses his co-commitment to their ideals through a good joke. It's a sentiment rock performers sought all through the decade, and Dylan says it only once.

"Hard Rain" is too overwhelming, too phantasmically aghast to stand alone—it needs "Talkin' World War III Blues" as a companion piece. If everyone shared the same dream of walking around alone after the holocaust, perhaps their dream lives could bring them together in ways their shrinks hadn't thought possible.

**Leadbelly, Sonny Terry,** Cisco Houston, and Woody Guthrie worked up a group number called "We Shall Be Free" during their travels together during World War II, a song Dylan adapts for his "I Shall Be Free." The Guthrie version mixes reassuring gospel refrains with barnyard hijinks:

> **I was down in the hen house on my knees**
> **I thought I heard a chicken sneeze**
> **Only a rooster sayin' his prayers**
> **Thank his God for the hens upstairs . . .**

Dylan simply drops the refrain ("We shall be free when the good Lord sets you free . . .") and reworks the number into a catalogue of contemporary ills with tabloid flair. President Kennedy calls him up, asks him what the country needs to help it grow. Dylan pops back "Brigitte Bardot, Anita Ekberg, Sophia Loren . . . Country'll grow." For some reason, the punch line to that verse as printed in *Lyrics 1962–1985* ("Put 'em all in the same room with Ernest Borgnine!") goes unsung. This kind of free-roaming, off-the-cuff satire can give you the impression that Dylan could make this stuff up on the spot, although the number was clearly a well-etched set piece, with a few interchangeable lines he inserted as needed. There's even a sidelong jab at his off-stage partner Joan Baez: "She's a humdinger . . . Folk singer."

**For a generation** caught up in the giant "now" of its size and political potential, "Bob Dylan's Dream" rings ominously prophetic of what will become of sixties ideals—with its flush of unrealized idealism, the song is like a seed for *Blood on the Tracks*. Like "My Back Pages," it looks back before its time and draws a lot of tension from the awareness that youth's immediacy can't last. It has a nostalgia for youth and easy times that helps make *Freewheelin'* less naive than *The Times They Are A-Changin'*, and gives Dylan's presence a sense of wise-beyond-his-years insight that matches his affinity for the blues. While "Blowin' in the Wind" and "Hard Rain" work off folk associations—not only in form but in tone—there's a streak of subversiveness at work in "Masters of War" and "Oxford Town" that springs more from American sources than from European traditions. And Dylan's love of trash culture starts to act up: the Lone Ranger and Tonto in "Bob Dylan's Blues," Rock-A-Day Johnny's song on the record player in "Talking World War III Blues," Little Bo Beep, Mr. Football Man, and Mr. Clean in "I Shall Be Free"—a cast of characters that will soon burgeon into a surreal burlesque.

As an emblem for the album's social and artistic ideals, "Bob Dylan's Dream" has a modesty that belies its insight—there's no question that songs like these will hold their own well into the future, passed on beyond their context to the point where a self-professed airhead like Edie Brickell can sing "Hard Rain" for the soundtrack to *Born on the Fourth of July* and remain as detached from the period she's singing about as the movie itself, and yet still not come off completely falsified; songs like "Hard Rain" have grown even more symbolic than their content would suggest.

For all practical purposes, *Freewheelin'* is the first Dylan album that conveys the enormity of his talent, with his debut a kind of primer, a set he might have sung to friends in living rooms and coffeehouses before he got to Greenwich Village—the kind of songs friends might exchange in the situations set up in "Bob Dylan's Dream." Holed up in rooms, making music, exchanging political views, searching out injustices, contradictions, hypocrisies, the singer and his friends revel in "laughin' and singin' till the early hours of the morn," in a time and place where "we never thought we could ever get old."

# hard rain

• • •

**The recording sessions** for *Freewheelin'* span a period of months between summer of 1962 and spring of 1963 and include a string of unreleased demos Dylan made for M. Witmark and Sons. Collectors cherish this material not only because a lot of the songs are still hard to find but because there are often differing performances of familiar songs that allow for telling comparisons. Many of these songs come to light on *Ten of Swords* on 1985, but it takes until *The Bootleg Series* in 1991 for some other *Freewheelin'* outtakes to surface: Dylan's version of the Village standard "House Carpenter," and "Kingsport Town," based on Woody Guthrie's "Who's Going to Shoe Your Pretty Little Feet?"

Dylan's first single was recorded on November 14, 1962, under the guidance of John Hammond. The song they cut was "Mixed Up Confusion," a nutball barb that wouldn't sound out of place on *Highway 61 Revisited*. On "Mixed Up Confusion" (which was backed with *Freewheelin'*'s "Corrina, Corrina") you can hear Dylan deliberately trying to shed his white-midwestern inhibitions, if only symbolically. It's the sound of someone seeking a common ground between his love for Woody Guthrie and his love for Robert Johnson, fantasizing a folk music for his generation where the gap between such indisputable greats wouldn't necessarily evoke the sexual primacy of Elvis Presley.

"Whatcha Gonna Do" is a gently ambling blues that bridges timidity with devotion, a morality list song that prefigures "Did They Know" and "Gotta Serve Somebody." "Seven Curses" pits the love of a daughter against a corrupt legal system: Old Reilly, a stallion thief, is caught and sentenced to hang. But when the judge gets a load of his daughter, who's come to bribe for his salvation with gold and silver, he tells her that he wants her, not the money. When she awakes the next morning, she sees her father hanging from a tree and damns the judge's deceit with seven curses: ". . . That six diggers will not bury him, / And that seven deaths shall never kill him."

In a pressing snafu that makes cultists swoon, fewer than three hundred copies of *Freewheelin'* (reportedly in a bulk shipped to the West Coast) contain four songs that were struck from the album's final edit: "Talkin' John Birch Paranoid Blues," "Rocks and Gravel" (which contains a verse he later used for "It Takes a Lot to Laugh, It Takes a Train to Cry," and would have made a fine B side to "Mixed Up Confusion," from the same session); and "Let Me Die in My Footsteps," a song about bravery in the face of death, and the relentlessness of history, which was probably left off *Freewheelin'* because of its similarities to "Blowin' in the Wind" (one howler reads "The meaning of life has been lost in the wind"). Greil Marcus will later dub the text "an anti–fallout shelter song"; a variation on Dylan Thomas's "Do Not Go Gentle into That Good Night," it becomes a highlight of the Manfred Mann–produced Coulson, Dean, McGuiness and Flint Dylan–tribute record, *Lo & Behold*.

Other Dylan songs from this period include selections on *Broadside Ballads, Volume I*, which features a version of "Blowin' in the Wind" by the New World Singers; "John Brown" done by Blind Boy Grunt (a Dylan pseudonym); "I Will Not Go Down Under the Ground," done by Happy Traum; "Only a Hobo"; and "Talkin' Devil."

## The Times They Are A-Changin'
Released: January 1964

*Freewheelin'* **bends** the folk-blues arrows of Dylan's first album and charts as alluring and unprepossessing a sentimental tone as folk would ever attain. By turns menacing and sprightly, Dylan's second record is so robust, so consistently vital, it's easy to forget it's the sound of a self-accompanied singer. But if the world on *Freewheelin'* is rife with possibility, subject at any moment to a sudden prank or an outburst of intemperate romantic anger, the emotional life of Dylan's third album is relatively severe—he sounds like a self-absorbed grad student who's grown weary not just of the world, but of himself. The charismatic title track, as hopefully incisive as anything Dylan has written so far, is un-equaled anywhere else on the record—only "When the Ship Comes In" trucks in hope beyond shortsighted troubles, and it wouldn't sound out of place on *Freewheelin'*. It's symptomatic of *The Times They Are A-Changin'* that Dylan turns only one of its songs (the beautifully understated "One Too Many Mornings") into a bruising rocker with the Hawks in 1966.

For too much of the record, Dylan succumbs to folkie social preening and black-and-white moralism; it's "Masters of War" stretched out into a concept album. Sulky, skeptical, and unfor-giving, songs like "Ballad of Hollis Brown" and "The Lonesome Death of Hattie Carroll" color Dylan's idealistic streak with strict pessimism. Framed by an insistently fatalistic guitar ostinato that echoes "Masters of War," "Hollis Brown" tells the story of a man who kills his family and himself out of desperate poverty. The last verse's tit-for-tat "seven new people born" sounds forced, tacked on for symbolism's sake.

Some of these songs soon re-emerge in better form: "With God on Our Side," a song that slows during each verse as it grinds to its war-is-inevitable conclusion, comes back as the finely bal-anced essay on the price of innocence in "Gates of Eden" on *Bringing It All Back Home*; "Restless Farewell" is the unsteady portent for "My Back Pages"; "Boots of Spanish Leather" is Dylan stealing the melody and sentiment of "Girl from the North Country" from himself. And if humor is the litmus test of Dylan's best work, *The Times They Are A-Changin'* is pretty grim stuff. The cockamamie glint of "I Shall Be Free" has vanished, and the upbeat songs don't flesh out his serious side the way his hoots

and freckles do in "Honey, Just Allow Me One More Chance."
And even the best songs ("Only a Pawn in Their Game," "When
the Ship Comes In," "One Too Many Mornings," the title cut)
don't sound like they have "A Hard Rain's A-Gonna Fall" behind
them. This third record is devoid of any surrealist experiments,
and along with the lack of humor, that makes it sound like a step
sideways, as though *Freewheelin'* might have been a fluke.
(Much of Dylan's career will have this fluky air.) Compared with
the openly naive expression on the cover of his first album,
where he looks prepubescent (which only makes the death
themes he sings about all the more charming when he apes an
older man's voice), his third album's cover-photo demeanor is
folkie stern and New York cynical, as though he takes the world's
injustices personally and holds a self-righteous grudge against
those not as correct and enlightened as he is. As Joan Baez
recounts, this is only partially true:

> You know when he wrote "When the Ship Comes In"? That
> was amazing, the history of that little song. We were driv-
> ing around the East Coast, we were out in the boondocks
> somewhere, and I had a concert to give. I don't even know
> whether he was singing with me at that point, but he and
> I were driving together and we stopped. I said, "Run in and
> see if this is the right place," so he went in and came out
> and said, "Hey there's no reservations here." I said, "You
> sure?" and I went in and they said, "Hello, Miss Baez,
> we've been waiting for you." And I said, "Hold it for a
> minute. I want an extra room, please," And then Bobby
> walked in, and he was all innocent and looking shitty as all
> hell and I said, "Give this gentleman a room." And they said,
> "Oh certainly," but they wouldn't talk to him. He had said,
> "Does Joan Baez have a room here?" and they had said "No."
> And he went out. So then he went to his room and wrote
> "When the Ship Comes In": "Your days are numbered."
> He wrote it that night, took him exactly one evening to

write it, he was so pissed. "Hey, hey I'm writin' something. Hey, I'm writin' something." I couldn't believe it, to get back at those idiots so fast. (Scaduto, p. 208)

In retrospect, this record has the most Old Testament imagery of his first three efforts and sketches the roots of conversion to Evangelical Christianity in the late 1970s. Christian humanism is the subtext of the racial parables, and the funniest song, "When the Ship Comes In," is laced with Old Testament imagery ("Oh the fishes will laugh . . . / And the seagulls they'll be smiling"). "With God on Our Side" is a political potboiler that negates the rationalizations of twentieth-century history; it's like Paul Goodman's coming-of-age-under-Eisenhower account, *Growing Up Absurd*, set to song, a generational gauntlet tossed to expose the speciousness of the Cold War mentality. Next to the other social-minded efforts (the title song, "Ballad of Hollis Brown," "Only a Pawn in Their Game," "When the Ship Comes In," and "Hattie Carroll"), "With God on Our Side" draws the line for those born long enough after World War I to find its issues blurry ("the reason for fightin' / I never did get") and who view the forgiveness of the World War II Germans as a farce. With six million murdered, fried in ovens, the numbers alone are numbing. This song manages to voice political savvy mixed with generational naiveté, just as Tom Hayden and the Students for a Democratic Society would when challenging the fervid anticommunism of the Old Left by drafting their Port Huron Statement. "With God on Our Side" gets a fine cover from the British band Manfred Mann in 1965, and the Neville Brothers give it a hymnlike setting for Aaron Neville's angelic tenor on *Yellow Moon* in 1989.

With all the righteous indignation in the air, you'd think Dylan's lovers might want to duck for cover. But the personal songs here are less assaultive than "Don't Think Twice, It's All Right." "One Too Many Mornings" casts a ruminative spell; it's the sound of someone too smitten by love to harbor regrets, grown too independent to consider a reunion. Compared with the black-and-white stridency of some of its predecessors, the performance is ineffably soft and lithe, even when he clips the ends of words or his harmonica shifts suddenly from chord to chord. "One Too Many Mornings" becomes a staple of his concerts from here on: tight-fisted rage against loss with the Hawks during their tour of England in 1966; a seasoned standard by the time the Rolling Thunder ensemble gets a crack at it in 1976 on *Hard Rain*. "North Country Blues" shows off Dylan's flair for making the traditional seem contemporary. An autobiographical piece that captures the dead-end sensibility of mining ghost towns all across the northern Midwest, this is the closest Dylan brings his narrative skills and social insight to bear on his own background.

"North Country Blues" is about working-class destitution, like Bruce Springsteen's "Seeds" (from *Bruce Springsteen and The E Street Band Live: 1975–85*, 1986), only disguised just enough to keep it from being about Hibbing specifically. (The second part of "11 Outlined Epitaphs" is graphically explicit.) And since the voice of the song is female (a turn of gender, the way Baez sings male voices), it allows Dylan to dramatize the demoralizing effects of the mining company's decision to hire cheaper labor in South America. Dylan later devotes a whole song to this subject in "Union Sundown" on *Infidels* (1984). The verse where the narrator's husband takes flight in despair over his unemployment is the most writerly: "As he talked to himself, / This silence of tongues it was building."

"Boots of Spanish Leather" is a whipped-puppy farewell; "Restless Farewell" bids good-bye with lingering hesitancy, like someone who knows it's time to move on but who insists on one last song, which turns into an evening's sad reverie. In retrospect, the good-byes Dylan is offering turn out to be salutations to folk and its more narrow-minded followers. But in the context of this record, it sounds like Dylan is so weary of bawling out the

government and the relentless tides of history, he's too dogged
to light into his women.

**Most Dylan records** resist sequential interpretation—individual
ideas take precedence over song order. But his third album
comes in with a rousing generational emblem of 1960s youth
culture, a clarion call to idealism, and goes out with a resigned,
self-pitying epitome that can be read as a placard on the decep-
tive security of fame ("Restless Farewell").

Dylan's title song belongs to its era: the sit-ins, the Freedom Rides through Mississippi, the brash hope of young civil
rights workers like Bob Moses, who volunteered to help the
South's voter-registration drive amid life-threatening conditions.
"This was definitely a song with a purpose," Dylan says in the
liner notes to *Biograph*, where he acknowledges that it was based
on Irish and Scottish folk songs, most notably:

> "Come All Ye Bold Highway Men," "Come All Ye Miners,"
> "Come All Ye Tender Hearted Maidens." "I wanted to
> write a big song," Dylan said, "some kind of theme song, ya
> know, with short concise verses that piled up on each other
> in a hypnotic way. . . ."

By this point, the civil rights movement and the folk movement were combined. Dylan played "The Times They Are
A-Changin' " the night John F. Kennedy was shot and it became
his opening song.

These ongoing ties between folk and civil-rights movements
went beyond convenience; they were the link between the left-
wing Jewish intellectuals and the black-consciousness activists
that would procure a student organizer–leftist like the Students
for a Democratic Society's Al Lowenthal on the one hand, and on
the other, Martin Luther King, Jr.'s deputy Stanley Levison,
who was mistakenly hunted as a Communist by J. Edgar

Hoover's FBI. Although wary of becoming too closely identified with leftist causes as a guitar-toting crank, Dylan did join Pete Seeger on a trip to Mississippi for a demonstration in 1963.

Like "Blowin' in the Wind," "The Times They Are A-Changin' " is allusive rather than specific, and utopian in a way that tapped—and fueled—the people-power spirit that grew into the War on Poverty and the antiwar demonstrations. With its allusions to biblical ideals, it's part of what saved Dylan's cynical side from its overbearing tendencies: because this record conformed to the social-protest hopes of the folkie crowd Dylan had conquered and would soon outgrow, you might think Dylan had nothing on his mind but the failure of the American dream (equal rights) and his own romantic riddles.

But the song did more than voice the call to action: it defined a generation's values simply by articulating its potential. If its listeners deserved songs as good as this, and performers as good as Dylan, then the society they might shape together deserved the same ideological heights. It's a measure of this song's sure sense of craft and uplift that it throws a positive shadow on the laundry list of social ills it precedes. John Herdman writes about the line "As the present now will later be last":

> Its implied corollary is that the future, in which the reversal of fortune which is the theme of the song will take place, will then be the present, as immediate and real as now seems the present which will then be past. The contrast between present and past is focused by the ending of three lines with the word "no," each time preceded or followed, or both, by rhymes ending in "-ast." The sense of insecurity induced by this menacing stress on the present is now intensified by the most ominous and far-reaching statement of all—"the order is rapidly fadin'. . . ." (pp. 86–89)

Herdman goes on to defend the reggae version of this song on the *At Budokan* album (1978), an example of Dylan's radical reworking of a standard never getting off the ground. Other revivals of the song also tend to ring hollow: Graham Nash, Carly Simon, and others try it out at the No Nukes concerts in 1979, but their celebrity posturing gets in the way of the song's relevance. It's like they're summoning the ghosts of the irreproachable sixties to sanctify their antinuclear cause with the beatific afterglow of an ageless epoch. The song is not a civics lesson.

**Medgar Evers was an NAACP** field secretary in Jackson, Mississippi, who was shot down outside his home after the spontaneous nonviolent demonstrations he oversaw in June of 1963, in the weeks following Martin Luther King's breakthrough in Birmingham. His murder occurred on the same day that a Buddhist monk named Trich Qhan Duc publicly immolated himself in downtown Saigon. The events link not only the civil rights strife with the elevating tensions that would soon see U.S. troops all over Southeast Asia; they serve as a microcosm of the racial and political upheaval that held the world in its grip during the early 1960s before stateside Beatlemania erupted and the counterculture heated up, identified itself, and became a news item all its own. As a key civil rights activist in the days preceding Martin Luther King's pre-eminence, Evers was the first person sought out by the civil rights contact in the Justice Department, John Doar. Doar came to Mississippi in April of 1961 to interview black voters as part of Robert Kennedy's campaign for equality through the courts.

Evers was also on call for a number of spontaneous demonstrations: he advised Air Force veteran James Meredith on his initial application to the University of Mississippi in 1961 and counseled him before he made his historic confrontation with Governor Ross R. Barnett the next fall; Evers joined members of the Student Nonviolent Coordinating Committee and comedian Dick Gregory in Greenwood, Mississippi, in April 1963, for a registration march after a dog attacked and bit a black minister during a peaceful protest march to the courthouse.

"In the racial picture things will never be as they once were," Evers said in Jackson's first direct television broadcast from a black, weeks before his death. "History has reached a turning point, here and over the world." The speech was a response to Mayor Allen Thompson's steadfast refusal to appoint a biracial committee to negotiate the same grievances that had just been settled by King in Birmingham: segregation of public facilities and discriminatory hiring in municipal jobs, like the police force. Soon, Jackson had its own spontaneous nonviolent lunch-counter protests going, which made the national office of the NAACP wary of wildcat protests they couldn't efficiently organize, and further raised the stakes of those already involved in confronting government authorities. Evers oversaw the Jackson uprisings with a mixture of forbearance and encouragement: aware of the limitations of his organizational resources, he nonetheless singled out protesters as heroic and watched in horror as six hundred schoolchildren were sent to a makeshift jail at the state fairgrounds in garbage trucks on May 31. By this point, death threats against Evers had grown common: he was the students' local leader, admired for his friendly caution. With Jackson quickly inflamed by the fervor that followed the Birmingham settlement, Evers himself was arrested outside Woolworth's with King's aide Roy Wilkins, who had flown in to show support, on June 1.

Two weeks later, with Alabama's Governor George Wallace doing his best to physically block integration by standing in the entrance to the University of Alabama, and Evers and hundreds of his protesters released from their cells with no promising advances in their cause, President Kennedy received a pleading telegram from King, accompanied by a front-page article in the *New York Times*, and was moved to deliver a nationwide speech on civil rights in an effort to calm the violent outbursts. That night, June 12, Evers was murdered in front of his house in Jackson after returning home from a strategy session; his wife and three children had waited up for him to celebrate Kennedy's extraordinary broadcast.

In "The Lonesome Death of Hattie Carroll," a rich tobacco-farm owner slays a black servant. The target is easy, and the message point-blank. But more than simply memorializing Evers, Dylan's point of view in "Only a Pawn in Their Game" out-radicalizes even King's nonviolent campaign: the lyric makes the connection between the systematic racial injustice in the South and economic oppression, where racism meets classism. In this way, it overleaps both "Oxford Town" and Phil Ochs's "Ballad of Medgar Evers." Evers, whose name in the news became the most potent symbol of civil rights martyrdom until King himself was shot five years later as he was supporting a garbage workers' strike in Memphis, is not the expendable pawn in the song: the pawn is the killer, the white man who is conditioned to lash out against an illusory black enemy. Evers is lowered into his grave as royalty; the *killer's* gravestone will bear the song's title. A line like "And the Negro's name / Is used it is plain / For the politician's gain" was no less true in 1988, when Roger Ailes's revolving-door Willie Horton ads stirred racial fears to help George Bush defeat Michael Dukakis, than it was in 1964.

Dylan took his first trip south in July with Pete Seeger and Theodore Bikel, and sang "Only a Pawn in Their Game" in Greenwood, Mississippi, to some of the same organizers who had worked under Evers's leadership. Bikel told Robert Shelton: "Bob was observing everything down there. He was also watching the reaction to himself. He was very humble to the farmers, admitting that there wasn't such a problem were he came from. Bob said he hadn't met a colored person until he was nine years old, and he apologized that he had so little to offer" (p. 179).

Civil rights activist Bernice Johnson told Shelton that " 'Pawn' was the very first song that showed the poor white was as victimized by discrimination as the poor black. The Greenwood people didn't know that Pete, Theo and Bobby were well known. They were just happy to be getting support. But they really liked Dylan down there in the cotton country" (p. 179).

At the end of August, Dylan shared the stage with Johnson, Baez, and Peter, Paul and Mary at the Washington Monument, to warm up hundreds of thousands who gathered to hear King's "I Have a Dream" speech. Peter, Paul and Mary sang "Blowin' in the Wind," and then Dylan performed "Only a Pawn in Their Game," as if to underscore the summer's events and keep the spirit of Medgar Evers alive as a symbol of what the thousands— black and white—had gathered to protest. "It was a rare moment in folk music," writes Taylor Branch in the first volume of *Parting the Waters*, "as the performers on the stage had gained celebrity status for themselves and celebrity for their overtly cross-racial tradition" (p. 877). "Think they're listening?" Dylan asked, looking toward the Capitol. "No, they ain't listening at all," he answered himself (Scaduto, p. 151).


**The general weariness** of the love songs on *The Times They Are A-Changin'* can be heard in retrospect as frustration with form, with the romantic notion of folksinger as social savior. Alongside the cheerless musical landscapes that predominate, Dylan sings to his lovers less as though they have disappointed him than as though he has disappointed himself. "Restless Farewell" is part apology, part equivocal self-abnegation that betrays a great degree of self-awareness about his insubordinate talent. The album's final words don't have the requisite sting and aren't as believable as the title track's golden-age zeal. ("So I'll make my stand . . . / And bid farewell and not give a damn.") Of course, the larger irony of Dylan's third record lies in whom he sings its title song to, which becomes not so much the journalists, parents, senators, and congressmen he addresses directly as it is the audience he will soon leave behind in a streak of poetic mind games and transmogrified rhythm and blues.

## hard rain

There were other songs taped in this period that might have balanced the moods of *The Times They Are A-Changin'*: "Eternal Circle" is a self-conscious song about self-consciousness. The singer flirts with an audience member while singing a song, and finishes only to find she has left. It's one of the clearest examples we have of Dylan's awareness of the head games that go on between artist and audience, and more revealing in that he gets inside the head of the performer's flirtatious fantasies: "My eyes danced a circle / Across her clear outline . . ." Unreleased until *The Bootleg Series*, perhaps because of a chuckle partway through, the song stands out among better-known Dylan efforts on the Coulson, Dean, McGuiness, and Flint tribute. "Paths of Victory" is an early, whittled-down version of "Chimes of Freedom" and sports an irresistibly condensed hook.

"Only a Hobo" is another Guthrie-style exercise about stumbling onto a dead man in a gutter that Rod Stewart saves from obscurity on 1970's *Gasoline Alley*. "Guess I'm Doin' Fine"— some of its guitar patterns foreshadow "Chimes of Freedom"— creates a mood that juggles melancholy with cautious cheer, and winds up a much greater count-my-blessings song than its lyrics alone would imply. It rolls by as if stubborn self-justification won't cheer him up, but untempered optimism might work against him.

**The two most** important songs from this period are laid down as demos but not released, and wind up being popularized by others. (Dylan's versions, recorded in New York City on October 24, 1963, don't appear until *Biograph* in 1985.)

The Byrds remake "Lay Down Your Weary Tune," which is even more fluent in images than "A Hard Rain's A-Gonna Fall." It's a pivotal song in his development from a political polemicist into a minstrel-mystic, a poet who has discovered that "message" songs need not be political to be potent.

As Stephen Goldberg writes, the song depicts nature "not as a manifestation of God but as containing God within its every aspect" (quoted in Gray, pp. 252–56). A hymn to music's instrumental spectrum, it approximates the suspended level of consciousness music delivers at its best—it's about the heightened awareness of nature and reality available to performer and listener in the course of a highly charged musical experience. (This theme is neatly ironic as a self-contained form, as a song being sung to a listener.) The natural imagery looks ahead to the musical transfigurations in "Chimes of Freedom": "The cryin' rain like a trumpet sang / And asked for no applause."

The other leftover is "Percy's Song," the haunting voice of a person who visits a judge to save his friend from a manslaughter charge and ninety-nine years in Joliet Prison—the accused was at the wheel when four people died in a car accident. Recorded at the same session as "Lay Down Your Weary Tune," the song borrows a melody from fellow folkie Paul Clayton, as Dylan discussed in the *Biograph* notes:

> "Don't Think Twice" was a riff that Paul had. And so was "Percy's Song." A lot of folk songs are written from a character's point of view. "House of the Rising Sun" is actually from a woman's point of view. A lot of Irish Ballads would be the same thing. A song like "Percy's Song," you'd just assumed another character's point of view.

Although the reactionary, corrupt judge is becoming a stock figure in Dylan songs ("Seven Curses," "The Lonesome Death of Hattie Carroll"), "Percy's Song" has a strong undercurrent of tragedy that rescues the cliché, even though the narrator comes off as a grief-stricken kid who's put out because a sentence can't be overturned by a sincere character reference ("But I knew him . . . he wouldn't harm a life / That belonged to someone else"). Even the repeats of "Turn, turn to the rain / And the wind" don't come off as fatalistic as they might—the song might be about the acceptance of misapplied justice if it weren't so busy fending off the acceptance of grief.

**down the highway**

We are people of this generation, bred in at least modest comfort, housed now in universities, looking uncomfortably to the world we inherit. When we were kids the United States was the wealthiest and strongest country in the world; the only one with the atom bomb, the least scarred by modern war, an initiator of the United Nations that we thought would distribute Western influence throughout the world. Freedom and equality for each individual, government of, by, and for the people—these American values we found good, principles by which we could live as men. Many of us began maturing in complacency.

As we grew, however, our comfort was penetrated by events too troubling to dismiss. First, the permeating and victimizing fact of human degradation, symbolized by the Southern struggle against racial bigotry, compelled most of us from silence to activism. Second, the enclosing fact of the Cold War, symbolized by the presence of the Bomb, brought awareness that we ourselves, and our friends, and millions of abstract "others" we knew more directly because of our common peril, might die at any time. We might deliberately ignore, or avoid, or fail to feel all other human problems, but not these two, for these were too immediate and crushing in their impact, too challenging in the demand that we as individuals take the responsibility for encounter and resolution.

While these and other problems either directly

oppressed us or rankled our consciences and became our own subjective concerns, we began to see complicated and disturbing paradoxes in our surrounding America. The declaration "all men are created equal . . ." rang hollow before the facts of Negro life in the South and the big cities of the North. The proclaimed peaceful intentions of the United States contradicted its economic and military investments in the Cold War status quo.

> **—Students for a Democratic Society**,
> the Port Huron Statement, June 11–15, 1962

To understand the Port Huron Statement, you have to understand Bob Dylan. . . .

> **—Richard Flacks**,
> Students for a Democratic Society, in Jim
> Miller, *Democracy Is in the Streets*

## Another Side of Bob Dylan
### Released: August 1964

**In a single** recording session on June 9, 1964, with a small circle of friends, writer Nat Hentoff, and a nearby table stocked with Beaujolais wine, Dylan lays down all the tracks for his fourth record. He tells his producer, Tom Wilson, "We're going to make a good one tonight, I promise," before he says to Hentoff: "There aren't any finger-pointing songs in here, either. Those records I've already made, I'll stand behind them, but some of that was jumping into the scene to be heard and a lot of it was because I didn't see anybody else doing that kind of a thing. Now a lot of people are doing finger-pointing songs. You know—pointing to all the things that are wrong. Me, I don't want to write *for* people anymore. You know—be a spokesman."

*Another Side of Bob Dylan* works off both the fallen innocence of *The Times They Are A-Changin'* and the expectations that that record stirred in its hero-lusting audience; it's a rejoinder that doesn't sound reactionary. As a set, the songs constitute a decisive act of noncommitment to issue-bound protest, to tradition-bound folk music and the possessive bonds of its audience. The love songs open up into indeterminate statements about the emotional orbits lovers take, and the topical themes pass over artificial moral boundaries and leap into wide-ranging social observation.

Framed by lighthearted morning-after retractions ("All I Really Want to Do" and "It Ain't Me, Babe"), these cold-feet turnarounds also work as songs about "Bob Dylan," the self-invented mass-media troubadour who discovered only too well how to stir his listeners' social consciences. In between, "Bob Dylan" unmasks his talent as too fertile—and too alert to life's paradoxes—to be hemmed in by his listeners' preconceptions. "Black Crow Blues" is a clumsy barroom blues done alone at a honky-tonk piano, goaded by a jesting harmonica (the number is a musical premonition of the blues skeletons in "She Belongs to Me" and "It Takes a Lot to Laugh, It Takes a Train to Cry"). And as Dylan's ranting version with the Hawks would soon dramatize, "I Don't Believe You" is hard-rock revenge packed inside the skin of the solo acoustic tradition.

To the 1964's true believers, this record's shift was troubling—it seemed as if he might have abandoned the ministry. To unsuspecting ears it epitomized what would come to be called "acoustic rock." The rock 'n' roll possibilities were tempting. The Turtles used "It Ain't Me, Babe" as a career launcher; the Byrds leapt onto "All I Really Want to Do," which reached number forty in August 1965 (they picked up "My Back Pages" for a number thirty in April 1967). These transformations make you wonder how some of the songs on *Freewheelin'* might have fared with rock settings: a song like "Don't Think Twice, It's All Right" would still be fine rock material for a drummer witty enough to play bull to the singer's matador.

Dylan's *Freewheelin'* songs took traditional forms as their models, but they discarded the notion that a socially conscious statement had to be tied explicitly to current events or situations. In the orations of Martin Luther King, civil rights issues had already taken on larger symbolic and historical dimensions, and the nonviolent struggle had passed from a sequence of individual strikes and speeches to a mass movement. Already, student activists like Tom Hayden, the leader of the Students for a Democratic Society (SDS), whose voice dominates the Port Huron Statement, understood the broader impact of collective action. By early 1964, the volunteers in the Freedom Rides were organizing towards voter-registration drives and a renegade delegation to the Democratic National Convention. Dylan's muse championed this activist groundswell: with "Only a Pawn in Their Game" as a first strike, he began to transcend the surface issues the way the movement's ideals led from nonsegregated lunch counters, bus seats, and public restrooms to enforceable voting and economic rights and eventually the anti-Vietnam protests. Dylan's poetics of implication grew to make his piquant suggestion ring more ominous than his straightforward "protest" lyrics—his targets began to include language itself. The second verse of "My Back Pages" flexes "foundation" into a verb.

The album's tone upends the chagrin of *The Times They Are A-Changin'*. The compassion that laces all the complaints in "All I Really Want to Do" and "It Ain't Me, Babe" is round with idealism and humor, and the baroque surrealism that gilds "Chimes of Freedom" flaunts an imaginative grasp of social subjects that returns to the visionary core of *Freewheelin'*. These "protest" songs are cut loose from topicality. That "All I Really Want to Do" and "It Ain't Me, Babe" work off a pure Jimmie

Rodgers yodel only makes their ties to wide-open American optimism that much more enticing (even though they are both essentially reluctant good-byes). "Chimes of Freedom" is the baroque-idealist flip side of the minimalist humility of "Ballad of Hollis Brown." Although less hyper, the humor is back as well: "All I Really Want to Do" may be more easygoing than the rockabilly inanity that steers "Honey, Just Allow Me One More Chance" on *Freewheelin'*, but it's breezier and more openly flippant than anything on *The Times They Are A-Changin'*.

Dylan is too often pigeonholed as an angry young man when more often—right up through *Oh Mercy's* "Disease of Conceit"—he's a strident moralist whose saving grace is a disarming self-deprecation. As many critics point out, *Another Side* atones for the rectitudes of *The Times They Are A-Changin'*, and "My Back Pages" stands out not just because it's his only unhedged apology but also because it's a thorough X-ray of Dylan's former social proselytizing. Targeting academia as the latest symbol of all that's wrong with institutions in general, and wrongheaded knowledge in particular, Dylan renounces his former over-serious messianic perch, and disowns false insights (he calls teachers "mongrel dogs"). As the ever-factional Left continues to learn, "equality" is anything but a hard-and-fast term. (Unfortunately, "My Back Pages" will become emblematic in an unflattering way—Dylan's moralist streak will need more hemming in than a few refrains of "I was so much older then / I'm younger than that now" can accomplish.)

A bridge between folkie rhetoric (albeit superior) and his troika of electric rants, *Another Side* is a rock album without electric guitars, a folk archetype that punches through the hardy, plainspoken mold. Built on repeated riffs and coaxed by the controlled anxiety of Dylan's voice, the songs work off one another with intellectually charged élan. It's a transition album with a mind of its own.

• • •

# hard rain

**"All I Really Want to Do"** is a gentle fear-of-commitment song that fans out in several directions. As a missive to the audience he's been busy building for three years, Dylan plays coy as to what this record will be about: on the heels of *The Times They Are A-Changin'*, the message comes through a hedging love song—a devotion that's riddled with frets about obligation. When he sings "I ain't lookin' to compete with you . . . Simplify you, classify you / Deny, defy or crucify you" in the first stanza, he could be prophesying his contentious electric set at Newport the next year.

Dylan is singing to several sets of listeners: his folk audience; those outside the folk crowd who may have been suspicious of his earlier self-righteousness; his own muse, which is carrying him afield of the folk domain; and to "Bob Dylan," his popular image, which, hatched as a Newport sensation a year before, was wary of how the movement expected folk's great white wonder to outdo himself. Linking Jimmie Rodgers's concluding title-line yodel up with the rampant Chuck Berry complaint list (as in "School Days" or "Too Much Monkey Business"), Dylan cracks himself up in the last verse as he sings about mindless mimicry in the name of emulation. It's a kindhearted putdown of idolizers who would remain stubborn about which kinds of message songs were worthy of his talent.

"From now on, I want to write from inside me," Dylan tells Hentoff,

> and to do that I'm going to have to get back to writing like I used to when I was ten—having everything come out naturally. The way I like to write is for it to come out the way I walk or talk . . . Not that I even walk or talk yet like I'd like to. I don't carry myself yet the way Woody, Big Joe Williams, and Lightnin' Hopkins have carried themselves. I hope to someday, but they're older. They got to where music was a tool for them, a way to live more, a way to make themselves feel better. Sometimes I can make myself

feel better with music, but other times it's still hard to go to sleep at night.

**With "Spanish Harlem Incident,"** Dylan begins evoking narrative through a collection of images that convey the quixotic spell love can cast, and his siege on the language fares better than his literal storytelling of a doomed affair in "Ballad in Plain D" or the cloying "Boots of Spanish Leather." "Spanish Harlem Incident" is a three-verse miniature, with a melody that fills in gaps that the words leave unspoken, that the voice implies but does not articulate. After laying down "Spanish Harlem Incident," Dylan turns to a friend and asks "Did you understand it?" The friend nods enthusiastically. "Well, I didn't," is Dylan's reply.

Like "To Ramona," "Spanish Harlem Incident" is a new romance that pretends to be short and sweet, but it's an example of how Dylan begins using uncommon word couplings to evoke the mysteries of intimacy. Its surface melodic cool is studded with loopy, love-struck detail: her "rattling drums" play off his "restless palms"; her "pearly eyes" and "flashing diamond teeth" off his "pale face." The imagery is oddly specific, yet Dylan's calmly suggestive vocal allure cues the listener to a heightened world of interior emotions, the slightly cocked way her affections make him feel ("On the cliffs of your wildcat charms I'm riding, / I know I'm 'round you but I don't know where").

"To Ramona" is sweeter, a waltz that extends the romance from ideals of emotional honesty out into issues of conditioned conformity: "From fixtures and forces and friends, / That you gotta be just like them." Not your typical tongue of seduction. Dylan has more than one agenda in these two songs: in "Spanish Harlem Incident," he's using flattery as a front for the singer's own weak self-image; in "To Ramona," he's trying to save his lover from herself if only because he knows he may soon need the same comfort he's giving her.

# hard rain

. . .

**The protest-song** ideal is rendered two-dimensional—even anachronistic—more by "Chimes of Freedom" than by "My Back Pages." Dylan talked to Nat Hentoff about his shift in attitude: "I looked around and saw all these people pointing fingers at the bomb. But the bomb is getting boring, because what's wrong goes much deeper than the bomb. What's wrong is how few people are free. Most people walking around are tied down to something that doesn't let them really *speak*, so they just add their confusion to the mess. I mean, they have some kind of vested interest in the way things are now."

"Chimes of Freedom" equates the civil rights movement's moral breakthroughs with the incandescent flash of a lightning storm. Swelling with natural imagery, the song metamorphoses thunder, lightning, and hail into transcendent bells of freedom that peal for all occasions and, more important, across social classes. "Starry-eyed an' laughing as I recall when we were caught" refers to civil-disobedient Freedom Riders, whose arrests and jailings fed the publicity machine and mocked the South's biased judicial system. It's an indirect way of fashioning a communal viewpoint: "We ducked inside the doorway as thunder went crashing . . ."

Dylan doesn't need to be explicit about his references: all ears instantly identified with the dream of democracy in his list of exalted peaceful figures: the gentle, the kind, the guardians of the mind, the poets and artists perpetually ahead of their time. It's a hallucinatory list of natural forces that achieves the same pastoral reverence as the vast geographical space of Guthrie's "This Land Is Your Land." The swell of feeling in the refrain defines the youthful fervor that fueled the civil rights protests.

Dylan dropped the song from his live sets before the year was out; and even though the Byrds turned in a softly glowing version on their debut album (in 1965), the song remained a towering sleeper until Bruce Springsteen covered the Byrds's cover to trumpet his Amnesty International tour at an internationally broadcast concert in Stockholm on July 4, 1988.

**Like "Talkin' John Birch Paranoid Blues,"** "I Shall Be Free No. 10" upends the Far Right's anticommunist hysteria—extremist attitudes that were easily parodied until Ronald Reagan was twice elected by landslides in the 1980s. In 1964, the *Sputnik* scare was still hanging in the air; Johnson's mushroom-cloud ads against Barry Goldwater made explicit the hard rain that grazed the popular subconscious. Joseph Heller's 1955 World War II novel *Catch-22* (which became a sixties totem) and Stanley Kubrick's film *Dr. Strangelove, or How I Learned to Stop Worrying and Love the Bomb*, both outrageously black comedies, went too far for some and got lost on others. Madness satirized only seemed to mock sanity.

In "I Shall Be Free No. 10," Dylan's buffoonery isn't as free-falling as it is in "I Shall Be Free," where sexual farce mingles with political satire, Willie Mays with Yul Brynner, Charles de Gaulle with Robert Louis Stevenson. The most startling he can get here is to grow his hair, gallop out to Omaha on a horse, and hang out at the country club.

But he gets off some sharper attacks, even if the approach doesn't sound fresh: "I ask you how things could get much worse / If the Russians happen to get up there [heaven] first." The *Sputnik* scare and Kennedy's space program were both about domination of the heavens, the frontier beyond the bomb. And the younger generation was having trouble taking all the Cold War bluffing seriously. The way Dylan concludes this verse— "Wowee! Pretty scary!"—exemplifies the Young Left's cocky impatience with the Old Left's maniacal anti-Stalinism, the brick wall the Students for a Democratic Society ran up against when seeking approval for their Port Huron Statement from their parent organization, the League for Industrial Democracy (LID). The LID was affronted that the SDS had seen fit to seat a former

## hard rain

Communist at its convention; Hayden and the other leaders couldn't imagine how such a gesture constituted a transgression of principles. "I Shall Be Free No. 10" is the kind of sarcastic wink at Russky paranoia that defined the generation gap—and the kind of hoot that *The Times They Are A-Changin'* could have used.

Another imaginary-electric prank, "Motorpsycho Nitemare," is a stab at the flamboyantly irrational parables that spew out onto his next three records in the form of "Maggie's Farm," "Tombstone Blues," and "Leopard-Skin Pill-Box Hat." A rock 'n' roll spree just waiting for a band, "Motorpsycho Nitemare" indulges Dylan's fondness for schlock archetypes: inside his traveling-salesman-joke parody, "there stood Rita / Lookin' just like Tony Perkins," and later, "Oh, no! no! I been through this movie before." The closing lines echo "Talkin' John Birch Paranoid Blues": "Without freedom of speech / I might be in the swamp."

**Instead of directing** his miffed, left-behind resentments to his ex-lover, Dylan aims "I Don't Believe You (She Acts Like We Never Have Met)" to an unsuspecting third party—us (note the shift from third to first person in the subtitle). With the advantage of hindsight, it would be easy to nail this song as a premonition, the sting he must have felt playing to a bewildered Newport crowd in 1965. But in the string of love songs that shoot off signifiers in directions outside love-'em-and-leave-'em heartache, "I Don't Believe You" gets dressed up in several different attitudes. Dylan's acoustic reading is somewhat agape, the emotional chill of a suddenly bereft lover. "It Ain't Me, Babe" is the sound of a lover whose epiphany brings release, someone who can walk away from a relationship without remorse; "I Don't Believe You" is the sound of the person left behind, which demonstrates that Dylan can identify beyond the perpetrator. With the Band, "I Don't Believe You" becomes a gale-force howl of wrath in the face of rejection. Greil Marcus goes so far as to fantasize that if Buddy Holly had lived, he might have duetted on this song with Dylan (or played pin-the-tail-on-the-melody with him). Despite their differences, Dylan and Holly share important traits: wiry frames, sweet smiles, swaggerless stage presence, keen musical intelligence, and often deceptively simple songwriting. To Dylan, Holly represented a particular rock 'n' roll archetype as a strange but nervy songwriter from nowhere (Lubbock, Texas) who dared to flaunt his insecurities, his differentness. And Dylan was certainly drawn to the way Holly drew out his vowels, lingered coyly on words and chewed up mispronunciations ("My Peggy Su-hu-hue, huh-hu-huh-hue-hue . . ."). But Holly was bitter in ways that only reinforced his inner sense of self-esteem: in "That'll Be the Day," he dares his girl to leave him, and reaches a biting assurance because he's certain she won't; "Love's Made a Fool of You" and "It Doesn't Matter Anymore" are frank about the humiliation of getting dumped, but more reassuring than defiant. Holly was the most unusual fifties rocker because he made such subversive sentiments lyrical and touching. Odd, yes—but Dylan would have shouted him down. And there's no sense in Holly's songs that he's singing to anyone but his ideal girl; Dylan will soon idealize his women—in "Love Minus Zero (No Limit)" and "Visions of Johanna"—but "I Don't Believe You" is the unalloyed sting of a romantic perfidy.

**Except for "I Don't Believe You,"** *Another Side*'s movement from "All I Really Want to Do" to "It Ain't Me, Babe" demonstrates how Dylan's romances have grown more implicative, less intransigent. His voice still cuts matter-of-factly through his more frantic word combinations, but there's less ambiguity at work here, and it's as if Dylan has graduated from the solo acoustic tradition in everything except the solo acoustic format. His language is so dynamic he doesn't have to put any spin on his delivery; the opening couplet of "My Back Pages" doesn't need any extra verve; it turns heads on its own. His songs operate poetically because he's singing about more than one subject, but you take him at his word; the invective resides more in the poetry.

Of course, Dylan's radical relativism worked a lot better in song than it did in action. "I know a lot of the kids in SNCC—you know, the Student Nonviolent Coordinating Committee," Dylan told Hentoff. "That's the only organization I feel a part of spiritually. The NAACP is a bunch of old guys. I found that out by coming directly in contact with some of the people in it. They didn't understand me. They were looking to use me for something." His brush with Clark Foreman's Emergency Civil Liberties Committee, the organization that gave him the Tom Paine Award in December 1963, is one Dylan's biographers love to detail. His slurred, off-the-cuff remarks embarrassed the cause and the organization:

> I'll stand up and to get uncompromisable about it, which I have to be to be honest, I just got to be, as I got to admit that the man who shot President Kennedy, Lee Oswald, I don't know exactly where—what he thought he was doing, but I got to admit honestly that I, too—I saw some of myself in him. I don't think it would have gone—I don't think it could go that far. But I got to stand up and say I saw things that he felt in me—not to go that far and shoot. [*Audience boos*] You can boo, but booing's got nothing to do with it. It's a—I just, ah—I've got to tell you, man, it's Bill of Rights, it's free speech, and I just want to admit that I accept this Tom Paine Award in behalf of James Foreman of the Students Non-Violent Coordinating Committee . . . (quoted in Shelton, p. 201)

Dylan was apparently unaware that the dinner crowd, which included author James Baldwin, expected a formal speech; and his drunken mumble about identifying with Lee Harvey

Oswald rattled the civil rights organization to its coffers. Thousands of dollars in fund-raising were lost after Dylan's ill-timed speculations on the universality of evil.

Dylan's swings of temper were conspicuous in other ways, too. At the Forest Hills Music Festival in August of 1964, he joined Joan Baez onstage to duet, and Robert Shelton reports he "never heard him in such poor shape. Dylan seemed to be struggling on one wing, never quite able to leave the ground . . ." (p. 263). He broke attendance records at that summer's festival, performing "It Ain't Me, Babe" and "Mr. Tambourine Man" at the Friday-afternoon topical-song workshop. His Sunday-evening solo set, which included "All I Really Want to Do," "To Ramona," "Mr. Tambourine Man," "Chimes of Freedom," and then "With God on Our Side" with Joan Baez, was also reportedly shaky. Still, just two months later, he performed a date at New York's Philharmonic Hall that is recalled as one of his greatest concerts. The program notes were Dylan's cackling prose-poem, "Advice for Geraldine on Her Miscellaneous Birthday," which was also used for the program of his October 1965 Carnegie Hall gig with the Hawks—"Do not create anything, it will be misinterpreted. . . . When asked what you do for a living say you laugh for a living." (Earlier in 1964, he appeared on Steve Allen's TV show to play "The Lonesome Death of Hattie Carroll." He also played harmonica on a record by his friend Jack Elliott, billed as Tedham Porterhouse, and piano on a Blues Project record, as Bob Landy.)

**Before going electric** and recording *Bringing It All Back Home* with rock musicians, several other songs are recorded and held for later release. "If You Gotta Go, Go Now," a single recorded twice (once with the same session men as on *Bringing It All Back Home*, once with the Hawks) is a raucous yet modest seduction that rivals "Lay, Lady, Lay" as erotic overture, "I'll Be Your Baby Tonight" as chortling conquest. "You know I'd have nightmares / . . . If I kept you from anything," Dylan beckons, all manners, feigning a guilty conscience. It's a protest-too-much invitation, and he gives it just the right veiled-smirk confidence. (Audiences ate it up.) It gets a cover from Manfred Mann; Dylan's version with the Hawks finally shows up on *Ten of Swords* and *The Bootleg Series*.

"Playboys and Playgirls" is a pro forma protest song that Dylan never releases, although he includes the text in *Lyrics 1962–1985*, and his listeners sing along with the tune at a 1964 Newport songwriting workshop. "Mama, You Been on My Mind" is the echo of a left-behind affair that rebounds off a couple of self-aware curves ("I am not askin' you to say words like 'yes' or 'no,' / . . . I'm just breathin' to myself, pretendin' not that I don't know").

"I'll Keep It with Mine" is taped on January 14, 1965, as a demo for Judy Collins, or for Nico (for her *Chelsea Girl* debut in 1967), depending on whom you ask; and until it showed up on Dylan's *Biograph*, it was one of the most sought-after Dylan performances. He's alone at the piano (in what sounds like the same session as "Denise" and "Black Crow Blues"), and his piano-vocal timing in this heady devotional is remarkable—his vocal rhythms float atop his piano playing with dreamy disconnection, and yet the combination evokes a fluid tension so airily seductive that it goes beyond druggy mysticism. (You can hear his back-up players get lost in bliss on the *Bootleg Series* take.) The song is simplistic, sincere; the performance delirious-erotic. Most people get to know this song through Sandy Denny's erotic white-soul reading with the Fairport Convention, on *What We Did on Our Holidays* (1968).

> There is a stage of hard luck that turns into fun, and a stage of poverty that turns into pride, and a place in laughing that turns into fight. . . .
> **—Woody Guthrie**,
> *Bound for Glory*

## Bringing It All Back Home
Released: March 1965

**Although Dylan's first** single, 1962's "Mixed Up Confusion," had a similar hornet's-nest buzz to it, the sound of "Subterranean Homesick Blues" was a trapdoor for most Dylan followers. *Bringing It All Back Home* unleashed wide resentment among those who saw electric instruments as the tools of commercialism, their hero suddenly a consenting pawn of interests he once snubbed. Much of the folk crowd comprised listeners looking for alternatives to dance trends like Little Eva's "Loco-Motion." True believers were flummoxed, but the emerging rock culture was taken by surprise, and the record captured a whole new audience for Dylan. The royal endorsement of Dylan's prophet status came when the Beatles sanctioned him in the pages of England's *Melody Maker* in early January of 1965. The article, headlined BEATLES SAY—DYLAN SHOWS THE WAY, was reproduced on the sleeve to the album's first single, "Subterranean Homesick Blues." And Dylan made the link between bandleader and self-contained minstrel baldly confronting the Newport folk types he would soon defy in person: with side one electric and side two acoustic, the record thumbed its nose at formula with the crudest possible layout.

*Bringing It All Back Home* seems titled to remind the rock audience where rhythm and blues began, and to point to its most promising native son. This competition between American and British musicians had not yet been approached as a subject in the music, and Dylan doesn't bother to get any more explicit about it—he lets the music make the argument. The record trumps the cocky, self-conscious irony of English R&B outfits like the Rolling Stones and the Animals as it outflanks the soft curves of the Byrds' West Coast "folk-rock." Dylan's rock doesn't sound like a response to either of those prevailing pop currents—it's decidedly edgier, less suave than Roger McGuinn's trademark twelve-string-guitar wash. Dylan's wire-brush textures accent his brash intelligence, his commitment to nonconformity, and his penchant for craggy, asymmetrical verbal rhythms. His affinity with the sources he shares with the Yardbirds and Van Morrison's Them coaxes entirely different moods from the obsessions they have in common, and he doesn't dwell on the tensions between white and black (never mind American and British) cultures. For one thing, Dylan, with a voice that outdistances his twenty-three years, already sounded older during his "protest phase," so his rock move sidesteps the teen lust that drove most of his English cohorts.

Instead, Dylan invents his own fixed contradictions: on the cover, he lolls in front of an urbane fireplace with a swank brunette (his manager's wife); albums are strewn about—Lotte Lenya, Robert Johnson, the Impressions, Eric Andersen—and on the back, the cover to *Another Side of Bob Dylan* peeks out. Dylan's impenetrable, eye-fixing gaze touts an extraordinary vanity posing as decadence, and the songs make a poetic leap towards heady insinuation with daring, deliberately unfinished similes. It's as though when he lets go of other people's folk-savior expectations, Dylan's language mushrooms, and the way he carries himself in front of a band brings him closer to an authentic, original voice, the sound of intellectually infatuated modernism that the beat poets sought first in the firefly streaks of bebop jazz.

Roping backup musicians into the charged world of Dylan songs might have been a sterile affair (witness *Self-Portrait*) had Dylan not had such a lackadaisical, just-play-whatever-comes-out attitude towards these 1965–66 sessions. Listen to Judy Collins's "high art" version of "Just Like Tom Thumb's Blues" (on *In My Life*, 1967) and you get an idea how much mystery and chance are involved in pulling these songs off—Collins's deliberate enunciations sound silly. With first takes the rule, Dylan got a spontaneous tension from his players, who hung on his every word just to keep up with a voice that juiced his hyper-beatnik verse with ironic manipulations.

Dylan's laissez-faire attitude tweaked expressiveness from unusual places. After his players learned the chord changes from his read-throughs, they were on their own for the one or two takes he had patience for. This meant that whoever he hired to back him up (be it the Mike Bloomfield–led ensemble he assembled for the Forest Hills date or the Nashville session men he hired for *Blonde on Blonde*) would basically be learning his songs *as they played*. This is like learning how to drive during freeway rush hour—reaction is all, and every moment is charged with a sense of nervy anticipation. The musicians didn't know what the next line was, never mind what sort of sardonic topspin Dylan's delivery would give it. It's gut-charged music-making without a net.

Inscrutable, oblique, balancing comic vagaries off odd spe-cifics, Dylan plumbs left-field emotions from improbable juxta-positions: the "frozen leaves, / The haunted, frightened trees," which distends into "the twisted reach of crazy sorrow" in "Mr. Tambourine Man"; the stubborn, cross-contextual identity per-plex of "I might look like Robert Ford / But I feel just like Jesse James" in "Outlaw Blues." And Dylan hinges entire verses on ambiguous conclusions ("She's a hypnotist collector, / You are a walking antique" as a symbol of captive affection in "She Belongs to Me"). "On the Road Again" is a series of dysfunctional do-mestic characters—mama, daddy, a pet monkey, grandma and grandpa, a wayward uncle, a milkman, and a mailman—in search of a structure, of situations in need of a theme, snagged by verse-clinching lover's rebuffs ("You ask why I don't live here / Honey, how come you have to ask me that?"). Dylan snubs jazz as the language of squares and elitists; it's no coincidence that his first electric nonprotest number is called "Outlaw Blues," or that his absurdist-comic streak hitches itself up to various forms of blues shuffles, like "On the Road Again." It's arty suggestiveness pumped out as primal truism.

## hard rain

As his rhythms get more insistent, Dylan's tone gets lighter. The romances ("She Belongs to Me," "Love Minus Zero") by-pass his earlier bitterness in favor of pedestaled devotion, with "It's All Over Now, Baby Blue" functioning as a veiled, albeit forgiving, signal to his audience. But the social songs trade accusations for comic affront with outrageous metaphor ("Subterranean Homesick Blues," "Maggie's Farm"), and the acoustic numbers extend the poetic sophistication of *Another Side*: "Mr. Tambourine Man," "Gates of Eden," "It's Alright, Ma" all inflate his message songs into broad social observations, the double-edged promise of dissident youth, and Madison Avenue's propaganda machine. With "A Hard Rain's A-Gonna Fall," Dylan flips the switch that turns dusty "folk" models into vigorous contemporary parables. Suddenly, these parables become as woolly and far-flung as the culture they reflect.

**In the opening sequence** of *Don't Look Back*, a deadpan Dylan stands in a deserted back alley—garbage cans punctuated by fire escapes—and drops single-word cue cards to a recording of "Subterranean Homesick Blues." Allen Ginsberg hovers off to the left, and stalks off with Dylan's professional sidekick Bobby Neuwirth after Dylan drops the last card, "What??" A minefield of street language wedded to the beat of an urban junkyard, the song's run-on spray of found images catalogs characters and transactions in a microcosmic detail of street-corner life (four verses streak by in less than two and a half minutes). Its shorthand characterization and throwaway tone hot-wires the album like the getaway car between a crime and the nearest state border. The song was recorded on January 15, 1965, along with nine other tracks for the new record.

"Subterranean Homesick Blues" ignites several unfinished stories at once, and the narrative voice streaks between Skid Row novice and omniscient overseer. Instead of the dilettante Dylan dresses down in "Like a Rolling Stone," the song is delivered to the every-gamin who takes in flashes of a hand-to-mouth street life, lines darting out like switchblades. Dylan's blank-stare delivery captures not just the tone of the score-freaked corner junkie, but the pace: the words go by so fast he's racing just to get them all out in time. His ashen-faced reading belies a jaded hipster's smarts.

The song opens with the image of an underground chemical mixer, sardonically named Johnny, an update of Chuck Berry's all-American everykid Johnny B. Goode, who's now dabbling with dope. The opening lines give us the duo's racket (they mix their own drugs), the hard turf they work (the streets are the sixties' handiest metaphor for action, protest, involvement), and the dawn of youth politicization (the song picks up where Berry's "School Days" leaves off: "Out of your seats and into the street . . ."). Robert Shelton notes how this string of lines is reminiscent of how Woody Guthrie and Paul Campbell (aka Pete Seeger) set up the song "Taking It Easy":

> **Mom was in the kitchen,**
> **preparing to eat**
> **Sis was in the pantry**
> **looking for some yeast**
> **Pa was in the cellar**
> **mixing up the hops**
> **And Brother's at the window, he's watching for the**
> **cops.**

In the second verse, Dylan's purview pans out to take in the surrounding character players, beginning with a laid-off cop on the take. Wariness of authority mingles with the dealer's search for quick customers. The first verse leaves off with this concise image of a failed drug deal in the street sty. The day's take is a dollar short of tomorrow's high.

In verse two, Maggie, a quickly sketched renegade revolutionary, rambles on paranoid about the bugs planted in her

bedroom. Indeed, the armed underground revolutionary guer-
rillas the Weathermen took their name from the end of this
verse. Dylan's alter-ego narrative voice keeps slinging warnings;
on the streets, the heat will nab you simply because you're
suspect—even if you're innocent, you're guilty. But the narrator
is always landing on words of caution: Keep your nose clean, and
beware of undercover (plainclothes) narcs.

Work is scarce, door-to-door pavement pounding the grind
even for a dope peddler. Life keeps slapping the singer in the
face, with the military as the only safety valve—government-
sanctioned murder is always the "respectable" way out. Authority strikes again: in *Don't Look Back*, this is where Dylan's cue
card reads "Watch It! Here They Come!" Night-life loitering is
summed up in a few deft images; hookers prop themselves up in
front of a laundromat; and the verse concludes with two terse
lines of cautionary wisdom, which doubles as a message from
Dylan to his unquestioning followers.

This "be wary" message is the thrust of "It Ain't Me, Babe,"
and "My Back Pages" expanded to include all leaders, not just
Dylan; here his references lump in Martin Luther King, Jr. (that
"fire hose"). As heroes, pop stars are no less fallible than nonviolent leaders.

"Parkin' meters" has aged into a symbol of mindless bureaucratic measure, but in this anxious dealer's world it's also a
metaphor for knowing when your number comes up.

Verse four sketches a cynically cackling history of the baby-
boom generation:

> **Ah get born, keep warm**
> **Short pants, romance, learn to dance**
> **Get dressed, get blessed**
> **Try to be a success**

The punch line to a "life lived well" within these parameters
point toward the thin rewards such values supply. The insistent

warnings about authority—the "Look out kid" couplets lacing all four verses—uncover the hypocritical veil of moral decency. The song skitters out with a return to the chaotic and unpredictable thrills of street-life vandalism.

As comically off-kilter as the song sounds, there's a great deal of scheme work involved. Everything is told in breathless glimpses: impressions come by in chaotic flashes; there's no time for pleasantries on the lam. Dylan's deadpan delivery is unsentimental in the best kind of way: he isn't trying to get us to feel sorry for these characters. It's a story of a homesick initiate interrupted by the hard-luck voice of experience.

This song gets a lot of tributes, both direct and oblique. Elvis Costello writes a song called "Pump It Up" that draws on Dylan's monotone word-frenzy as a model, and points up the minimalist debt of punk and New Wave. By the eighties, "Subterranean Homesick Blues" gets covered by the libidinous Red Hot Chili Peppers. But they don't measure up to the rhythmically daunting rap cover by Wack Attack in 1986, a highly unusual conciliatory move considering the state of black-Jewish relations in Manhattan by that point: 1984 presidential candidate Jesse Jackson's inflammatory "Hymie town" remarks, and Mayor Ed Koch's race-baiting tactics during the 1988 campaign. As an example of how rhythmic Dylan's words are, Wack Attack uses a novelty conceit to argue that rap starts here, with melody-free protest draped in urban clatter. Another song, R.E.M.'s "It's the End of the World As We Know It (and I Feel Fine)," cops from "Subterranean Homesick Blues" as a run-on (and not as funny as it tries to be) tour of the over-the-hill counterculture on 1987's *Document*.

**Among Dylan's mock epics,** "Bob Dylan's 115th Dream" is the most patriotically sarcastic in a category where even Dylan abuses easy targets like judges, preachers, and police. The subject is merely the history of the United States, an eleven-verse

comic saga starring Dylan as a pilgrim sailor—call him Ishmael—
who seeks in vain to spring his mates and their Captain Arab
(subbing for Melville's Ahab) from jail with tall tales, Huck Finn
fibs, and slapstick ingenuity. (That captain is a sly turn, mod-
ernizing Melville's hunt-obsessed Ahab into a pulpish Arab). The
theme is how the (ongoing) American adventure is as much experiment as accident, so take one dissolves into laughter when
the band misses its cue. The clinched, rickety sound of the band
as it responds to this yarn, stuffed to the gills with oddball types
and chance getaways, matches the indeterminacy of events that
shape the story.

The minute the *Mayflower* lands, Captain Arab begins is-
suing land deeds, but a cop intercedes by throwing everyone in
jail for carrying unlicensed harpoons. From there the song is a
series of slapdash vignettes, as the narrator sees his good luck
squandered via exploding kitchens, lost hats, pants (as collateral
for the sailors' bail), and boots. "They refused Jesus, too," he
protests at the door of a flag-bearing house; "You're not Him,"
comes the answer. (Not many who hurl Dylan's Christ complex
back at him take note of instances where he takes digs at it
himself.) "This Englishman said, 'Fab'" is a loving poke at
quickly dated Liverpudlian slang. At a funeral parlor, his friends'
plight fails to move a mortician, who simply hands him a card and
tells him to call if they die.

A come-on from a French girl leads to more shenanigans: a
bowling ball rolls down the street and knocks him off the pavement; a foot comes through the receiver of a ringing telephone.
Finally, the helpless innocent gives up any hope of springing the
sailors, so he sells his suit and flips a coin to decide his fate. By
now the ship has earned a parking ticket, so he tells a coast guard
boat that he's been sent by the Pope of Eruke. The last he hears
of Arab, he's stuck on a whale. When he meets someone named
Columbus on his way out of the bay, good luck is all he can say.

There aren't many better examples of America's cascade

through history that plumb the tension between the noble face patriotism gives itself and the wild, uncontrollable urges the newfound land inspired in its settlers. In Herman Melville's own words in a letter to Nathaniel Hawthorne, "Genius is full of trash." "Bob Dylan's 115th Dream" is another of Bob Dylan's dreams of self-realization, parading as the luckless hero in the thankless role of bailing his peers—and superiors—out of their self-imposed delusions. (Bruce Springsteen had a go at a *Mayflower* farce with "Stand on It," a single from his *Born in the U.S.A.* [1984] sessions, which glances towards Dylan's effort: "Well, Columbus he discovered America / Even though he hadn't planned on it.")

**Part of *Bringing It All Back Home*'s** coherence lies in the way these songs talk to one another from different sides of the same vinyl, making the connections between electric and acoustic material all the more synergistic. At fifteen verses, the dark, ambulatory psychological matrix of "It's Alright, Ma (I'm Only Bleeding)" is the intense acoustic complement to the run-on slapstick of "Bob Dylan's 115th Dream," and it makes about as much emotional sense. Snagged by a sour, pinched guitar riff, the song has an acerbic tinge, like the vicious retort of someone who is angrily shaking off maternal encumbrance—which works as a metaphor for larger social conditioning—and Dylan sings the title rejoinders in mock self-pity. If "Bob Dylan's 115th Dream" is about the meaninglessness of historical fact, "It's Alright Ma" is about the futility of philosophy. It's like a phantasmic bad-luck charm, and it bypasses logic so persuasively you're tempted to buy into the song's nihilistic certainties. Like "Gates of Eden," it comes close to expressing the dream life of Dylan's audience, only this time through circuitous emotional flashes instead of highfalutin surrealistic language.

The verses build in patterns of three towards a terse three-line varying refrain that works like a deflating punch line; it's a list song with summations so inconclusive that they only pry more frustration from what they follow.

Dylan has gotten so good at exploiting his song forms that sifting through these shards of psychic displacement becomes another chance to drop-kick the odd glimmer of truth: "Money doesn't talk, it swears / Obscenity, who really cares?"

Verse twelve may be the best expression of Dylan's obsession with the Madison Avenue's mass coercion towards sameness:

> **While one who sings with his tongue on fire**
> **Gargles in the rat race choir**

Part of what steers "It's Alright, Ma" is Dylan's angered determination to expose the hypocrisy that induces such mass-media inebriation; and part of what keeps these crap-shoot images afloat is their very potency as seductive illusion. It's less an indictment of the system than a coil of imagery that spells out how the system hangs itself with the rope it's so proud of.

**Recorded in June** of 1964, and the centerpiece of his live set long before a recorded version was released, "Mr. Tambourine Man" is Dylan's pied-piper anthem of creative living and open-mindedness ("Maggie's Farm" is the counterculture's war cry, "Gates of Eden" its epitaph). "Tambourine Man" incites folk-rock: the Byrds have their first hit with it three months after the Dylan version appears. On the heels of his "don't follow leaders" message, the song assumes an ironic glow: Dylan is himself the "Tambourine Man" whom people are looking to follow, and "Mr. Tambourine Man" is the number that best describes the imaginative places Dylan's songs carry them to. Only Dylan, who is busy poeticizing the streets, could make the claim "the ancient empty street's too dead for dreamin' " and make you realize how much mileage he's getting from them.

The song's method is slyly at cross-purposes: with an honest-to-gosh refrain, it fulfills a formula as it continues to subvert the language. A lot of these lines are evocative without holding up to logic, even though they ring worldly. Trippy and cut-loose as this adventure is, it's clearly directed at the establishment squares who take umbrage at liberated behavior. The song is a don't-worry bromide to the unenlightened that admits a good deal of the new bohemians' shortcomings ("With all memory and fate driven deep beneath the waves / Let me forget about today until tomorrow").

These overtones are lost in the Byrds' cover, arguably their best work (even though electrifying this song seems redundant). Like a Day-Glo painting dipped in glitter, the Byrds' version seduces you into the Tambourine Man's con, and misses the art of the con in the process. In their hands, it's less a song about questions than one about influences—which makes it a rare Dylan cover that both transcends and informs Dylan's original.

**On the heels** of tribute covers by the Specials and U2, Dylan's return to "Maggie's Farm" in England in the 1980s made the allusion to Margaret Thatcher inevitable. It's a good example of how Dylan's grab-bag imagery suits flexible interpretations, and how well his plain-speak delivery and old-world characterizations stand up to the recontexualization a lot of listeners impose on them. (The song had been read variously as a rock star's gripe to his record company, a songwriter's gripe to his publisher, and a singer-as-commodity's gripe to his audience-as-market.) "Maggie's Farm" is a list of complaints, from everyday chores and employer hassles to bureaucratic oppression. Maggie makes you scrub the floor; her brother fines you for slamming the door; her pa snuffs his cigar out in your face; her ma lectures workers. It's Dylan's stubborn individuality persisting above the din of society's manic-absurdist regimentation: "I got a head full of ideas / That are drivin' me insane."

But of all the songs about sixties self-consciousness and generation-bound identity, none forecasts the lost innocence of an entire generation better than "Gates of Eden." "Aladdin and his lamp" and "the motorcycle black madonna" shoot off signifiers in all directions: towards the idealism of the civil rights movement (the song is a second chapter to "Chimes of Freedom"), the bloated utopianism of Woodstock, the riot at the 1968 Democratic National Convention in Chicago, and the Cain and Abel tragedy of Altamont. "Gates of Eden" resonates far into its third decade as part of Dylan's live sets.

Sung with ever-forward motion, as though the words were carving their own quixotic phrasings, these images seem to tumble out of Dylan with a will all their own; he often chops off phrases to get to the next line. The closing lines serve more as convenient stanza-closers than as summations.

The opening verse sports images of free-flying youth with foreboding Icarus metaphors ("The cowboy angel rides / With his candle lit into the sun / Though its glow is waxed in black"). A catalogue of classical imagery, cloaked in bright psychedelic colors and fantastic verbal turns, gets clamped down by a foreboding sense of inevitable fall at the end of each verse. Eden is the predominant image of American naturalism, the field on which the Puritans planted their notions of rectitude on the new land ("There are no sins inside the gates of Eden . . ."), the symbol that "Bob Dylan's 115th Dream" helps to tear wide open.

"Gates of Eden" has its easy targets: in verse seven, a princess and prince discuss the gap between reality and fiction, plain double-talk for a Dylan-Baez bull session, which echoed across campuses in a million variations. But the next verse bestows a global consciousness with the fervent utopianism of cosmic youth ("free / To do anything they wish to do but die"). A world that is totally free, of course, has no need for laws or courtrooms: hence, there are no trials within Eden's gates.

In the last verse, the singer's lover tells of her dreams, without attempting to "interpret" their meaning, and these dreams provide the key to the song's strategy. Truth—the opening image of a song intoxicated by fantasy, illusions of power, luckless, self-deceiving soldiers and "Utopian hermit monks"—is a gliding "curfew gull" that twists itself to suit what each individual sees, feels, and hears.

**You'd think going electric** would galvanize the pent-up recrimination and bitterness in Dylan's love songs; but just to stay unpredictable, he bunts tenderness into the mix. "Love Minus Zero / No Limit" is hallucinatory allegiance, a poetic turn that exposes the paradoxes of love ("She knows there's no success like failure / And that failure's no success at all") and goes out with a shrewd poetic pirouette. After the lofty hype and concrete comparisons (he compares her spirit to ice and fire), the closing couplet sponges both humor and affection from what it follows—it upends the song's unguarded praise and points toward the dual vulnerabilities that steer "Just Like a Woman." In both cases, a woman's susceptibility is linked to the singer's defenseless infatuation.

John Herdman underscores how the concluding raven image establishes a "vulnerability-within-strength," how "it establishes her humanity: this is no goddess and no abstraction, but a woman who lives out her values in the world" (pp. 25–26). But it's not clear from Dylan's lyric *how* this is a woman who lives out her values in the world—or whether those values are noble except to the singer.

The final song, "It's All Over Now, Baby Blue," is one of those saddened good-bye songs a lover sings when the separation happens long after the relationship is really over, when lovers know each other too well to bother hiding the truth from each other any longer. What's intriguing about these romances is what they share lyrically with the social-minded songs: "reindeer armies" could just as easily show up on "Maggie's Farm" or "Bob Dylan's 115th Dream." Ordinary language has become inadequate to the sentiments Dylan is after. What shines through "Baby Blue" is a sadness that blots out past fondness, and a frustration at articulating that sadness at the expense of the leftover affection it springs from. "Yonder stands your orphan with his gun / Crying like a fire in the sun" casts the singer as an orphaned lover, with tears that would burn a hole within the largest star. Whether this is an externalization of the singer ("*your* orphan" with "*his* gun") or some fabricated character projected onto his lover's feelings (the orphan within *her* who is rejected, isolated within a fireball of pain) is left ambiguous. And the first verse's capping line (a play on "When the Saints Go Marching In") is one of those perversely comic images of death—this is a funeral, there must be a jazz march; it only makes the final wilting conclusion of the title line that much more despairing.

There's not much question whom the singer is addressing in this song: the forsaken lover. But the words rebound back onto the author—it's pretty clear that the singer is bound up in the feelings he projects as well. He may be the agent of the breakup, but that doesn't mean his heart is in it.

The version of this song Dylan sings on *Biograph* (from Manchester, England, May 1966) demonstrates the power he could hold over an audience, how he could put across these strange, convoluted verses to listeners without losing them. In the liner notes Dylon acknowledged its reference to a favorite Gene Vincent song, "Baby Blue."

Van Morrison's version with his group Them, from 1966, is as ardent and forcible a cover as Dylan will ever receive (it ranks with Hendrix's demonization of "All Along the Watchtower"), and it makes the point of how much compassion Dylan himself leaves unexpressed. The instrumentation is lulling (a Mellotron echoes Morrison's voice); but the performance captures the blues sensibility Morrison heard in Dylan's writing (not to mention singing)—the misunderstood outsider's struggle to be heard.

By this point, Dylan was also procrastinating a finish to "Love Is Just a Four-Letter Word," which he never released (Baez sings it on *Any Day Now* [1968]), a song that makes the bridge between his end-of-relationship blues and his giddy poetic streaks even more apparent. It's like "She Belongs to Me" crossed with the cynicism of "Don't Think Twice."

**Retrospect makes too** much sense of Dylan's flight from acoustic-only material. Looking back, the transition seems natural, and the backlash from the folk faithful wasn't so much about Dylan's plugging in as about his apparent flight from social themes. The audience that made him a star at Newport in 1963 wanted him to be the new Woody Guthrie, and songs like "The Lonesome Death of Hattie Carroll" and "Only a Pawn in Their Game" filled that expectation only too well. But Dylan had other ideas—or, perhaps, simply *bigger* ideas—than his audience. For Dylan, to master the leftist agitprop tunecraft that so impressed Pete Seeger was to outgrow it—he found the topical song too much like aspirin, as inadequate and shortsighted a response to the questions of Dylan's era as Frank Capra's screen good-guy John Doe had been to those of Guthrie's audience.

It's also clear on looking back that *Bringing It All Back Home* was the album that *Another Side* looked towards, and that solves the frustration with form that hampered songs like "Ballad in Plain D" and compensates for the absence of farce on *The Times They Are A-Changin'*. Once again Dylan has managed a redefinition—with a cunning acoustic-versus-electric layout, if his listeners wanted to get confrontational about it—that plays down transition as the least provocative of its qualities. Going out with "Baby Blue" is the most pat thing about his record, even though it works as more than a farewell to protest, a (temporary)

## hard rain

farewell to two-dimensional morality plays, and a farewell to direct language. Dylan had long been tempted by the surreal end of the blues that tied earthly experience with otherworldly vision, but this is his first step towards fashioning a sound to match his verbal fever.

## Don't Look Back
(Filmed April–May 1965; released May 1967)

> Bob Dylan's greatest initial dive into the rock 'n' roll domain, "Like a Rolling Stone," represents an attempt to free man by rescuing him from meaning, rather than free man through meaning.
> —**R. Meltzer**,
> *The Aesthetics of Rock*

**Compared with the other** pop movies that capitalized on sixties icons, *Don't Look Back* is self-consciously layered, unscripted, and has the erratic comic pace of a scrambled Dylan put-on like "I Shall Be Free No. 10." Its running themes echo the scope of Dylan's layered delivery: the relationship between Dylan and his young fans (seen waiting anxiously below his hotel room); Dylan and his coterie (Bobby Neuwirth, Albert Grossman, Joan Baez); Dylan and the press (he follows the papers avidly, and delights in their fabricated contest between himself and the newcomer Donovan); and, finally, the jocular, disaffected Dylan offstage versus the mercurial Dylan onstage—the two are almost irreconcilable. As a frantic tour through the bubble of fame popstars glide around in, *Don't Look Back* doesn't provide any primers; it simply begins with his arrival at London's Heathrow Airport in April 1965, and proceeds through stops for eight solo concerts.

The film stars Dylan as the beleaguered but game popstar, Bobby Neuwirth as Neal Cassady (sidekick as inspirational jester), and manager Albert Grossman as Colonel Tom Parker (there's a telling dance between Grossman and a British agent, Tito Burns, that's a businessman's analog to British cricket and American hardball). The footage, shot in newsreel black and white, projects a voyeuristic sensation of visually eavesdropping on backstage antics, private parties, and limo rides—there's not nearly enough performing sequences to offset the three-ring circus offstage. Director D. A. Pennebaker manages in documentary form what the Beatles' *A Hard Day's Night* does as narrative comedy: it shows Dylan as the center of an uncorked youth scene sent reeling over the celebrity surrounding Dylan's talent, with Dylan as the bemused center of the storm. His celebrity is as much a mystery to himself as to anybody else; but his hip smoke screen makes the rest of the world, especially the press, look hopelessly hypocritical and square. Dylan's songs are the cause of public uproar, but he can only be alternately oblivious and aghast at his effect on his public. "He is not so much singing as sermonizing," says a journalist for the *Manchester Guardian* as he reads his review into a pay phone. "His tragedy perhaps is that the audience is preoccupied with song . . . so the bearded boys and the lank-haired girls, all eye shadow and undertaker makeup, applaud the song and miss, perhaps, the sermon. . . ."

Shifting from hotel rooms to backseats to dressing rooms, the film conveys the discontinuous transience of life on tour, and Dylan's gentle, introverted quietude plays off of his angry outbursts. Onstage, he looks waiflike, younger than his twenty-three years, but offstage he acts much older. The brief clip of a scrawny young Dylan singing "Only a Pawn in Their Game" at the civil rights rally in Greenwood, Mississippi, the previous summer makes it seem as though *Don't Look Back* is the British arrival of a young backwoods troubadour. At one point, in the middle of a rambling discussion in which he jabs and intimidates a nerdy young science student/journalist before going out on-stage, Dylan says, "If we wanted to knock you we could put you on," and suddenly a flash of honesty appears on his face—he's just put his victim on about putting him on.

As the king and queen of folk, Dylan and Baez enjoyed their limelight, but Dylan conquers England unfazed about his debt to the star who all but handed him her audience. Baez follows him over to England for his last all-acoustic performances, when *Don't Look Back* is being filmed, and there is a long hotel-room scene where they trade songs. Baez sings "Percy's Song" as Dylan pecks away at a typewriter. Then she starts up "Love Is Just a Four-Letter Word," which Dylan has not yet finished. "Oh, God, you finished it about eight different ways," she says, and then, "Oh, it's beautiful. If you finish it I'll sing it, on a record . . . or something"—which by that point is no longer the dangling carrot it once was. Then Dylan requests Bill Anderson's "She Died for Love at Three A.M.," Neuwirth calls for "In the Shadows of the Warm Red Wing," and Baez begins Hank Williams's "Family Reunion." Dylan begins "Long Black Veil" (a Lefty Frizzell song the Band will cover for their debut), then a beguiling version of Leon Payne's "Lost Highway," and then Williams's "I'm So Lonesome I Could Cry," with Baez adding harmony in the background (Neuwirth prompts Dylan on the last verse). It shows how much mainline country Dylan had in his blood; it's his only gesture so far that admits as much of his debt to Hank Williams as to Woody Guthrie.

The way this scene gets treated in Dylan's biographies, you'd never know there was a musical discussion taking place. Dylan's snubbing of Baez for their signature encored duets is all that gets mentioned. Dylan was adamant:

> She came on with me, man, and I didn't owe her nothing. As far as I'm concerned, I paid her back. I told her while we

were in the States—that she couldn't sing with me. I told her that before we left. And she came on like a little kitten. . . . She's done everything I've done, man. She liked to watch and see what I do. . . . There is no place for her in my music. . . . She don't fit into my music. Hey, I can fit into her music, but she doesn't fit into my music, my show. It would have been dumb. It wouldn't have added to me, and it would have been misleading to the audience. (Shelton, p. 296)

In one sequence, Dylan is seen chastising his own guests at a hotel party. A drunk has created a disturbance by heaving a glass out the window onto the street, and Dylan refuses to take responsibility for it. Reasoning with drunks is hopeless: "I'm a small noise . . . I'm a small cat," the drunk insists. Dylan finally says, "You are what you think you are." "I am nothing," the drunk retorts. Later on, after the liquor has worn off a bit, Dylan leans down to explain to him, "I just didn't want any, I didn't want that glass . . . if you're sober, I didn't want the glass to hurt anybody"—and the early-hours song exchange with Donovan begins. Pennebaker told Robert Shelton:

Dylan's great strength is in the questions he leaves unanswered. It never occurred to me to supply *information* in the film. Dylan asked me if I could take out the fight in the hotel room. . . . He didn't want it to indicate that was the way he lived. I understood, but thought there were more important considerations. "You are what you think you are." What a marvelous thing to say! It's the fundamental existentialist concept. And Dylan's doing it, not like Norman Mailer, writing about it; that's what the film's about, so it couldn't be left out. (p. 299)

The party scene might be a parody of a beat-crowd reunion, with Jack Kerouac's friend Derroll Adams defending the disorderly drunk and suggesting Dylan read Behan. "Listen, man, why don't we get together and I'll turn you on to some things," Adams says to Dylan. "Dominic Behan is a friend of mine."

"No, I don't wanna hear nobody like Dominic Behan, man, Dominic Behan," Dylan answers.

"Dominic Behan is a friend of mine," Adams responds.

"Hey, that's fine, man. I just don't wanta hear anybody like that, though."

At the party of his hero, Donovan is beside himself, happy just to be in Dylan's presence. He offers up "To Sing for You," a generically innocuous ditty that brings squishy smiles to the faces of the listeners, as much from childish pleasure as from embarrassment. The guitar is handed to Dylan, and Donovan requests "It's All Over Now, Baby Blue." Dylan goes into the first verse, emphasizing the lyric "Yonder stands your orphan with his gun" as though correcting somebody's misinterpretation of the line, smiling it right. It's a masterful trump of Donovan's overpleasant minstrel, and the mood in the room changes instantly to one of fond respect (Donovan looks like he's just gone ten rounds).

**"Ballad of a Thin Man,"** the generation-gap diatribe that appears on *Highway 61 Revisited*, doesn't come out of nowhere. Late in the film, before his Royal Albert Hall appearance, Dylan confronts the London correspondent for *Time* with a speech that sums up his position against corporate journalism, and voices the youth culture's impatience with the establishment's recherché orthodoxies:

> Are you going to the concert tonight? . . . Okay, you hear and see it and it's going to happen fast. Now, you're not going to get it all, and you might hear the wrong words, and then afterwards, see I can't . . . I won't be able to talk to you afterwards. I got nothing to say about these things I write, I mean, I just write them.

After *Time* treats Dylan and Baez like a tabloid subject, Dylan comes out swinging for his interview with the news weekly. But *Time* magazine also symbolizes everything Dylan hates about the way he is presented by the "straight" press; and with the cameras rolling, he lights into its generic approach and style to its correspondent. "They've just got too much to lose by printing the truth, you know that," Dylan scowls. "There's no *ideas* in *Time* magazine, there's just these facts." After biting his lip nervously and shifting his eyes momentarily off to the side in discomfort, the correspondent gives his best shot at slinging a question in sideways, a stock interview potboiler: "Do you care about what you sing?" Dylan leaps on the question—it's even worse than he expected: "How can I answer that if you have the nerve to ask it?! I mean, you've got a lot of nerve asking me a question like that. Do you ask the Beatles that?"

Dylan makes his way out of this tense exchange by picking up the interviewer's bait: "Well, you appeal to your audiences in some sense as a pop singer," he tells Dylan. "Even if it's Caruso, he's . . . uh, you know, appealing to a popular, you know . . . this is a—"

"I'm just as good a singer as Caruso," Dylan announces. "Have you ever heard me sing? Have you ever heard me sing?"

"I like Caruso better," the interviewer dodges.

"Ohhh . . . well, you see right there now, right there we have a little disagreement." Dylan is smiling, victorious. "I happen to be just as good as him . . . a good singer. Have to listen closely . . . but I hit all those notes and I can hold my breath three times as long if I want to."

In the concert montage that follows, he makes his point. "The Times They Are A-Changin' " is still opening sets; "Talkin' World War III Blues" is as spontaneous and hilarious as ever, and allows another sideways swipe at T. S. Eliot and Donovan.

"I looked in the closet, there was Donovan" (laughs). "I'll let you be in my dream if I can be in your dream," he sings, even though everybody (the autograph hounds, the hangers-on, the newspapers) seems to miss the point.

"I don't like your new album," a young fan tells him in a hotel lobby.

"Oh, you're one of those, I can tell right away," Dylan says, signing his name for her.

"It's just not you," she protests.

"Yeah, but those are my friends playing with me—you don't mind me giving some work to my friends," he responds innocently.

The concert sequence at the Royal Albert Hall (attended by the Beatles) features "It's Alright, Ma (I'm Only Bleeding)," "Gates of Eden," and "Love Minus Zero / No Limit."

The film ends with Dylan, Grossman, and Neuwirth driving away from the concert giggling over the latest Dylan press tag: "anarchist," or British shorthand for his new antiprotest lyrics. Dylan takes a quick holiday in Portugal (which he will mention later, in "Sara"); tapes two half-hour segments for BBC-TV from June 8 to 24, 1965; and returns home to write and record "Like a Rolling Stone."

**While recording his** next album, Dylan made two celebrated appearances. On July 25, 1965, he appeared at the Newport Folk Festival with members of the Butterfield Band (guitarist Mike Bloomfield, drummer Sam Lay, bassist Jerome Arnold, with organist Al Kooper and pianist Barry Goldberg) to play "Maggie's Farm," "Like a Rolling Stone," and "It Takes a Lot to Laugh, It Takes a Train to Cry." This became the fabled public betrayal, where the audience booed a commercial sell-out from the previous season's folkie hero. But the stories that make their way out of this concert are by no means in accordance with each other— you can't hear boos on the bootleg tapes. Apparently, the sound system buried Dylan's voice, and many of the audience's protesters were simply yelling to fix the sound mix; the crowd behind them joined in the booing, and the scene mushroomed into what was generally taken as antielectric purism. After Dylan left the stage, Peter Yarrow implored him to return with his acoustic guitar: he gave them "Mr. Tambourine Man" and the fatefully emblematic "It's All Over Now, Baby Blue."

As knowingly ironic as that closing song choice may have been, Dylan might have gone further: that same month he cut a song called "Positively 4th Street," his strongest fallout with an ex-lover (it makes "Don't Think Twice," "Ballad in Plain D," and "It Ain't Me, Babe" sound meek). Twelve-verses of bombast that gains in incisiveness via its lack of a refrain, the song is one long tirade of unreleased tension, a complaint pushed uphill to a two-stanza, fist-shaking slur that turns the "stand inside another's shoes" adage into insult: "You'd know what a drag it is / To see you." The song incensed the Greenwich Village folk crowd, which felt it had given him his start—everybody was beginning to take Dylan songs personally.

On August 28, Dylan appeared at the Forest Hill Music Festival in Queens, for an acoustic set ("She Belongs to Me," "To Ramona," "Gates of Eden," "Love Minus Zero," and the debut of "Desolation Row," and then "It's All Over Now, Baby Blue" and "Mr. Tambourine Man") followed by an electric set with the Hawks' guitarist Robbie Robertson and drummer Levon Helm, organist Al Kooper, and bassist Harvey Brooks for a set that would stand as his boilerplate set on through his 1974 tour with the Band (except for his Nashville period circa 1969): "Tombstone Blues," "I Don't Believe You," "From a Buick 6," "Just Like Tom Thumb's Blues," "Maggie's Farm," "It Ain't Me, Babe," "Ballad of a Thin Man," and "Like a Rolling Stone."

If I told you what our music is really about we'd probably all get arrested.

> **—Dylan to an interviewer**,
> 1965 (quoted in Greil Marcus, *Mystery Train*)

Bob will suddenly ring me up and say that he's got a
whole new batch of songs together, which he'd like to
record. The studios are usually well booked, but it's
quite easy for me to get another group, no matter how
big, to vacate the studios. Everyone has so much respect for Dylan. The studio session men may be guys
Bob has heard and wants to use. . . . With Dylan,
almost everything is done live, with a minimum of
overdubbing. This way we can get things done in just
a couple of takes. I can work a week on the mixing,
and if it's wrong as far as he's concerned, I would do
it again. The sequencing lies with him. He's the boss,
but we work together. Dylan is a perfectionist. He
won't settle for second best. Dylan is so intense, he is
quite unlike any other artist I've worked with. I don't
really "produce" his albums, but just do my best to
make him smile when he leaves the studio.

> **—producer Bob Johnston**,
> (quoted in Robert Shelton, *No Direction Home*)

**Highway 61 Revisited** is Dylan at his most mercurial: misan-
thropy veiling compassion, obsessive and romantically plaintive,
the songs bounce off the walls of emotional extremes. From the

embittered insider cynicism of "Ballad of a Thin Man" to the gut-crazy, love-struck ruse of "Queen Jane Approximately," he touches more bases on *Highway 61 Revisited* than on the previous two records even though he's not shaking up his instrumentation as much. There's enough humor and self-consciousness lurking in the last verse of "Just Like Tom Thumb's Blues" alone to make his trademark evasiveness just another myth propped up for target practice: "But the joke was on me / There was nobody even there to call my bluff . . ."

This is the first Dylan record to posit protest as a way of life, a state of mind, something as psychologically bound as it is socially incumbent. To crude physical rhythms—square and stiff, undancelike yet brash, gripping—these backhanded potshots at history and the seemingly irreducible aspects of commonplace reality take on a hurdy-gurdy, maniacal ring and become raw, inscrutable emotional statements that touch on social themes by way of everyday banalities. This music sounds border-free—there are an infinite number of windows to enter these songs through, and they shoot off meanings like sparks off an anvil.

"The songs changed all the time," recalls Al Kooper. "We would try different tempos, he would try other words. Most of the songs had different titles. It was a long time, for example, before I realized 'It Takes a Lot to Laugh, It Takes a Train to Cry' was not called 'Phantom Engineer.' "

**A drum shot,** then a high, soaring organ, flanked by electric guitar and honky-tonk piano on the left, tambourine on the right. Before Dylan begins to sing "Like a Rolling Stone," the band's swagger only hints at the harangue that follows. Scorning its subject, and lobbing the hardest sounds to hit radio in the preceding six months—no small feat, considering the Beatles' "Ticket to Ride," the Four Tops' "I Can't Help Myself," and the Rolling Stones' "(I Can't Get No) Satisfaction"—the song smiles its threats. "Once upon a time . . ." is the most sarcastic fairy-tale entrance ever to kick off a prolonged insult. And Dylan's first-take serendipity pays off in spades: the best parts of this recording are accidental. Al Kooper wandered into the June 15, 1965 session uninvited, and his organ playing becomes the lead instrument, the shiny edge atop the band's energy, toiling away above Dylan's voice like the sweat on his brow. His delivery is the vocal equivalent of staring down both his subject and his listeners: the mood of Dylan's most enduring rock tour de force acquires the tone of a brutally incisive and vengeful interrogation, and the music bears down even harder than in "Positively 4th Street."

The opening stanza's nose-thumbing taunts prefigure the prevailing question that the entire song plunges toward: "How does it fee-uhl?" And as he heads for the first refrain, Dylan lingers for the drawn-out punch line ("about having to be scrounging . . . your next mea-uhlll"); and his players—a hodge-podge of New York sessionists and hangers-on—begin to hug the curves in the groove he's set in motion, feel out its direction as well as its implications on their way towards its inexorable conclusion. It isn't until Dylan finishes that line that he puffs on his harmonica, as if to say, "Stick around—there's more." (Dylan refused to cut the song's 6:13 length, thereby exploding the three-and-a-half-minutes standard timing for a radio single.) "Like a Rolling Stone," his greatest rock 'n' roll clenched fist, "the poor boy's put-down" (Robert Christgau), is a sneer at innocence so full of verbal facility and deeply felt betrayal that it remains a pinched nerve on classic-hits radio formats some twenty-five years on.

The rest of the song follows this same course, Dylan jabbing at the band's increasingly angered contours with sharp innuen-does and offhandedly surreal metaphors of class and privilege ("You used to be so amused / At Napoleon in rags and the language that he used . . ."). Because the players feel the song's meanings out spontaneously, they gain on its insinuations as every refrain rolls by. Each time that question returns—"How does it *feel?*"—the words not only shoot off a myriad of inferences and targets (How must the song's target feel? How do the million or so eavesdroppers feel? How do these players feel to be goaded by this music for the very first time?), they become embankments for the musicians to rebound off of after verses of free-falling accusation. As with *Blonde on Blonde*'s "One of Us Must Know (Sooner or Later)," with its tension-release avalanche at the top of refrains, the act of playing the song is the act of inventing it.

Dylan's delivery pushes through everything in full contradictory gait: arrogant intimidation laced with compassion. As "Like a Rolling Stone" rises on those glaring questions, the song has a built-in lift that in anyone else's hands would ring duplicitous. Dylan's delivery incorporates a compelling opposition: the bitterness of his attack belies an underlying affinity. After all, if he meant to humiliate his subject (the repeated "you") so thoroughly, why is he doing it so poetically, so obsessively, so knowingly? The very extent of the tirade is an index of care, an ascription of value. In its straightforward rejection, "Positively 4th Street" is a much harsher song; it suffocates its subject in derisiveness and delights in the overkill. "Like a Rolling Stone" feeds on a telling paradox: by stripping away all falsity and class duplicity, Dylan strips his subject of pretense while exonerating what remains; he celebrates an essential condition as he mocks the former arrogance. Its meanspiritedness is undercut by empathy; the singer sees his former self in his subject's shoes.

Dylan didn't tell his players what the song was about before they played it—how could anyone explain class resentment in ecstatic, dynamic motion? He must have been gunning for the haphazardness that keeps the recording alive, and the shape it ultimately achieves: a journey from spite to knowing acceptance, from accusation to release, as well as from denial to exposure ("Do you want to make a de-uhlll?").

## hard rain

• • •

**"Ballad of a Thin Man"** is the signal antijournalist song, ironic only to the extent that Dylan is the most critically celebrated rock figure ever. Mr. Jones is a pedigreed archetype, a person to whom knowledge is a class distinction: "You're very well read / It's well known." As usual, there's more to it than that. When Dylan notes his pride in having read the complete F. Scott Fitzgerald, he's saying that the 1960s scene makes the Roaring Twenties look quaint, even though Gatsby's parties had their share of "hot" jazz and cocaine. It's the same point Dylan makes when he sings about Miss Lonely in "Like a Rolling Stone." Schools, especially universities, are concrete metaphors for the larger power structure, which is why administration building sit-ins at Berkeley in 1964 and Columbia University in 1968, and the Kent State murders in 1970, were such potent symbols of student rebellion. And the isolated brand of academic knowledge leads Dylan to the verse in "Desolation Row" that begins with a reference to the *Titanic* and goes on to lampoon the very poets whose canons are synonymous with modernism:

> **And Ezra Pound and T. S. Eliot**
> **Fighting in the captain's tower**
> **While calypso singers laugh at them**
> **And fishermen hold flowers**

Pop singers command such a vast audience, and practice such liberated forms of verse, they can laugh at ivory-tower "high art" masters whose sanctity has grown stuffy. More than this, when "poetry" and bookishness are so removed from everyday life as to be inconsequential, they become as escapist and morally dangerous as any drug.

As Dylan will dramatize, especially on his tours with the Band in 1966 and 1974, "Ballad of a Thin Man" juts out in other directions as well. Like "Positively 4th Street," and "Like a Rolling Stone," "Ballad of a Thin Man" taunts its subject so thoroughly it almost makes you sympathetic toward the poor scribe. It's Dylan the outsider flaunting his sudden authority as an insider prophet, which makes the comically subversive songs on this record all the more balancing. In his leering salute to America's heartland, "Highway 61 Revisited," he goes after authority with a broad stroke, evoking his own father's name ("God said to Abraham, kill me a son / Abe said, 'Man, you must be puttin' me on' "). The last verse of the song ropes in a bored "rovin' gambler"—and finds his accomplice in a rock promoter. And the grand, flippant sweep of "Tombstone Blues," a gleeful sprint through some of the same historical ills that pervade the contemporary comic gloom of "Desolation Row," uncoils to a final verse that denounces bookishness as "useless and pointless knowledge."

Like a lot of Dylan songs that sound patched together from many sources of dialogue, found quotes, and discarded ideas, "Tombstone Blues" is Dylan stealing from others for a distinctive style. He says in the *Biograph* notes:

> There was this one bar I used to play where cops would always come and hang out, mostly off duty, they'd always be talking stuff, saying things like "I don't know who killed him or why, but I'm sure glad he's gone," that kind of stuff, you'd hear things like "the guy should have stuck to ripping off his own people," you'd hear stuff like that all the time.

*Highway 61 Revisited* performs a wedding of distinctive contemporary subjects to radicalized folk forms, Dada references and guileful verbal stunts to scraggly blues patterns. Of course, Dylan's strategy—anarchic rebellion as a response to overindustrialized bureaucracies—is an index of how square the world seemed to the youths who responded to this music. These songs spring from the same television imagination that could cross-contextualize to make the most distant historical events rub against each other naturally, like so much video footage. Characters talk across centuries: "Tombstone Blues" stars not only Belle Starr handing down her wits to Jezebel the nun but Ma Rainey and Beethoven unwrapping their bedroll. Loco jokes spar with cubist images like "the geometry of innocence flesh on the bone"; notions like existential tour maps roll out packaged and sold as commodities to nursing homes and universities.

The title track features a signal train whistle, like the old Roy Acuff tracks, as though the song and the album it gives its names to fly in hot pursuit of the folly of modern "progress." The record fuses the personal, political, and cultural connections Dylan has been making all along to produce even more casual effrontery for his first all-rock stance. The acoustic closer, "Desolation Row," functions as anything but a conclusion. This apotheosis of the list song is a rock marathon stripped to its core essence; and as a double-edged apocalypse-complaint song, it points more forward than backward.

**In October 1965,** Dylan records his first tracks with the Hawks, recommended to him by John Hammond, Jr., who used them on his record *So Many Roads* that year. A healthy collaboration begins: "Can You Please Crawl Out Your Window?" (released in November) is a hilarious elopement sales pitch, the sound of a young man wooing his girl from below her window, pleading for the chance he's afraid somebody else might get ("You can go back to him any time you want to"). The stop-time cymbal beats could be the overheated pulse of his heart pounding its way out of his chest. "You gotta lotta *nerve* to say you are my friend," Dylan squeals, hijacking a line from "Positively 4th Street," "if you won't crawl out your window!" (The song was released in an earlier version with the *Highway 61* players, then pulled.)

These sessions with the Hawks include run-throughs of

several other songs, one of which shows up a year later on *Blonde on Blonde* with a different arrangement: "I Wanna Be Your Lover" casts a love as bumper-car ride that resembles the hot-rod derangement of "Highway 61 Revisited." (The liner notes to *Biograph* mistakenly call this the only song released by both the Rolling Stones and the Beatles, which slights their tellingly characteristic recordings of Barrett Strong's "Money"; but it *is* a clear homage to Lennon and McCartney's "I Wanna Be Your Man"— the Stones' first hit. "I always thought it was a good song," said Dylan, "but it just never made it onto an album.") Also from these sessions: "Number One," an instrumental demo waiting for lyrics; "Seems Like a Freeze-Out" (the rehearsal title for "Visions of Johanna"), which takes on a creepy pace with the band feeling out what they can for themselves in between the stanzas—the song hadn't quite jelled; and "She's Your Lover Now," which remains among the great unreleased long-winded breakup songs and tempers the revenge motive of "Positively 4th Street" with humor: "Now you stand here expectin' me to remember somethin' you forgot to say" and "Yes, you, you just sit around and ask for ashtrays can't you reach?"

# 3: mona lisa's highway blues

## Blonde on Bonde
Released: June 1966

In *Blonde on Blonde* I wrote out all the songs in the studio. The musicians played cards, I wrote out a song, we'd do it, they'd go back to their game and I'd write out another song.

—**Dylan**,
   January 1968, *In His Own Words*

I always hear other instruments, how they should sound. The closest I ever got to the sound I hear in my mind was on individual bands in the *Blonde on Blonde* album. It's that thin, that wild mercury sound. It's metallic and bright gold, with whatever that conjures up. That's my particular sound. I haven't been able to succeed in getting it all the time. Mostly, I've been driving at a combination of guitar, harmonica and organ. . . .

—**Dylan**,
   January 1978, *In His Own Words*

**Nineteen sixty-six goes down** as Dylan's Promethean year. In the first three months he records *Blonde on Blonde*, his tour de force of obscurantist rock poetics; in the next two months he makes some of his (or anybody's) greatest rock 'n' roll onstage with the Hawks in America, Australia, and Europe; and, in August, he suffers multiple head injuries from a motorcycle crash that leads to an eighteen-month sabbatical from public appearances. It's difficult to overstate the significance of this stage in Dylan's career. For many, it signals the end of his great early period: nothing after would ever shatter the same illusions, flaunt the same hip authority, create the same grand, chaotic beatnik philosophy. The made-for-television film of his English tour with the Band, *Eat the Document* (the follow-up to *Don't Look Back*), suggests that Dylan's frantic, sleepless pace was as driven and wracked as the music that drove him; all signposts point towards a fall. Dylan edits the choppy *Eat the Document* with Howard Alk; D. A. Pennebaker cuts the same footage as *Something Is Happening*, lauded by the lucky but still unavailable.

A sprawling abstraction of eccentric blues revisionism, *Blonde on Blonde* confirms Dylan's stature as the greatest American rock presence since Elvis Presley. The recording sessions move to Columbia Studios in Nashville after a fruitless January session in New York, and the project is broken up by solo concert dates in White Plains, Pittsburgh, and Montreal. Over the course of two records, the longest stretch of music yet produced by a rock star, Dylan delivers inane verbal spectacle atop a stylistic range (New Orleans marches, Chicago stompers, dead-of-night waltzes) that makes *Bringing It All Back Home* and *Highway 61 Revisited* sound like functions of a larger design. The opening three sides are looser, more seductive, and more danceable than what Dylan attained previously in his New York sessions, and the music seems to goad and buoy the lyrics, which are more difficult to get a clear emotional fix on. As Greil Marcus writes in *Stranded, Blonde on Blonde* is "the sound of a man trying to stand up in a drunken boat, and, for the moment, succeeding. His tone was sardonic, scared, threatening, as if he'd awakened after paying all his debts to find that nothing was settled" (p. 267).

Producer Bob Johnston, who had taken over from Tom Wilson during the *Highway 61* sessions, encouraged Dylan to record in Nashville, where musicians he had used before (like Charlie McCoy, lead guitarist for "Desolation Row") earned their living as session men. This was a highly unlikely move: rock figures recorded in Los Angeles or New York (though the Rolling

Stones recorded wherever they were so inclined, like the Chess Studios in Chicago when they passed through). In the mid-sixties, the country scene was relatively hipless, a market for rednecks that the emergent counterculture could take seriously only as an opposition to free-thinking values. Country-and-western music itself was beyond passé until a later incarnation of the Byrds (in the person of Gram Parsons) adopted it affectionately, doting fondly on the style's simplicities without sacrificing any of its fatalistic beauty (*Sweetheart of the Rodeo*, 1968).

Dylan wasn't intent on recording country (yet); he just wanted to exploit a few of its unsung studio heroes for a spell, and perhaps baffle his audience again. Johnston signed up Bill Aikins, Kenny Buttrey, Jerry Kennedy, Charlie McCoy, Wayne Moss, Hargus Robbins, Joe South, and Henry Strzelecki. But more than this, as biographer Bob Spitz writes, Johnston promoted a creative atmosphere, removed the sound dividers that blocked the musicians' eye contact, and allowed Dylan free rein on how the songs were taped. The first track they recorded was "Sad-Eyed Lady of the Lowlands," a lumbering romantic analog to the political apocalypse of "Desolation Row," which was laid down in a single take immediately after Dylan finished the lyrics at four in the morning. The musicians, not accustomed to waiting on songwriters, never mind leaping into an obsessive *eleven-minute* song, were stupefied. "I have to admit," Buttrey remembers, "I thought the guy had blown a gasket and we were basically humoring him" (Spitz, p. 337).

By the second day, when Dylan's New York cronies Al Kooper and Robbie Robertson proved to be valuable musical companions, the Nashville attitudes had changed. The divider-less studio "made all the difference in our playing together," Buttrey says, "as if we were on a tight stage, as opposed to playing in a big hall where you're ninety miles apart. From that night on, our entire outlook was changed. We started having a good time. We started eating together, we took breaks together—that never happened on any album I'd worked on in the past. Dylan made us feel as if we had a personal stake in the album, and we began to play our asses off for him" (Spitz, p. 339).

This combination of session camaraderie and Dylan's deadpan conviction gives these absurdist word puzzles a mercurial tinge that keeps them contemporary. Next to "Lily, Rosemary and the Jack of Hearts" (from *Blood on the Tracks*), "Stuck Inside of Mobile with the Memphis Blues Again" may be rock's grandest costume piece, balancing displacement and alienation with the offhand hatchet job (Shakespeare hitting on a French girl, the preacher "dressed / With twenty pounds of headlines / Stapled to his chest"). In her 1967 *Cheetah* overview, "Dylan," Ellen Willis chalks it all up to making fun of drugs. R. Meltzer calls "Memphis Blues" a "warning about *mixing*," and dubs "Rainy Day Women #12 & 35" "the 'How Dry I Am' of grass" (*The Aesthetics of Rock*, p. 280).

It's a rare entry in Dylan's catalogue where his studies in sexual ambiguities actually sound sexy, where the haze of ideas doesn't smother desire so much as prod it, balancing postromantic bitterness ("Most Likely You Go Your Way and I'll Go Mine") with anticipatory bliss (the knowing befuddlement of "Absolutely Sweet Marie," the trippy submission of "I Want You"). "Obviously Five Believers" is a randy excuse to take a galvanizing guitar lick, set the band into cant orbit, and juice it all at the end of each stanza with the first coital afterthoughts that spring to mind ("You know I can if you can, honey / But, honey, please don't"). "Pledging My Time" uses prison jargon to express commitment; Dylan's wearied pleas drag each verse to a dead end, where the song squirms at the tip of some existential rope ("Somebody got lucky / But it was an accident"). His vocals on this record deliver not only the requisite side-angle detachment such allusiveness calls for but a new seductive enticement, as though his heart is held for ransom by these vagaries, and he believes in them no matter what they may come to mean to the listener.

## mona lisa's highway blues

•   •   •

***Blonde on Blonde*** works off the opening hook to "Rainy Day Women #12 & 35" ("Everybody must get stoned!") in ways that sink in only after the comic residue wears off. The song extends into ribald explicitness what Ray Charles's hit "Let's Go Get Stoned" toys with as double entendre. In a fit of wry, offhanded dispassion, Dylan plays barnstormer, carny barker, ringmaster, snake-oil salesman, drunk-tank crank, and weary bail bondsman all in one breath. The Salvation Army street-corner brass band—bass drum, slurping trombone—tromps out a pungent, bawdy romp that sounds even more inebriated next to Dylan's wry eccentricity. Along with the opening line ("Well, they'll stone ya when you're trying to be so good"), it snubs the antielectric backlash—there's not even a drum kit here. He delivers his paranoid diatribe with a mixture of self-deprecation and sarcastic indifference, and his hip detachment from everything around him makes him sound gone as gone gets before losing the will to complain.

But in a larger sense, "Rainy Day Women #12 & 35" sets the tone for an album about rock's encroaching "respectability," the changing nature of the relation between pop artist and audience, and the new ground rules being written (largely by Dylan) that allow drug talk to surface as the counterculture's argot, a new mass idiom. Drugs and the music world have always cross-pollinated, but they used to be an open secret that measured the distance between a hidden network of backstage hipster life-styles and the audience's vicarious, look-the-other-way titillations. (Think of Cab Calloway's "Reefer Man" and "Minnie the Moocher.") By 1966, even though rock stars as huge as Dylan remained sheltered, the life-styles they sang about were widely imitated, and subversiveness became a public style. It's doubtful that "Rainy Day Women #12 & 35" would have reached number two during the Reagan administration, the way it did in 1966.

Dylan puts drug references to work as metaphors for re-

**131**

bellion and fun, to the point where simply sharing antiestablishment fervor on a mass scale *means* fun, and the raciest pop pleasures define themselves against straight values. But the narcotic metaphor doesn't stop there. "They'll stone you when you're trying to keep your seat" can be read as a reference to the Montgomery, Alabama bus strikes, with the attendant overtones of religious martyrdom that was developing around civil rights activists like Bob Moses. "Visions of Johanna" plays drug slang ("a handful of rain," "conquer my mind," those newfangled "highway blues") off erotic power plays, and works as a metaphor for the dope culture's fractured idea of itself. The next song, "One of Us Must Know (Sooner or Later)," finds strength and release in its vengeful admonishment—it sends "Don't Think Twice" back to charm school. Throughout the album, Dylan turns hallucinated abstractions into symbols even when they point towards vagaries; non sequiturs take on meaning as they leap out of their elastic contexts: "You know it balances on your head / Just like a mattress balances on a bottle of wine," he sings in "Leopard-Skin Pill-Box Hat," which can mean both "very artfully" and "ridiculously lopsided." Not many listeners fully comprehend the ins and outs of "Stuck Inside of Mobile" (we're not meant to); but not many misconstrue the line sung by honkytonk Ruthie, about how your debutante knows what you "need" but Ruthie knows what you "want": it's either sex or drugs—or both.

The musical-emotional tone of *Blonde on Blonde* shows just how highly Dylan esteems a mentor like Jimmy Reed as a guru of electric-blues texture—it's like he's graduating from the rural-acoustic South to urban-electric Chicago. Listen to the lazy perseverance of Reed's "Honest I Do," or his personification of a clowning ham during the shaggy-dog sarcasm of "Shame, Shame, Shame." Reed lets his guitar talk a bit more than Brownie McGhee did, and there's more of a comic at work in his music. Dylan flexes entire verses—not to say songs—adopting Reed's brand of cavalier vocal glint, to the point where these songs' very ambiguity becomes a subject in itself. Side three's "Absolutely Sweet Marie," "Temporary Like Achilles," and "Obviously Five Believers" are a string of backhanded arguments about the manipulative tactics of art, the limits of song craft, rock credulity, and message-bound sentiment. These bilges-as-songs bear the test of time a lot better than dozens of overearnest folkie rants: Paul Simon's weak-kneed parody "A Simple Desultory Philippic (Or, How I Was Robert McNamara'd Into Submission)" (produced by Tom Wilson) takes smug aim and wilts in the face of its target.

As a grand cosmic farce, *Blonde on Blonde* strings along half-baked plots and ramshackle discourse not only for the thrill of getting away with it—a key rock principle—but to demonstrate, like Picasso or Braque, how rife with implication nonsense can be made to sound, how seemingly slapdash methods can yield unforeseen expressive vitality.

If "The Times They Are A-Changin' " reinvigorated the traditional formulas for the contemporary protest song, *Blonde on Blonde* is both a blues homage and a model of antitraditionalism; it's a rock version of art's postmodernism, where pretexts function as portals for meanings to escape every which way. In anyone else's hands, this material would sound unfocused. With Dylan's impassivity posing as commitment, it's a postromantic joyride, steeped in the blues, with sour-grapes romance thrown in to spite the intellectuals.

Despite its amorphous metaphysical charge, *Blonde on Blonde* spawned four charting singles: "Rainy Day Women #12 & 35" peaked at number two in April; and its follow-up number "I Want You," hiked to number twenty in July. "Just Like a Woman" hit number thirty-three in October; and "Leopard-Skin Pill-Box Hat"—a minefield of near-clichés, and so a tonic to the rest of pop—landed at eighty-one in May 1967. And one more thing: the album prompted Pete Seeger, the epitome of Newport's old guard, to turn in his authenticity badge and record with the Blues Project.

## hard rain

. . .

**Dylan's overzealous wordplay** can delve into comic imperviousness, but his devotional romances make use of the same verbal ploys to convey a dreamlike obsessiveness. Through the quixotic conviction of his deliveries (rarely sardonic in tone, like "Motorpsycho Nitemare"), his linguistic heat translates into deeply felt desire, a quicksand passion that flirts with madness. The imagery used to stress how much he cares for his lover in "Love Minus Zero / No Limit" brushes up against the offbeat insight: "In ceremonies of the horsemen / Even the pawn must hold a grudge." In other romances, he resorts to bizarre analogy to sustain a heightened mood: "She's a hypnotist collector / You are a walking antique" works as an ironic possessive compliment in "She Belongs to Me."

In "Visions of Johanna," these strategies grow more convoluted and disorienting, even though nothing seems to happen in the course of the song; it's a static rumination rich with psychological peril. "Johanna" is herself absent from the narrative (except for her persistence in her ex-lover's hallucinations); the emotional texture is suffused with hazy duress. The "rain" that Louise holds out in the third line is double-talk for heroin, and the lovers' chemical addiction works as a metaphor for a compulsive emotional bond.

The opening line—"Ain't it just like the night to play tricks when you're trying to be so quiet?"—foreshadows the song's nocturnal riddling. With the singer as the mired central figure, struggling simply to express what he sees and feels, Dylan spins a phantasm of isolated torment around a narrative that steps in and out of the first person. The first verse describes a drug den, where lights glimmer from a nearby loft, the heat pipes cough, a country station plays quietly, and the lovers sit estranged—from each other, and their interior selves. The first verse's last two lines shift from Louise's lover to these visions of Johanna that "conquer *my* mind," as though the protagonist is seeing the situation from outside himself as he reacts to the scene he's describing. He wants it to be someone else's tragedy. (This cinematic ploy is picked up in "Just Like a Woman.")

From a literal standpoint, the song is a confessional thicket described by Johanna's ex-lover, now in the arms of his fallback, Louise. But the narrator adds crucial bits of scenery: the emotionally barren urban playground of the neighborhood hookers, the nightwatchman absentmindedly clicking his flashlight on and off, musing on who's loonier, he or they. Louise appears comparatively desirable, but her hollowness reminds him that he's only looking at himself, that Johanna is missing. These perceptions clue not just the hyperactive psychological awareness that this song inhabits and expresses but the self-negating despair as well—the protagonist no longer feels his own presence in his own story: "The ghost of 'lectricity howls in the bones of her face / Where these visions of Johanna have now taken my place." With Louise's face in the flickering light, the organ line filtering through the band's claustrophobic texture, all he can see and feel is Johanna, whose visage takes not just Louise's place but also his own. With all conscious thought overtaken by the absence of Johanna, his obsession has overwhelmed his perception of what is real.

Verse three throws confusing arrows into play: "Little boy lost, he takes himself so seriously" could be a gnawing self-reflection, as could the line about being so gallingly useless; but the same figure makes small talk with the wall, which makes the shift between omniscient narrator and protagonist-confessor all the more blurred. The question of whose name he brings up is also left ambiguous (both Louise and Johanna are plausible), and it winds up emphasizing what we already know: a one-sided love triangle is suggested but not acted out (Louise is oblivious to Johanna).

What with "jelly-faced" females who sneeze, and the guy with the mustache hopelessly groping for his knees, verse four is out-and-out self-parody, but it works as a platform for two key statements about the overidealism of romanticism, and modernism's response. "Inside the museums, Infinity goes up on trial" joins Dylan's ambitious self-worth as a durable songwriter (must art be defined by its *eternal* merits alone?) with a punch line about the transparency of art's supposedly redemptive effects. "Salvation" goes stale in a culture that miscomprehends and thus underrates these cross-contextual leaps of modernity (songs that use cinematic devices, mediums as themes, detached observations that weave in and out of unrestrictive narratives). Museums were a favorite target in Dylan's 1965 *Playboy* interview, where he mocked them as "sexless." It's a point he follows up on with even more levity in the next line (a drug ruse): "But Mona Lisa musta had the highway blues / You can tell by the way she smiles"—or, modernism holds classical art in highest esteem by returning to its sense of fun (enter jelly-faced women, sneezing). The closing couplet (where jewels and binoculars hang from a mule) arches back towards the narrative, turning this verse into the vindictive joke that modernism makes of its subjects.

If verse four simply prolonged the quietly anxious mood (while gently laughing at itself), the last verse does nothing but intensify it. The protagonist is now "the peddler" (or "fiddler," as Dylan sings in the live *Biograph* version), who fesses up to his dependency while defending it (everybody is parasitic, he says). Louise is compared to a countess making preparations as she mocks the protagonist's innocence towards either sex or the next fix, or both. The tilt towards insanity is underlined by the elongation of the final verse, where two extra lines are wedged into the twelve-line format to emphasize how the song's voice has come unglued: the narrator's conscience bursts.

Michael Gray holds that "if the 'rain' of verse one is indeed heroin, Louise's gesture in 'temptin' you to defy it' seems positive" (p. 32). But holding out a handful of heroin and tempting the addict to resist can hardly be called a "positive" image. It's almost like Dylan set out to write the darkest, most dissuasive ode to drug abuse imaginable, and then cloaked it in relationship metaphors.

Part of the song's allegorical allure is its resilient inconsistency, the way it lunges between comedy and depression.

*Biograph*'s live take intensifies most of these lines with deliberate, almost overenunciated vocal punctuations. He stresses the gently descending triplets on the words "op-po-site loft," harmonica outbursts flooding the space between verses, and he skips the occasional bar in anticipation of the next line. Another live version, from the bootleg *On the Road, 1974–1975*, is much faster, adrenaline subverting subtlety; and Dylan plumbs anger and hostility from his thwarted will to express.

It's been said that Dylan's chief talent lies in conveying subliminal feelings, insinuating emotional nuances by a turn of inflection, or pasting over a scatological conceit with mock indifference. "Visions of Johanna" sustains a bereft mood without drama or interplay, and largely without motion or climatic tension: only three voices are quoted in the entire song; the two lovers speak their only lines in the final verse. The overriding device is a keenly felt sense of place and a vocal delivery that transforms surrealist imagery into something disturbing, ominous yet self-mocking. How would a trip to a museum help these lovers? It's romantic estrangement parading (with a knowing smirk) as the inadequacy of art.

**The dialogue that** developed between groups in the mid-sixties became a theme in its own right. The Byrds covered Dylan and invented folk-rock. The Beatles imitated Dylan's psychological introspection and found a bridge to adult themes ("You've Got to Hide Your Love Away"). The Stones went pop and came off even more scathing than if they had simply mimicked Dylan's temper ("Under My Thumb," "Get Off of My Cloud"). The Animals covered "House of the Rising Sun" and gave Dylan as much if not more of an incentive to go electric as the Byrds. And the British Invasion bandwagon led to all manner of delightful idiocies—like Donovan, the "Scottish Dylan."

As a folkie who enjoyed a crossover hit when Peter, Paul and Mary recorded "Blowin' in the Wind," Dylan was an album act in a prealbum era, who got pressured into writing singles by Columbia despite his aversion to pop gestures. In sound and spirit, "Mixed Up Confusion," from his first single session, was a dry run for "Subterranean Homesick Blues," his first successful single. Come 1965, "Positively 4th Street" was the most mean-spirited onslaught to hit the top ten since Elvis sang "Hound Dog"; "Like a Rolling Stone" was a natural hit even though it ran six minutes and thirteen seconds. But despite its hilarity, "Can You Please Crawl Out Your Window?" didn't reach the Top 40.

"I Want You" is the antisingle follow-up that climbs to number 20 three months later. A colorful beckoning with freck-led lyrics and a jaunty refrain, the song is as innocuous as it is incisive, and it makes fun of every fun-in-the-sun bromide on the charts it inhabited ("Hanky Panky" by Tommy James and the Shondells, "Sunshine Superman" by Donovan). Dylan pinches the Byrds' own self-satisfied chart sheen as he undercuts their folk-rock tone with his inimitably dry smirk. The bridge retraces its own steps and comes up smiling. To paraphrase: Fathers have been without true love, but their daughters "put me down," 'cause "I don't think about it." Even the hawklike Dave Marsh finds pleasure in being perplexed: "Having studied the disc in detail since I was sixteen," he says in *The Heart of Rock and Soul*, "I can now state that this most likely means two things: 1) Dylan had found a clever rhyme; 2) he thought about it all the time, maybe even too much" (p. 66).

This kind of rapt absurdism is impossible to write off as foppish; its indecipherability mocks all the ornate "rock poetry" that was flying around the time everybody began to realize that Dylan lyrics were as easily excised from his music as newspaper headlines, and catchy one-liners for sign-offs. When he sings "But it doesn't matter" in the third verse, he may or may not be singing about whether his chambermaid knows where he'd like to be; but it's a sure thing Dylan wants you to wonder about it. (Then again, when Dylan belabors the Grateful Dead with the song some thirteen years later, he doesn't worry about it too much.) He makes enough insipid sense to free up lines from their context, even from within a jingle that parodies everything from overbearing recrimination ("I wasn't very cute to him / Was I?") to shopworn Rolling Stones (via Irma Thomas) clichés ("time was on his side").

If "Desolation Row" is at once the portent and parody of the sixties long-form album track, "I Want You" is a paradigm of the glib cartoon single, a clownish pastiche of what Top 40 radio takes for granted. "I Want You" is how a character in "Memphis Blues" might break into giddy song, entreating a lover to play at romance, if only because romance staves off more tedious games. It's a jingle confection of off-the-rails wordplay, with an aloof Dylan delivery at the center, grounding it with bohemian benignity.

**Feminist critics take** justified umbrage at Dylan's Mr. Sensitivity rebounds and overdefensive outbursts when his relationships come to an end. He doesn't break up with girlfriends, he lectures them, and when they leave him unexpectedly, he feigns innocence (albeit with righteous zeal, in "I Don't Believe You"). But "Just Like a Woman" has been strangely labeled an antifemale song when it more than atones for some later misogynist clinkers, and lays bare a male vulnerability that is still radical by pop standards. It straddles an almost inconceivably thin line between compassion and scorn, forgiveness and retribution. It's a breakup song without his trademark sting, but he still gets his licks in. "One of Us Must Know (Sooner or Later)" and "Most Likely You

Go Your Way and I'll Go Mine" close in on the rock possibilities that stem from "Don't Think Twice," and prove that the electric version of "I Don't Believe You" was no accident.

As an exaggeration of the closing broken raven's wing image of vulnerability in "Love Minus Zero / No Limit," the refrain to "Just Like a Woman" strips bare the adult masks lovers don when coping with leftover pain: "And she aches just like a woman / But she breaks just like a little girl." Even though this is a marginal putdown, what's stressed in that last line is not his lover's girlish games or dependency but her honest vulnerability. The song is delivered with such care, such evidence of trust, that it hardly condemns Dylan of treating women as a subspecies. This point is drawn out in the last verse, where Dylan unveils his own hungering vulnerability in sizing up the end of the affair.

This song courts critical perplex. Michael Gray calls it one of Dylan's bad songs, but John Herdman points out how the last refrain switches from "she" to "you" via the connecting bridge, where "And *your* long-time curse hurts" prepares the shift to direct address at the end.

When Dylan revives it at his 1971 Bangla Desh concert appearance, "Just Like a Woman" takes on something more than a nostalgic glow—it's like he's wooing his audience back into his charms as he tells them that the sixties are over ("I believe it's time for us to quit"). Perhaps because it's placed next to a lumpy reading of "Eleanor Rigby," Richie Havens's sadder-but-wiser reading of this song on *Mixed Bag* (1968) is underrated. The other key cover of this key track is by Van Morrison, who still sings the song as an uptempo R&B devotion onstage.

"Just Like a Woman" is more grown-up than "Ballad in Plain D," but it works as a respite from *Blonde on Blonde*'s wilder fantasies. The "fog . . . amphetamine and . . . pearls" wouldn't have sounded out of place on *Bringing It All Back Home* or *Highway 61 Revisited*. "One of Us Must Know (Sooner or Later)" and "Most Likely You Go Your Way and I'll Go Mine" follow up on the arrested rage of "Positively 4th Street": one-liners that are so condescending you wonder what made Dylan get involved with these lovers in the first place. "I didn't mean to treat you sooooo baaaad / . . . You just happened to be there, that's all" is his entrance to "One of Us Must Know (Sooner or Later)," which swells to a pitch of torrent mixed with rationalization at each refrain. For all his cockeyed exuberance, Dylan knows how to set up a line, and follow through with the requisite surge of feeling: "I really did try to get close to you."

Dylan strings out words with knowing condescension as the band begins its descent, and in the second verse you sense that it doesn't matter what she whispered in his ear as much as how it was whispered, and that this remembered moment probably has only so much to do with the naivete of the lover he's singing to.

The opening and closing number for most of his 1974 tour shows, "Most Likely You Go Your Way and I'll Go Mine" is Dylan's most dramatic antilove letter to his audience, the number that flaunts his self-assurance even as it vents injury. "Probably written after some disappointing relationship where, you know, I was lucky to have escaped without a broken nose," he says in the *Biograph* liner notes—in other words, Newport. The tune has a singsongy spitefulness to it, and lines land on pitiless twists ("You say you love me / And you're thinkin' of me / But you know you could be *wrong*"). The bridge has a sly dig at faulty justice, which could be either a slap at the new boyfriend who shows up in the next verse or a scathing self-admonishment. The way Dylan backs off from these lines, sings them with an air of remote indifference, gives them even more burn—once again, his anger charts his commitment, but by not letting on he ups the ante.

**The most impressive feature** of "Sad-Eyed Lady of the Lowlands" may be the withheld intensity Dylan sustains in order to keep some of the lyrics afloat. It's even coarser, and less meek,

than "Desolation Row"; and until "Wedding Song" (on 1973's
*Planet Waves*) and "Sara" (on 1976's *Desire*), it stands as the
apotheosis of allegiance. Mapping out the course of a romantic
mystery as if it could be charted comprehensively, as though the
entire range of feeling summoned by one-track love could be
fueled into song, Dylan winds his way through situations and
visions so vivid and yet so allusive that they end up only skirting
the feelings he's trying to get a handle on. "With your mercury
mouth in the missionary times," its frank alliterative *m*'s not-
withstanding, is a cryptic gauntlet tossed at those criticizing Dylan's language as too eccentrically evasive (this from a song that
lauds a woman's "curfew plugs"). Like the enthralled waltz of
"4th Time Around" ("Everybody must give something back /
For something they get"), "Sad-Eyed Lady" is loaded with enigmatic pronouncements that insinuate like crazy but don't really
go anywhere. It's not only a song about weariness; it's a performance that defines nervous exhaustion, weary with the weight of
the affection it means to express. You can hear his players loping
behind his deliveries—it's like they're daring one another to see
who can sing or play more behind the beat.

Verses end with exalting questions (like "Who among them
do they think could carry you?") answered only by a repeated
five-line verse-ending riddle.

It's a list song of serene attributes offset by passing farmers
and businessmen with their own dead angels; its subject is someone whom scoundrels confide in, who despite her broken marriage has a gentleness which belies her many masks. The words
take pains to enshrine this woman—exotic, mysterious,
prevailing—but at the center of things lies the singer as suppli-
cant, questioning not only this fantastic creation of an unreach-
able, unknowable woman but his own inexplicable desires.

**With *Blonde on Blonde*,** Dylan completes his transformation into
a rock deity of vague but undeniable powers, the undisputed

heir to the fast-break life-styles that Jack Kerouac and Allen Ginsberg championed on the page. Undaunted by fame and completely at home with the profound-sounding absurdities he bores into, Dylan tosses off this cubist-minded music with blithe cavalierism, as though the underground world had been lying in wait for his clever-inscrutable sensibility to update individualist beat attitudes.

With "Visions of Johanna" a murky entanglement of romantic envy and artistic disillusionment, a centerpiece that takes the druggy opening pratfall and turns it into loaded symbol of emotional disarray, these songs overleap the pretensions of folk poets like Paul Simon and shove rock into the forefront of postmodernist debates (baiting even Susan Sontag in *Against Interpretation*). When Dylan's latest romances aren't flaunting a gift for inhabiting the opposite sex's consciousness ("Just Like a Woman"), they stand at polar extremes to the typical pop attitudes. "I Want You" is as tongue-in-cheek as "Most Likely You Go Your Way and I'll Go Mine" is irrevocable. And his tightrope walks between the vengeful and the comic (the layered putdowns in "One of Us Must Know" and "Leopard-Skin Pill-Box Hat") cut a fine line of piqued hilarity.

As the counterculture's anointed bard, Dylan remains strangely aloof from the trends he set in motion (folk-rock, rock poetry, rock modernism, high-spirited nonsense posing as baronial pretension). When he sends up Shakespeare's pointed shoes and bells, he's also sending up modern costumes, long hair, and boho love beads, as well as his own frankly passive role as ambivalent trendsetter. The irony of all this throwaway brilliance, of course, is that *Blonde on Blonde* remains among the most listenable of sixties relics—its incidental qualities only enhance its staying power. *Blonde on Blonde* is a triumph of a pop tactic that turns the tempting kiss-off into a classic gesture.

The word is not "international phenomenon"; the
word is "parental nightmare."
   —**Dylan**,
      1966, *In His Own Words*

As far as folk and folk-rock are concerned, it don't
matter what kind of nasty names people invent for the
music. It could be called arsenic music, or perhaps
Phaedra music. I don't think that such a word as folk-
rock has anything to do with it. And folk-rock music is
a word I can't use. Folk music is a bunch of fat people.
I have to think of all this as traditional music. Traditional music is based on hexagrams. It comes about
from legends, Bibles, Plagues, and it revolves around
vegetables and death. There's nobody that's going to
kill traditional music. All these songs about roses
growing out of people's brains and lovers who are
really geese and swans that turn into angels—they're
not going to die. It's all those paranoid people who
think that someone's goin' to come and take away
their toilet paper—*they're* going to die. Songs like
"Which Side Are You On?" and "I Loves You,
Porgy"—they're not folk-music songs; they're political
songs. They're *already* dead. Obviously, death is not
very universally accepted. I mean, you'd think that
the traditional music people could gather from their
songs that mystery is a fact, a traditional fact. . . . But
anyway, traditional music is too unreal to die. It
doesn't need to be protected. Nobody's going to hurt
it. In that music is the only true, valid death you can

feel today off a record player. But like anything else in great demand, people try to own it. It has to do with a purity thing. I think its meaninglessness is holy. Everybody knows that I'm not a folk singer.

**—Dylan,**

January 1966, *In His Own Words*

**Dylan's collaboration with** the Hawks, which began with sessions in late 1965, would prove to be the most lasting bond he developed with any musicians. They play on *Blonde on Blonde*'s "One of Us Must Know Sooner or Later," accompanied him on his first electric tour (even though the first half remained a solo acoustic set), and then retired with him after his motorcycle accident to Woodstock, New York, to make song demos and their own debut album (as the Band) while the rest of the rock audience fawned over the Beatles' *Sgt. Pepper*, the Monterey Pop Festival, and the flower-power spectacle of mass bohemia.

Robbie Robertson, the Hawks' guitarist and nascent songwriter, succeeded Bobby Neuwirth as Dylan's foil, at his side through all-night songwriting sessions on the road. Dylan's praise was generous: "He's the only mathematical guitar genius I've ever run into who does not offend my intestinal nervousness with his rear-guard sound" (Shelton, p. 316).

Along with organist Al Kooper and bassist Harvey Brooks, Robertson and drummer Levon Helm had backed Dylan up at the 1965 Forest Hills concert. Some say they met him through John Hammond, Jr., who used the band on his 1965 record *So Many Roads*. Whatever the connection, the Hawks (Robertson, Helm, bassist Rick Danko, pianist Richard Manuel, and organist Garth Hudson) sounded like Dylan's songs made their fingers itch. They did more than simply back Dylan up; they ambushed his music the same way Dylan swarmed his lyrics. Once a song got kicked off, it took command of these players, and nothing was safe as long as the number lasted. At their best, the Hawks sustained the peculiar quality of allowing the music to be in charge instead of Dylan, which allowed Dylan to surrender control and succumb to the words. The Band grew into the closest North American equivalent to the Beatles, a quintet that blended five players into a unified voice, individual lines shaping a larger whole. Arkansas pride kept Helm from playing a backup role to anyone, and he opted out of the tour, and when it continued overseas, Mickey Jones (formerly with Johnny Rivers) and Bobby Gregg filled in.

As seamless and tart as the Band's playing could be, Dylan was growing into an ideal bandleader and emotional arsonist; having laced the songs with gasoline, he knew where to strike the match. Playing the odd mixture of narrator and protagonist, Dylan made these songs sound cagily insinuative, and a far cry from tame. The bootleg tapes from this period—Dylan rehearsing *Blonde on Blonde* songs, reimagining them onstage—remain some of the most cagey and unsettling music made in the rock era.

**When the *Blonde on Blonde*** sessions wrapped, Dylan and the Band flew to Australia in April and gave a typically absurdist press conference, including one in Sydney in which Dylan interviewed himself:

Q: How long is it since you saw your mother?

A: About three months.

Q: Why don't you see her more often? Doesn't she approve of your music?

A: Well, my mother doesn't approve of it but my grandmother does.

Q: I see you've got about twelve people there with you: What's that, a band? Don't you play pure music any longer?

A: No, man, that's not a band with me. They're all friends of my grandmother. . . .

## mona lisa's highway blues

If anybody knew how to put over unreleased material to an audience lured by familiar hits, it was Dylan. Since the tour took place the spring before the June release, listeners were hearing some of its now legendary songs for the first time, without the recorded versions to refer back to in their minds. On the many tapes that survive this tour, the silence during the first half's acoustic set is palpable. At first-time hearings of songs like "4th Time Around," "Just Like a Woman," and "Visions of Johanna," ears strained (understandably) simply to follow the narratives—which picked up where the psychological conundrums of "It's Alright, Ma" left off. "Desolation Row" was a mainstay by this point, an eccentric soap-opera parade of historical figures dangled to keep the audience dazzled between his latest inscrutabilities. The song became a kind of tease, as much an apparition of comic despair as a Fellini-esque workout (and skeleton for "Eve of Destruction," Barry McGuire's imitation, which leapfrogged its model to the top of the charts in 1965). "We forget how funny crowds found 'Desolation Row,' and how right they were," Greil Marcus writes in *Mystery Train* (p. 117).

Only four recordings from this period have yet been officially released. "I Don't Believe You (She Acts Like We Never Have Met)" from Belfast and "Visions of Johanna" from London lie side by side on *Biograph* ("This is called 'I Don't Believe You,'" Dylan announces. "It used to go like that. Now it goes like this"), which also features an "It's All Over Now, Baby Blue" from Manchester. A live version of "Just Like Tom Thumb's Blues" from Liverpool appeared as the B side to the "I Want You" single.

Still, these tracks are only well-polished upgrades of dozens of tapes that appear repeatedly on widely available bootleg titles like *The Great White Wonder* and the CD *Live in England, May 1966*. *Biograph* was supposed to quell the need for bootlegs and represent a kind of corporate response to all the illegal releases making money for other people; but, like Springsteen's *Live:*

**147**

1975–85, it wound up working against its own purposes, whetting people's appetite for more. Someday there will be a complete live set that does for these 1966 performances in sound fidelity what the bootlegs have done for Dylan's myth.

**The new songs** Dylan unveils on this tour are difficult, even more demanding than the streak of situations that is "Subterranean Homesick Blues," or the delightful ambiguities that blitz past in "Tombstone Blues," but Dylan's deliveries are anything but unintelligible. He sounds as though he respects the audience's concentration, and enunciates every word of his acoustic "4th Time Around" without getting in the way of the song's trance-inducing waltz. The *Blonde on Blonde* version which would soon hit the stores is arranged for band and has a wispy quality, as though its teary-smile lilt can do little to dispel the loss the song harbors. But in concert Dylan sustains the emotionally laden pulse while giving the words a careful going-over—the performance is as much a reading of the poetry as it is a singing of the song. (This belies the later excuses Dylan makes for performing his well-known hits into his lazy tours of the 1980s, sleepwalking through "Boots of Spanish Leather" and "Tombstone Blues" as obligatory, faceless staples from the past.) The response is a hailstorm of applause; these ears knew they were privy to a classic.

Still, the second half, when Dylan brought out the Hawks, led to even more rancor and dissent from the English audiences than Dylan had experienced at Newport and Forest Hills among his home-crowd faithful. Perhaps because British taste reveres the word, Dylan, the bard of youth, betrayed something more than the flames of social conscience he had ignited in his protest songs. This rhythm-and-blues move, although championed by British groups like the Animals and the Yardbirds, was heard less as courageous than as chaotic, misshapen—and the stage technology didn't help. Dylan observes in the *Biograph* notes:

> There's a couple things that people don't realize or say. Back then, the sound systems were not sophisticated like they are today. We used to carry our own sound truck just to boost up the sound in these halls. There were hardly any monitors at all. You could never really hear yourself.

Dylan's lyrics were hard to decipher; difficult to grasp when audible, they became confusedly unsettling amid the roar of the electric backing, as though the prophet of literate experimentalism was being drowned out by the electronic din he had so nobly spent the concert's entire first half proving he didn't need.

It's hard to listen to these electric sets without admiring Dylan's courage and tenacity for the sense this music makes in retrospect. The sound is chafing, chaotic—captive, furious, liberating, it bites back at both performer and listener. But its freneticism is simply an amplification of the wild flights Dylan takes on his harmonica during the first half, the winding, jittery tours he takes in "Desolation Row" and "Mr. Tambourine Man"—and some of the chancy skids his voice takes. The Hawks compound every element of Dylan's songs, enlarge them, and shoot them through with buckshots of force and free-falling thrills that his solo settings toss off as subtleties.

The bootleg, which captures the showdown between Dylan and his punchy audience, took place at the Free Trade Hall in Manchester the week before it was fabled to have occurred at the Royal Albert Hall. It contains the quintessential confrontation between Dylan and his audience, or between any rock star who's left his audience in the dust and rebounds in person fronting a fire storm. As in the bulk of the shows from this tour, the electric set groups an unusual mix of earlier acoustic songs and recasts them as magnificent rock cathedrals: his first album's "Baby, Let Me Follow You Down," his third album's once-reposing "One Too Many Mornings," his fourth's once-resigning "I Don't Believe You." Together with an as-yet-unreleased *Blonde on Blonde* number ("Leopard-Skin Pill-Box Hat"), three from *Highway 61 Revisited* ("Just Like Tom Thumb's Blues," "Ballad of a Thin Man," and the closing "Like a Rolling Stone"), plus the never-released "Tell Me, Momma," this set would bewilder the most ardent follower. And as with some Dylan moves yet to come, perplexity is both cause and effect.

But with his gift for harrowing stare-downs, and his latent talent for charging up a band onstage and taking them places they didn't know they had in them, this music would be singularly intrepid even if Dylan were singing "Barbara Allen." Not that the songs are secondary—these versions are often superior to the ones he recorded in New York and Nashville—but the spirit of the playing and the shocked response from the crowd (a turnaround from the first half's respectful silence) produces a tension that singes the mood with fear. The Hawks muster musical spirits in the face of more than an empty studio in the early-morning hours; they play to hostile, unforgiving expressions. In Dylan's free-for-all studio sessions, his bands played without a net; onstage, the Hawks played to an audience that might have cheered an unbroken fall. As Robertson would later say to *Rolling Stone* during the 1974 tour, "The first time we played with him, when we walked out there, people would actually start booing and throwing things, so this is actually like a big, big departure. This is nothing, to have a couple of people yell, 'Dylan!' " (*Knockin' on Dylan's Door*, p. 32). Dylan's voice is the sound of the songwriter held hostage by his own material, lucky to have a few accomplices along for the inconvenience, determined to match the heights his muse calls him to, and belligerently flippant about the consequences.

On *Live in England, May 1966*, the set begins with "Tell Me, Momma." The refrain peels around several upchucking kicks, lurching and lunging; Dylan is needling his lover (again), but this time he's more desperate for her to spill her guts than put her down: "But I know that you know that I know that you show / Something . . . is tearing . . . up your . . . *mi-yi-i-nd.*"

## mona lisa's highway blues

The stop-time breaks where Robertson triggers off some quick-draw guitar licks only rough up all the sniper fire around him. Garth Hudson's organ toils away on top, chasing the others down, gaining on them, falling behind, catching up again.

Between numbers, as Dylan puffs on his harp and Robertson tunes his guitar, you can hear the audience's restlessness. They begin to clap in unison, with the odd shout amid the roar. ("Cocksucker!" someone is said to have yelled out at Forest Hills. "Ah, it's not that bad," Dylan responded.) Dylan plows ahead, into "Baby, Let Me Follow You Down," arduous where his debut album's version of Reverend Gary Davis's song had pleaded. Robertson's stinging leads between verses match the cymbals thrash for thrash, and Hudson's organ solo uncoils from the center like a snake winding its way through a thicket; Richard Manuel scatters some high rockabilly piano frills. They hold back for Dylan's verses, assail the interludes, and send enough ripples across the song's surface to smother everything within earshot. Not a moment is left unscathed.

"Just Like Tom Thumb's Blues" gets counted off with a loud thumping of someone's boot, and gasps for a couple gulps of Robertson's guitar before heaving down into the song ("When you're lost in the rain in Juarez / And it's Eastertime *too*-ooh-ooh . . ."). Robertson turns in a vengeful lead that coaxes even more fervent cymbal splashes, and carries the entire song and band to a higher pitch than seems conceivable—even for a beatnik jaunt through the back alleys of Mexico. Hudson fills in the gaps of the last verse to the point where when Dylan sings about heading back to New York City, he sings it like he's seen the same ghost that spooked Angel from the song a verse earlier.

The next few moments are confusing. Dylan begins an introduction when he's interrupted by a disturbance that gets the crowd clapping. He stops, and then starts again, in a deliberate, schoolmarmish voice: "This is called 'Your Brand-New Leopard-Skin Pill-Box Hat'. . . ." The crowd isn't paying attention; they start clapping in unison again as Dylan talks briefly with his band. Suddenly, they forge ahead, and the song struts off with authority; instantly, nothing else matters—all crowd chatter is swallowed up by the obliterating noise.

By this point Dylan is working off the energy of what's around him—the heat pouring from the band, the cool tension in the audience—and he sings this forsaken lover's revenge directly to his listeners: ". . . Tell me . . . how your head feels under somethin' like that." It's as though by upbraiding his ex-lover in the song, Dylan is reading a hilariously condescending riot act to the crowd—he imagines catching them in the same compromising position with the garage door ajar.

After that, the mood is exacerbated: people are calling out insults as Dylan tries to get the next song off the ground, and the friction escalates into another group clap. Dylan greets heckling with heckling: he steps to the mike and begins mumbling in a quiet but unflappable voice. The audience can't hear him above their own noise, and slowly they realize they're missing something and begin to quiet down. Just at this moment, when the noise is receding, Dylan says "[*garblegarble*] . . . if only you wouldn't clap so hard," which shatters the crowd's impatience. They even applaud Dylan's ability to turn the tables on them. The occasional lone shout still leaps out, but Dylan has regained command, and his sarcastic sense of humor (retorting to the crowd's cacophony with a distracting prattle of his own) has won them over, if only until the next interlude. The sledgehammer downbeat of "One Too Many Mornings" seals his victory like a door slamming shut an argument: "we're both just too many mornings / And a thousand . . . mi-hiiiiles . . . be-hiiiind."

The clapping continues after the song's cutoff, and the mechanical piano chords to "Ballad of a Thin Man" start up. Hudson's organ fills up the sound like a smoke machine, and the band comes down on the verse-ending kicks like they were slamming the door behind the entire concert. Twisting his words, elongating his vowels, and whining the lyric like a hungry tomcat, Dylan spills antiestablishment torpor into this song as though the *Time* magazine correspondent in *Don't Look Back,* with his invidious Caruso comparison, was easy prey. In *Eat the Document,* Dylan cross-cut segments from this song with the mixed reactions from the crowd outside the hall after the concert, as though the attack applied as easily to fans as it did to journalists. Even though this groove is slower, less manic than what's come before, the players bear down on this music to the point where it doesn't seem to have any curves left to hug; the gears are stripped but the chassis plunges forward. The ending is more a fait accompli than a climax.

Surprisingly, there is silence in the hall between numbers as Dylan puffs on this harmonica again. Then a sudden burst of laughter erupts from an indecipherable joke, and a high-pitched cry of "Judas!" rips the air. It's what the crowd's agitators have been thinking all through the second set, and the strain has built to the point where the accusation punctures the tension like gunfire. Dylan's scornful but comic gibberish has only goaded more antirock dissent.

The crowd applauds, dissolves into debate. Dylan takes his time, then steps to the microphone. "I don't *believe* you," he says. "You're a *liar.*" The next and final song is bubbling up from beneath him. "Play fuckin' *loud,*" Dylan tells his band, and they grab hold of "Like a Rolling Stone" as though the hammer-shot downbeat to "One Too Many Mornings" were a blank.

It's not just that the crowd and the band have pushed each other into a confrontation, or that Dylan has already proved his unwillingness to back down and concede to demands for an acoustic contrition (the way he did at Newport by encoring with "It's All Over Now, Baby Blue"). It's a moment that defines Dylan's unwavering stance as an unrepentant R&B iconoclast, and his closing song choice makes the new image indisputable in ways that are even larger than Dylan may have had in mind. Instead of singing this song to an imaginary neophyte, a high-class loner who has fallen from privilege, or to himself (as Dave Marsh suggests), Dylan directs this assualt at his audience, and

## hard rain

confidently peels off layers of pent-up recrimination and shattered confidence that the song lies ready to unveil:

> **You never turned around to see the frowns on the**
> **jugglers and the clowns**
> **When they all come down and did tricks for you**

He's singing to his audience, accusing them of self-limiting expectations, but he's also singing about the pressured relationship he shares with them—his listeners, his critics, his medium, the pop world around him—and about who keeps the upper hand. There's no mistaking who wins—this time. The fact that a rock press has yet to exist, and that all this passes within the rock community as word-of-mouth legend, in tape exchanges and bootleg racks around the world, unreported until three years later in *Rolling Stone*, seals the mythical level of this exchange. It's the key defining moment of Dylan's early career: it articulates the gulf between what he expects of himself and the standards his audience, critics, and players misapply to his protean talents. It's also the last music he makes publicly for two years.

**clothesline sagas**

## The Basement Tapes
Released: July 1975

I was touring for a couple of years. That's a fast pace
. . . we were doing a whole show, no other acts. It's
pretty straining to do a show like that . . . a lot of
really unhealthy situations rise up . . . I was just going out there performing these songs. Everyone else
was having a good time . . . I did it enough to know
that there must be something else to do . . . It wasn't
my own choice. I was more or less being pushed into
it—pushed in and carried out. . . .
   **—Dylan**,
      Robert Shelton, *No Direction Home*

**After Dylan urbanized** folk, which led him to punch-drunk
rhythm and blues, his 1966–67 convalescence pointed him
straight back towards country. Having coaxed his audience into
the pleasures of renegade fantasies, he retreated towards prerock
styles as a reaction to both the mass psychedelic movement and
the social-activist values that were undercut in the process. As
long as Dylan's hipster raids on the establishment were outboard
attitudes that wangled their way onto the charts as much for
weirdness as for anything else, Dylan seemed pleased. But the
more Dylan's image evolved into an oracle of truth-for-youth
hype, his insecurities flared; you get the sense that he was bound
to withdraw from the rock scene even if he hadn't had a motorcycle accident. The sound of the resulting *Basement Tapes* is so
ripe with comfort that the mythical place where Dylan holed up
with the band—in the basement of Big Pink, a house in West
Saugerties, New York—becomes a haven that induces a secluded

state of mind, the site for a sequence of floating, tuneful confidences.

In a year when the Beatles released *Sgt. Pepper's Lonely Hearts Club Band*, and Jimi Hendrix doused American listeners with a hard, bracing guitar brew he'd been concocting in Britain, the climate of *The Basement Tapes* was not just foreign to prevailing pop currents, it was a classic statement of rural virtues. It's a credit to this material that as radically removed as it was from that of Dylan's colleagues, it's not simply reactionary, as if he were merely holing up as a way of acting superior to the foppish explosion erupting all around him. Instead, Dylan sounds relaxed, sure of his muse, and steeped in an imaginary Americana even when he's making up lyrics on the spot ("Odds and Ends," "Open the Door, Homer") and kicking out the kinks of outback life by heading for the honky-tonks ("Goin' to Acapulco"). *The Basement Tapes* rebelled against its context as much as the acoustic-electric tension on *Bringing It All Back Home* or the antipop delight of "I Want You," and gathered a long-lost mystique his other records hadn't simply by remaining a well-known secret for eight years.

While Dylan's elaborate escape fantasies circled around displacement as a defining symptom of modern culture ("Mr. Tambourine Man," "Memphis Blues"), they also called out for stability and tradition as only uncorked reveries can. Confronting the folk faithful with the electric rock he knew they would have trouble accepting, and touring to hostile audiences in England, Dylan must have felt even more like an outsider than he had to begin with. In retreat, these obsessions took root in the music, and played themselves out as yarns about domestic strife, half-remembered escapades, and lofty farces about the joy of music making.

Roots music turned out to be the void that rock was busy creating for itself, and one that would need filling for longer than anybody could have imagined. The sixties were such an onslaught of experimentation with new sounds, looks, and material, it was almost as if after darting off so far into so many directions some catch-up time was necessary. Bands like the Hawks, who had spent their lean years like everybody else—playing fifties music to bar crowds—did what a lot of other bands did when they were fishing about for new material: they turned to their live set to pass the time; and as adults going over the music that had inspired them as teenagers, they were rewarded with something more than adolescent kicks. Like all originals, the Band found their sound by piecing together influences, invoking shared experiences through patchworks of references—their sources make Motown, rockabilly, and doo-wop bells ring in listeners' heads as the players discovered something new from the compound.

The Band had a knack for creating cushions of musical support for Dylan to sit back in, and the tone on *The Basement Tapes* is prerock antique, a feel these players will chase through their first two independent projects (*Music from Big Pink* in 1968 and *The Band* a year later). It's as though Dylan and his cohorts deliberately set out to play against the outrageousness in rock that was beginning to turn into spectacle. Dylan's wilder capers celebrated the exuberance of the open road, the joy of casting off ties with the past and the prescribed values that government or society might place on a person. But by re-creating an imagined past, a fantasy of how things might have been if Hollywood's westerns had had rock 'n' roll soundtracks, Dylan and the Band created a sound that affirmed a yearning for stability that flows from rootlessness. In doing so, they created an imaginary past for rock while everybody else was chasing an empty psychedelic future.

**If *The Basement Tapes*** would have sounded out of place in 1967, it certainly didn't suit the disco-bound pop agenda of 1975, when it was finally released. It remains one of the most unselfconscious pieces of rock 'n' roll mysticism ever taped, as pertinent in its

## clothesline sagas

domestic-philosophic riddles as Presley's race-mixing Sun sessions, as involving in its casual flair and whimsical language as John Lennon's prose or Allen Ginsberg's poetry-reading jam sessions (*First Blues—Rags, Ballads & Harmonium Songs, 1971– 74*, dedicated "to Minstrel Guruji Bob Dylan").

The characters' names in these songs tell a story all their own—they evoke a nineteenth-century mining town, in the rock equivalent of an offbeat movie western like Robert Altman's *McCabe and Mrs. Miller*, where the formless narrative adds shape to the story. ("I got poetry in me," McCabe mutters at one point in the film. "I do. I got poetry in me. Ain't gonna try to put it down on paper . . . got sense enough not to try.") "Tiny Montgomery" alone features Skinny Moo, Lester, Lou, and Half-track Frank. Valerie and Vivian get rhymed with "salary" and "oblivion" in "Too Much of Nothing"; and Genghis Khan wanders onto the set of "You Ain't Goin' Nowhere." It's mountain music made by people who speak the same deadpan double-talk; people to whom life doesn't begin to make sense and never has, who take comfort in a full bottle and despair in an empty, who see life as a series of disconnected perplexities, grab hold of pleasure where they can find it, and submit themselves to the fate of the land ("Ain't No More Cain," "Down in the Flood")—and the omnipresent, epic-bender poker games. More often than not, they take cover from the hapless, openended world around them through song ("Million Dollar Bash," "Too Much of Nothing," "Open the Door, Homer," and "Clothes Line Saga").

Dylan's cryptic non sequiturs abandon the street language of *Bringing It All Back Home* and *Highway 61 Revisited* and the druggie double entendres of *Blonde on Blonde* for rustic allusions. The opening lines to "You Ain't Goin' Nowhere" set an outdoor scene that shorthands an imaginative pastoral:

**Clouds so swift**
**Rain won't lift**

## hard rain

The title couplet expresses the kind of kicked-back flirtation yokels surrender to when they're snowed in for the weekend or longer. Where Dylan's earlier rock 'n' roll was more explicitly urban—faster, slicker, in a manic vein—good-natured serenades like "Apple Suckling Tree" reflect the relaxed pace of small-town mores and modest means. This music harbors the roots of the folk Dylan started out with, as well as the strains of early rock and country that emerge on *John Wesley Harding* and *Nashville Skyline*, and balloons into a full-scale roots-rock movement well beyond punk.

The Band's six songs ("Katie's Been Gone," "Bessie Smith," "Ain't No More Cain," "Reben Remus," "Yazoo Street Scandal," and "Orange Juice [Blues for Breakfast]") provide snapshots of players beginning to find their voice as an ensemble, and follow the cues of their leader (and chief songwriter), Robbie Robertson. After hanging out with Dylan for just under two years, Robertson has sponged up everything Dylan has to teach about song styling—how inference can be more titillating than detail, how intriguing setups can alleviate the need for follow-through, how vagaries can stack up to pseudoplots. The idea of an American Beatles begins to make sense on these recordings; and when the Band comes into its own, the confluence of writers, voices, and players emerges as a distinct yet Beatles-inspired approach. Along with producer John Simon, Robertson is responsible for the pine-box tone of their early records, but he counts on Danko, Manuel, and Helm for the singing. Group refrains are the norm (even though backup vocal pairings are few), and Garth Hudson's organ-grinder flourishes dart in and out of the sound like whiffs of good snuff. What the Band learned from Dylan was how to let a song define a sound, so that the song (the lyrics, the chord changes) guides individual players towards instinctively felt counterpoints instead of saddling the singer with all the dramatic duties. Listen to the carefree control they achieve in "Don't Ya Tell Henry," or "Long-Distance Operator." What the Band learned from the Beatles was how to balance instrumental

## clothesline sagas

voices inside the ensemble, so that specific moments or inflections become just as enjoyable as the overall effect, the details as expressive as the whole.

Dylan's genius in following these ensemble arrows lies in how he exploits this method without ever trying to harness it, or manipulate it to his own devices—following his peculiar voicing is enough of a challenge even for these seasoned players. With sawed-off pleasure romps like "Million Dollar Bash" and the come-hither sexual smirk of "Apple Suckling Tree," he lets the music fill in the blanks, even when he's not sure just what those blanks are there for.

**A lot of the happenstance comedy** on *The Basement Tapes* sounds improvised. *Lyrics 1962–1985* catalogs most of the lyrics, but you get the feeling that they were largely words that just happened to pass through Dylan's mind as the verses kept coming around. *The Basement Tapes* is like an open spigot to Dylan's thought process, and it lets you know how much of a feel he has for twisting shopworn homilies into non sequiturs that sound as though they should make sense ("The louder they come, the harder they crack" in "Million Dollar Bash"). Some of these stabs at philosophy, especially the way healing begins with forgiveness in "Open the Door, Homer," point directly towards the ambiguities that lace *John Wesley Harding*.

There's a streak of the drunken poet in these songs, a resourceful soul fighting his way through a smog of fear, self-doubt, shame, and peer pressure towards affection and acceptance—(symbolic) trips to the bawdy house that restore more than the singer's (symbolic) libido. "Goin' to Acapulco" is the saddest song about rocks-off relief ever written; "Goin' to have some fun" is sung with such aching trepidation that the guitar squawks Robbie Robertson wedges in beneath the singer's held notes on those lines are like the throb of a hangover before the next drunk, the pangs of desire grinding against certain disappointment. Even good-natured jokes and pranks elude this love-starved man.

And the lanky, weak-kneed "Get Your Rocks Off," a hilarious outtake from these outtakes, sounds like a postlude to an exhausting orgy ("Get 'em off me!" Dylan sings). ("Rocks Off!" can't be so easily summarized: with a nod to Fats Domino's "Blueberry Hill," the song brushes up against the same ironic double entendres as "Rainy Day Women #12 & 35," and the final verse alludes to the Mississippi Freedom Rides: "Well, you know, we was cruisin' down the highway in a Greyhound bus / All kinds-a children in the side road, they was hollerin' at us, sayin': / 'Get your rocks off! . . .' ")

The *Basement Tapes* may be the most celebrated accident in rock since Presley's Sun sessions, but the songs hang together in delightful ways. "Goin' to Acapulco" is fleshed out by the careening earthy warmth of "Please, Mrs. Henry," in which a drunk who can't hold his jism begs for sexual mercy ("I'm down on my knees / An' I ain't got a dime," he pleads).

The drinking and womanizing are a front for the layered anxieties these binges conceal, fears that well up in confessions like "Too Much of Nothing," in the aftertaste of moral betrayal in "Tears of Rage," "Nothing Was Delivered," and "This Wheel's on Fire," and in a good-bye song that is equal parts condescension and threat, "Down in the Flood." As Greil Marcus points out in the liner notes, the forces that make this music ribald and liberating are tied to more private debates about debts and obligations—what people owe to one another, and how much can be assumed between lovers, friends, and adversaries. "She wrote last week and sent her love," Danko sings in "Katie's Been Gone," "I wonder what kind of love she's thinkin' of."

"Tears of Rage" (which Dylan writes with pianist Richard Manuel) is a soldier's curse upon his commander. It's the voice of a man who followed his leader into battle, saw his friends slaughtered for a cause he may never have fully believed in, only to return to find his superior running for political office, turning his back on the values that were so easily sacrificed. "We carried you in our arms / On Independence Day" is the kind of battle-scar allusion that Robbie Robertson will flesh out in songs like "The Night They Drove Old Dixie Down," on the Band's second album. "Tears of Rage" doesn't depend on the same associations, but it pursues the same memories, and voices a disbelief in and cynicism about authority so charged with resentment it can barely work up the steam to get pissed off. (On *Any Day Now*, Joan Baez turns this song into a robust a cappella spiritual, as though it had been written for Odetta.) Who knows how many Vietnam protesters—and veterans—might have called this song their own had it been released before the fall of Saigon?

This leader who was carried in the arms of his troops, who scratched his name in sand, must now hear the bitter voice of his dissenters. The song can be read as an allegory for the Vietnam experience from the side of the dispirited soldier instead of the peaceniks, the usual heroes of the antiwar songs written in this period (Neil Young's "Ohio," John Lennon's "Revolution").

"Tears of Rage" closes with a summary of how earthly riches (gold) corrupt spiritual values, and make love and honor go from bad to worse. This is betrayal of the most profound kind: having sacrificed everything for a cause, only to find that the leader of the cause never believed in the battle's purpose to begin with. Most commentators note the allusion to *King Lear*, but that passage is actually a measure of self-awareness coming from the accuser (to follow the allusion through, the song's narrator is identifying with Lear's daughter Cordelia and pointing out the manipulative snare the father figure lays for the children). This song is of a piece with "Nothing Was Delivered," which is sung from the same betrayed vantage point with a more forgiving refrain ("Nothing is better, nothing is best / Take care of yourself and get plenty of rest"). Again, it's a song that reads like a prophetic snub of Lyndon Johnson and Richard Nixon, a theme that Stevie Wonder made popular when he released "You Haven't Done Nothin' " in the early months of 1974.

## hard rain

Like a lot of the songs on the Band's first two albums, "Tears of Rage" paints a picture of frontier life that obliterates the myth of hardy pioneers settling scores and imposing a moral righteousness on uncivilized land. When he concludes refrains by bemoaning life's brevity, he says a lot about the flip side of the Woodstock generation's lust for heroes, and the communal blather that would spin out into biker fables like *Easy Rider*. In Dylan's imaginary West, which he inhabits through *John Wesley Harding*, moral righteousness is a concept that is slippery at best. The mythic West was shaped as much by betrayal, double-crossings, unremarkable men performing heroic feats, and average people caught up in extraordinary moments as by the lone gunmen with a score to settle. It was anything but a linear process.

**For all of** Greil Marcus's liner notes' talk about Americana in these sessions, the outtakes reveal a broader embrace of indigenous music running through these songs and would have rounded out *The Basement Tapes* with black styles—gospel and soul—had they been included. An uncanny Motown echo, "All You Have to Do Is Dream," gets clipped by guitar strokes that point towards the soul-based revivals the Band excel at on their oldies revue, *Moondog Matinee* (1973), and in covers like the Four Tops' "Loving You Is Sweeter Than Ever" and Marvin Gaye's "Don't Do It (Baby Don't You Do It)," both available on *To Kingdom Come* (1989). "All You Have to Do Is Dream" is a finished Dylan song, a farm boy's daydream with barnyard metaphors about unrequited love. The Band gives it the submerged feel of a lost B side, and Dylan sings with a teasing, affectionate quality that doesn't lack for intensity—he sings almost as well as he does on "Tears of Rage."

And if the *Blind Boy Grunt and the Hawks* bootleg culls tracks from different sessions, it shows how, despite their best efforts, the times did impinge on the world of Woodstock, New

York. Tiny Tim, whose granny soprano patronized the establishment's need for an emasculated hippie clown, drops in during the same period for vocals on four numbers with the Band, including an outsized, absolutely bloodless version of the Ronettes' "Be My Baby" that defines rock camp (the others are Sonny and Cher's "I Got You, Babe" and Chuck Berry's "Memphis, Tennessee," and "Sonny Boy"). There are working versions that show how the sessions toyed with a song's makeup, tempo, and delivery: a slow, unformed version of "Too Much of Nothing," an instrumental backing track to "Orange Juice Blues," and several other instrumentals and Garth Hudson keyboard snatches that make it sound like these men killed time by making music the way some people play checkers. There are also half-finished songs that were abandoned: "I'm Not There," a not-too-funky blues, "Down on Me," and "One Man's Loss"—an old saw that Paul Simon reworks in "One Man's Ceiling Is Another Man's Floor" on *There Goes Rhymin' Simon* (1973).

But even some of the remnants grab hold of the ear and refuse to be labeled throwaways. A drumless run-through, "One Single River," is a lost-love plea with a melody that's all reconciliation, a soulful antidote to the chewings-out Dylan used to subject his lovers to: "How come you shut me out as if I wasn't there / What's this new bitterness you've found?" Along with "I Don't Hurt Anymore" and "I Can't Make It Alone," it looks back with affection through shadows of pain.

Then, too, there are unfinished classics that beg for completion. As the Band's instruments slowly join in on what sounds like a first run-through of Dylan's ominous twelve-string saga "The Hills of Mexico," the song becomes a Spanish-tinged narrative that resembles the later "One More Cup of Coffee" (from *Desire*). The journey that in three verses only gets started never reaches Mexico; but Dylan's singing delves so far into these characters, especially on the held notes just before the title lines, that you fear for these people even before you get to know them. "We're wasting tape," Dylan says as the song collapses.

## hard rain

Neither "One Single River" nor "The Hills of Mexico" approaches "A Night Without Sleep," where bitterness returns in a slow, shame-ridden waltz that could be the hokum antithesis of the Band's "It Makes No Difference":

**If the ladies were squirrels with them fair bushy tails**
**I'd fill up my shotgun with rocks, salt and nails.**

Amid several gospel standards, among them "People Get Ready," is Dylan's cover of a song that Hank Williams sang under the name "Luke the Drifter": "Be Careful of the Stones That You Throw" is one part country parable about the boomerang evils of gossip, and one part TV evangelism, in which Dylan sends up his future born-again self. The narrator listens to a neighbor who has "gossip, not flowers" on her mind, as she calls down a girl living on her street. Later, the neighbor's daughter is saved from an onrushing car by the same girl, who gives her own life to rescue the child:

**A car speeded by and the screeching of brakes a**
**screaming that made my blood chill**
**My neighbor's one child had been pulled from the**
**path and saved by a girl lying still**
**The child was unhurt and my neighbor cried out**
**Oh, who was that brave girl so sweet**
**I covered the crushed broken body and said**
**That bad girl that lived down the street**

**So unless you have made no mistakes in your life**
**Be careful of stones that you throw. . . .**

In this spoken morality play, Dylan's delivery catches a plain-talk sincerity that put Williams over—it's the kind of sentimental ploy Dylan has spent a career deflating. But he clearly enjoys hamming up the thick end of country's moralism.

## clothesline sagas

As heartfelt gospel comedy, "Be Careful of the Stones That You Throw" does nothing to prepare you for "Sign on the Cross," which captures the deathless fatalism of gospel and country Dylan was after in much of his later born-again albums. While Hudson's velveteen organ rises to counter Dylan's voice on the opposite channel in the second verse, the song becomes a paradigm of gospel styling—unpretentious surface, unfathomable depth. During Dylan's spoken third verse, he lapses into self-parody and walks the unforeseen line between low farce and high religious humility: the players keep missing changes, and between chuckles, Dylan makes the last verse a summary of the musical rewards that "I Shall Be Released" and "A Night Without Sleep" have promised.

**Perhaps it's appropriate** that the two most famous songs from these sessions—"I Shall Be Released" and "Quinn the Eskimo (The Mighty Quinn)"—don't show up on *The Basement Tapes*. "I Shall Be Released" is an overpraised and overplayed potboiler about a man in prison who hears another man's cries of being framed, and the rock community latched on to it almost as warmly as it did "Knockin' on Heaven's Door" as an all-purpose sentimental finale. The Band are the first to release it, on *Music from Big Pink*; and as their *Last Waltz* closer it turns into an all-star blowout with Ringo Starr on drums and soon-to-be Rolling Stone Ron Wood, one of Dylan's closest friends, on guitar.

"Quinn the Eskimo (The Mighty Quinn)" eventually shows up on *Bob Dylan's Greatest Hits, Volume 2* in 1971, but it surfaces before that as one of this period's most notorious party odes. A drug song with a chorus that overtakes even the after-hours bacchanalia of "Rainy Day Women #12 & 35," "Quinn" is a half-cocked paean to impending renewal that works as a reveille for any kind of awakening—a second coming, a favorite blend of LSD ("everyone's gonna wanna doze"), a Tambourine Man's song. With barnyard yawps from cats and cows, it drops its share of blasé stingers ("I like to do just like the rest, I like my sugar sweet / But guarding fumes and making haste / It ain't my cup of meat"). (Manfred Mann jumped on it for a hit in 1968, and twenty years later the title got rewritten as a reggae cover by Sheryl Lee Ralph, with Cedella Marley and Sharon Marley Prendergast, for a comedy movie by the same name starring Denzel Washington, set in Jamaica.)

**That Dylan could** have released a lot of this material to great success even during the psychedelic era made the aroma of isolation and mystery on *The Basement Tapes* all the more puzzling. Dylan recorded some of the songs again later (*Bob Dylan's Greatest Hits, Volume 2*: "I Shall Be Released," "You Ain't Goin' Nowhere," and "Down in the Flood"), but not until they have become known through recordings by others: the Band began their career with "Tears of Rage" at the top of *Music from Big Pink* (which included "This Wheel's on Fire" and Richard Manuel's falsetto treatment of "I Shall Be Released"); Ian and Sylvia took a decent stab at "This Wheel's on Fire" on their *Nashville* (1968); the Coulson, Dean, McGuiness and Flint album of this material dramatized how ironies can seep through even unironic singing; and Fairport Convention, Britain's rough equivalent of the Band, picked up "Million Dollar Bash" and ran with it (as well as turned "If You Gotta Go, Go Now" into a sweet, French-language pub song; both are on *Unhalfbricking*, 1969); Sandy Denny took to "Down in the Flood" on her first solo effort, *The North Star Grassman and the Ravens* (1971). The Byrds picked up "You Ain't Goin' Nowhere" as an emblem for the back-to-the-country movement when it kicked off their *Sweetheart of the Rodeo* album in 1968 (the record went home with "Nothing Was Delivered"). Roger McGuinn sang this song for years and recorded it again with Chris Hillman on *Will the Circle Be Unbroken, Volume 2* (1989), the Nitty Gritty Dirt Band title that tried to cash in on the roots boom Volume 1 jump-started in 1972.

## clothesline sagas

But as on a lot of famous demos (take, for example, the out-of-body frankness of Hank Williams on *Just Me and My Guitar*, or the estranged air of Bruce Springsteen's *Nebraska*), recording for themselves instead of the public brought out different qualities in Dylan's vocals as well as the Band's playing—the performances reveal even more about these singers than about the songs. Instead of the deadpan flippancies that characterized Dylan's earlier rock, this is personalized music making, signals passed between musicians where language would fall short, where as much is expressed in a vocal harmony or a solo trade-off as in a knowing glance or facial guffaw. Since they're making music for one another and not for the millions of ears that the microphones usually symbolize, these sessions turn listeners into eavesdroppers after-the-fact, and the music becomes a shared private code of symbols and secrets. By now, with the proliferation of bootlegs, we're accustomed to hearing first takes, false starts, and unfinished songs. But these sessions reveal more than the typical camaraderie and open-spirited experimentation; they remain the most seductively underproduced sessions of the rock era.

Dylan's about-face between neurotic exhibitionist onstage with the Hawks in 1966 and reclusive hermit in a makeshift demo studio with the same players the following spring makes it hard to generalize about his temperament. The music he performed live in 1966 endures as a standard of challenge, confrontation, and vision by which rock performers still measure their relationship with their audience. But until *Biograph* (and then only sparingly), these widely circulated live tapes were officially unreleased, as if Dylan felt they were unpublishable. Whatever the reason, he insists on withholding some of his best recordings, both from his tour in England with the Hawks and from the music they returned to in New York. He made some of the best music of his career when he was certain his audience was not listening.

# retro man

*John Wesley Harding* is a profoundly egotistical album. For an album of this kind to be released amidst *Sgt. Pepper, Their Satanic Majesties Request, After Bathing at Baxter's*, somebody must have had a lot of confidence in what he was doing. . . . Dylan seems to feel no need to respond to the predominate trends in pop music at all. And he is the only major pop artist about whom this can be said. The Dylan of *John Wesley Harding* is a truly independent artist who doesn't feel responsible to anyone else, whether they be fans or his contemporaries.

   **—Jon Landau**,
     *Crawdaddy*, 1968

I ran into George Harrison some time after the record was out, and he told me the album was one of his all-time favorites, but he imagined it must have been a bitch to record. . . . He wanted to know how long it took to do the damn thing. So I looked at my watch and said, "About six hours." Then he said, "Well, how long did it take to mix?" and I said, "That *was* mixed!" We just put it down and Columbia threw it out. Nobody ever went into the studio to mix a note.

   —drummer **Kenny Buttrey**,
     in Bob Spitz, *Dylan*

**It's a credit to** Dylan's talent as a narrative impressionist that as the western becomes a metaphor for the rock experience, he turns it into a strangely appropriate backdrop for his comeback. On *John Wesley Harding*, all the western hero needs to be is a provocative and misunderstood outsider—the rest is pieced together by the listener. As a metaphor for his self-conscious relationship with the world of rock, *John Wesley Harding* is a finely honed satire of Dylan as the music's dry sage, the reputed gunslinger-in-exile who suddenly shows up back in town, downs psychedelia's show-biz camp with understated aplomb, and rides into the sunset with his woman at his side.

The record is remote on several levels: the lyrics are opaque-vernacular; the music—acoustic guitar, bass, and drums—is skeletal, yet inscrutable; the songs are riddles posing as revelation. The central mystery is the central character, John Wesley Harding, a symbol for Dylan himself: known throughout the land as an elusive troubadour, a "friend to the poor / . . . he was never known / To hurt an honest man." The legend comes from Texas: the real outlaw was called John Wesley Hardin (no g), who, after killing a Texas sheriff in 1877, studied law in prison—only to be gunned down by a constable a year after his release. Dylan updates the tale of Guthrie's "Pretty Boy Floyd," the outlaw who downed a deputy with a log chain for cursing in front of his wife. Floyd spent his days on the run from the law, but left Christmas dinners and thousand-dollar bills for the farmers who fed him. "You'll never see an outlaw drive a family from their home," Guthrie concluded.

Guthrie's way of thinking is basic: killing a corrupt sheriff on principle is nobler than a wealthy banker evicting families because of drought-induced shortfalls. Floyd's good deeds turn him into a figure that common folk look up to not because he's an outlaw, but because he represents the kind of decisive action against authority most people can't afford to take.

It's a theme brought out in *Bonnie and Clyde*, the Warren Beatty–Faye Dunaway movie that is to put-on comedy what Dylan is to deadpan doggerel. Beyond its mock-glamorized violence (and cheesy impotence subplot), *Bonnie and Clyde* fed the sixties' preoccupation with both resistance and innocence. Early in the film, after Clyde finishes target practice with some bottles atop a sign that reads "Property of Midlothian Citizens Bank—Trespassers Will Be Prosecuted," he's come upon by a farmer, who is startled to find a gunman on his farm.

"Y'all go right ahead," says the farmer, backing away. His family sits watching in his dust-bowl jalopy. "Used to be my place, but it's not anymore. Bank took it. Yessir, they moved us off—now it belongs to them."

"Well, that's a pitiful shame," says Bonnie.

"You're damn right," replies the farmer. "Me and him put in the years here," he says, looking over at his helper. "Yes, you all go right ahead—we just stopped by for a last look."

Clyde suddenly opens fire on the sign, then hands the gun to the farmer. He gives it a blast and passes Clyde a quick wink. "Ya'll mind? Hey, Davis," he calls to his helper, "come on over here." The farmer takes another shot through his window. "Go on," he tells Davis, who takes a couple shots for himself. "Much obliged," the farmer concludes. "My name's Otis Harris, and this is Davis—we worked this place."

"How're you," Clyde says, shaking his hand. "This here's Bonnie Parker, and I'm Clyde Barrow. We rob banks." The comic slur of that punch line is not lost on the farmer—or on the rock audience.

When the Barrow gang ambush a Texas ranger who has caught up with them in Missouri, Bonnie suggests they take a picture of the ranger with the gang for public relations. As Clyde hoists the ranger up onto the back of their car, he says, "Now, see what come of your mischief—from not doin' your job? You know, down in Duncanville last year, poor farmers kept you law away from us with shotguns. Now, you supposed to be protecting them from us—and they protecting us from you, that don't make sense, do it?" He might as well have said, "Something is happening here / But you don't know what it is."

At the next bank robbery, Clyde asks a man in overalls

whether the money on the counter is his or the bank's. "It's mine," the man says. "All right, then. You keep it," Clyde says, before nicking the cop in the corner with a warning shot.

"All I can say is, they did right by me," the farmer tells the press later. "And I'm gonna bring a mean mess of flowers to their funeral."

Dylan robs his banks by pilfering "straight" history and mangling stiff tradition. The fables in *John Wesley Harding* are bleached of detail: the image of the cowboy is so large in our collective imagination that he has no trouble pushing the right buttons and keying us in to the myth. The "situation" Harding is renowned for takes place in Chaynee County, where he took a stand with his lady at his side. That's all the listener gets. It's a three-verse nonstory that reads like a telegram—its subject is temerity in the face of danger, its method innuendo and suggestion. Dylan told Jann Wenner in 1969:

> I was gonna write a ballad on . . . like maybe one of those old cowboy . . . you know, a real long ballad. But in the middle of the second verse, I got tired. I had a tune, and I didn't want to waste the tune, it was a nice little melody, so I just wrote a quick third verse, and I recorded that. . . . I knew people were gonna listen to that song and say that they didn't understand what was going on, but they would've singled that song out later, if we hadn't called the album *John Wesley Harding* and placed so much importance on that, for people to start wondering about it . . . if that hadn't been done, that song would've come up and people would have said it was a throw-away song. (*Rolling Stone Interviews, Volume I*, pp. 314–15)

Some Dylan songs operate off circumstances that lie outside the narrative action (the broken relationship that prompts "Don't Think Twice," the betrayal that tweaks "Positively 4th Street"). *John Wesley Harding* fields subjects that the songs

barely point toward—the idea of the western Dylan plays off of
here is so pervasive he doesn't even need to fill out his sketches.
The writing on *John Wesley Harding* reduces the stabs at impressions from the *Basement Tapes* songs into shadow parables,
and shows how Dylan is at least as much a phrase turner as he is
a songwriter ("His tongue it could not speak, but only flatter" in
"The Wicked Messenger"). Not many people remember "Drifter's Escape," but the judge's ironically kind words to the pris-
oner he's about to sentence are emblematic: "You fail to
understand . . . Why must you even try?" That line juts out; and
in figuring up all these situations and fleeting impressions this
record has to offer, you can't help being thankful for it. Before,
Dylan streaked through rambling verses that did more to carry
the song forward than to spin out a narrative ("Memphis Blues").
On *John Wesley Harding*, the ersatz narratives are not only
evasive, they're barely even glimpses: blink and you miss everything that's happening off-screen.

History is written from dust and unfathomable chance
events that change people without cause or pity, and this process
intrigues the storyteller as much as anybody. That's why Dylan's
liner notes are so self-consciously revealing—the story of the
three kings in search of truth follows the same lines the songs do,
only the tale is openly hilarious in ways the songs aren't. It's a
Kurt Vonnegut (*Breakfast of Champions*) love triangle between
Frank; his wife, Vera; and Terry Shute, a mysterious reactionary,
who vents a tirade about creeping consumption.

After Frank chastises Shute's outburst, the kings ask Frank
if he is indeed the key to the new Dylan album—he consents.
Then in a parody of how Dylan imagines fanatics want him to
decode his own songs, he has Frank wave his shirt in the air and
break a light bulb and a window. When he sits back down and
calmly pulls a knife, his decoding is through.

When the kings leave before dawn, one's nose has been
"fixed," another's arm has "healed," and the last was "rich."

"Oh mighty thing!" Vera tells Frank afterwards, "Why

didn't you just tell them you were a moderate man and leave it at that instead of goosing yourself all over the room?" The leap this ending takes between serendipity and bogus revelation is a gap the songs pitch in more pious tones—the joke is, they only *sound* profound. There's a tension at work here, but you're hard-pressed to put your finger on where the friction is coming from. This kind of writing style is a stretch for Dylan—he's trying to see how much more he can get away with by limiting his resources. And by converting his antisong tactics into enigmatic vessels of innuendo, he stumbles upon a new form: the micro-epic.

Since nearly every song on *John Wesley Harding* conforms to a ridiculously rigid three-verse mold, it's as though Dylan means to manipulate surface events to hold more meaning than any interior explanation could approach—as if by mastering surface, content will follow. The feat is that to some extent—with the help of his ripe, implicative singing and acute harmonica work—the style becomes the content.

On one level, Dylan the demigod is trying to deflate his own mythic status, which only mushroomed after his accident. But this record is also the beginning of Dylan's detachment from his audience as a generational hero, as somebody listeners identify with as a spokesperson for their age group. What *John Wesley Harding* opens up (for Dylan, and for everyone else) is the idea that the racial, philosophical, and ideological mysteries that rock 'n' roll can traverse are as boundless as the secrets the music springs from and can't hope to explain. This is American music of a vintage that, as Paul Williams put it, sounds like it might have sounded just days before Elvis made his first record (quoted in *Stranded*). But because the lyrics are so flirtatiously subdued, Dylan makes an intriguing argument that's persuasive even when the "logic" of these songs evaporate: rock doesn't need to be bound by its audience's age, its past, or, by extension, its present. Not only can rock address adult concerns, Dylan is saying; its heroes can approach universal archetypes—a wayward immigrant, a naive pilgrim, a forgotten saint, a tragic fool—as they undo classic "conventions." The cowboy is America's idea of a classic, and his mission was always about the tension between imposing law on a lawless terrain and being true to his woman. Dylan taps the relentlessness with which nature subverts man's idea of order, and caves in to romance with an impassive smirk.

**When Dylan drew** on historical characters before, he toyed with them as abstractions that had lost some of their weight through the joyful surface-happy preoccupations of pop (Beethoven cavorting with Ma Rainey, Mona Lisa's "highway blues"). Here, the names he drops into the mix get used more for their associations: Judas Priest preys on Frankie Lee's weakness, then disappears; St. Augustine appears as a vision in a dream (it's patterned after the Union hymn "I Dreamed I Saw Joe Hill," which Joan Baez sang at Woodstock); a convicted drifter escapes captivity when a bolt of lightning zaps a court of law; a landlord is the object of a naked plea for respect and equal rights; a hobo utters a humble warning to those better off; the immigrant is a pitiful and fearsome specter; and a wicked messenger vows not to talk double-talk.

There are exceptions: "As I Went Out One Morning" has more to do with the temptations of a fair damsel who walks in chains than with America's first outlaw journalist, Tom Paine. But that hasn't kept some from diving into the song's spell; as Greil Marcus writes in *The Rolling Stone Record Review*:

> I sometimes hear the song as a brief journey into American history; the singer out for a walk in the park, finding himself next to a statue of Tom Paine, and stumbling across an allegory: Tom Paine, symbol of freedom and revolt, coopted into the role of Patriot by textbooks and statue committees, and now playing, as befits his role as Patriot, enforcer to a girl who runs for freedom—in chains, to the

*South*, the source of vitality in America, in America's music—*away* from Tom Paine. We have turned our history on its head; we have perverted our own myths. . . . (p. 530)

A lot of what's said on *John Wesley Harding* jibes neatly with the continuing saga of Dylan's relationship with his audience. Dylan is the only rock star in this period to make explicit his wariness of his audience's craving for heroes—the others who gathered at Monterey and Woodstock lapped up their listeners' adulation. When, in "I Dreamed I Saw St. Augustine," Dylan has Augustine say, "But go on your way accordingly / And know you're not alone," listeners scurried to interpret those words as signs that Dylan refused to be nailed on the cross for his audience (as if the sixties were starved for martyrs). But St. Augustine was an unlikely "martyr" for Dylan to choose: a cleric-philosopher who held the episcopal seat in Hippo Regius, a Roman port in northern Africa, he died when the city was besieged by Vandals in 430. Dylan twists his symbolic stature to signify anyone who has been put to death by a mob. Even if Dylan is not confused, there are innumerable ways of reading this song: after the fact, Augustine could be John Kennedy; or he could be Martin Luther King, Jr., who causes Dylan to hang his head in shame for being among the crowd that put him to death. (Along with the reference to Tom Paine in "As I Went Out One Morning," these lines trigger memories of Dylan's botched acceptance speech at the Tom Paine Award ceremony in 1963.) "What might possibly be relevant," suggests John Herdman, "is that St. Augustine was perhaps the first Christian thinker to see in the End of the World a figure for personal death" (p. 99). But Dylan is also singing about how it feels to be the target of mob psychology, and how confusing it is to identify with the throng's impulses to smother what it loves too much or destroy what it can't understand.

## retro man

Next to the Sturm und Drang that Hendrix will bring it, Dylan's version of "All Along the Watchtower" sounds like a wizened exchange with his record company (like "Dear Landlord"): "Businessmen, they drink my wine, plowmen dig my earth / None of them along the line know what any of it is worth." Coming from the joker, those opening lines establish a strong sense of distrust—and it's no mistake that the thief answers kindly.

As one of the first black superstars, Hendrix heard more in those words than Dylan probably expected: being branded a "psychedelic Uncle Tom" by Robert Christgau is a hideous cross for anyone to bear. A Seattle-born expatriate who had to be exported from England before he found success in his native land, Hendrix suffered the status of racial outsider even in his own band, the Jimi Hendrix Experience. He used traditional themes of voodooed romance as metaphors for his love affair with the electric guitar and the disfiguring stardom it brought, and turned his racial and cultural trials into the central subject of his blues. This makes Hendrix's take on Dylan's song the more clinching, the more difficult to sit through comfortably—if Dylan had such thoughts about the people who sold his records, imagine how Hendrix felt. Shaking this song by its roots, Hendrix torches the opening moments with one of rock's most arresting lead-guitar flourishes, an entrance that makes Dylan's sound shy. The solo sections between verses amount to tours of blues traditions: rhythmic jabs, slide bellows, piercing drill-work. Dylan's raw thematic material of bewilderment with Western values gives Hendrix his opening. There's no mistaking why the wind howls when Hendrix takes flight at the end: for Dylan it howls in place of talking falsely; for Hendrix it howls for what his guitar can't say.

It's a cliché to say Hendrix made this song his own when what he really did was set a new standard for Dylan covers, and transform what you took away from Dylan's original. There's a way in which the Hendrix performance of this song summarizes the way the counterculture felt about Dylan's presence, his return and the voice they claimed as their own. It's a benediction of sorts—from Hendrix to his hero (whom he trumps), from rock to Dylan, and from fate to both men. Each found in this song a thunder (both symbolic and realized) that rattled beyond the career-as-life metaphors.

(One of the minor jokes underlying this song is the way Dylan unwittingly invents the heavy-metal thunder vi-v-iv progression: Jimmy Page steals this cadence whole for the coda to "Stairway to Heaven, " and it's used for countless metal proclamations thereafter. Dylan returns to this same chord progression in "Hurricane.")

**Tracking down meaning** in the album's centerpiece, "The Ballad of Frankie Lee and Judas Priest," is another knowing odyssey of contradictions, philosophical patter, and open-ended suggestion, all couched in a mock-linear narrative with a punch line that sends home the comedy of phony truisms. What Dylan gets, though, is a clean, atypical sense of how events can keep you guessing at the storyteller's intentions.

In the first four verses, Judas Priest tempts his best friend, Frankie Lee, with a roll of tens. Frankie sits down to make his decision, but with Judas staring at him, his head starts spinning. Quit staring at me, he tells Judas. Judas leaves, telling Frankie he can be found at a place known cryptically as "Eternity," just down the road.

In the next four verses, Frankie Lee meets a clairvoyant stranger, who identifies Frankie as a gambler whose father is dead. This stranger tells Frankie that a man named (Judas) Priest has been asking for him. Frankie goes into a panic, and he runs to find Judas. When he comes upon him, at the mysterious house down the road, Frankie looks up to see a building with twenty-four windows, a woman's face in each pane.

The last three verses describe Frankie's downfall: after

sixteen days and nights of raving, he collapses onto Judas Priest, where he dies of dehydration. The death silences everybody.

Dylan shovels on two morals: "One should never be / Where one does not belong / . . . And don't go mistaking paradise / For that home across the road."

Nothing is settled here: Where does the neighbor boy's guilt come from, and why is it "concealed"? And why does Dylan have this unexplained fourth character, who appears in only one verse, utter the song's subtext, "Nothing is revealed"? It's clear from the beginning that Judas is holding something on Frankie Lee, that "the best of friends" is meant ironically. But Frankie Lee's downfall doesn't have a lot to do with Judas Priest—the raving nights Frankie spends in Judas's flophouse before dying of "thirst" are a flimsy rite of passage about spiritual bereavement. Did Dylan throw in the name "Judas" to divert our attention from Frankie Lee's self-administered debacle? Or is Frankie Lee betrayed by Judas's love of money and women, and glib talk of eternity and paradise and the difference between house and home? And if he is, what kind of hero is he?

**The notorious Dylan** garbage monger, an overbearing, self-styled Dylanologist named Al Weberman, read Albert Grossman manager-references into "Dear Landlord," but Dylan isn't that small. He may have written a song about Greenwich Village girlfriend Suze Rotolo ("Ballad in Plain D"), but he never devoted an entire one to Joan Baez. "Dear Landlord" is a one-sided argument with God, which at times seems explicitly about post-motorcycle-accident reconciliations:

> **And anyone can fill his life up with things**
> **He can see but he just cannot touch.**

"Dear Landlord" (along with "I Am a Lonesome Hobo") features some of his finest controlled singing. Above sparse piano chord changes, and dismissible bass lines, his voice etches everything the words leave out—and then his harmonica enters after verse two for a high-lonesome coyote wail. There are passages in this song when Dylan's voice resembles his harp's pinched whine the way Robert Plant's voice echoes the fuzzy ballast of Jimmy Page's guitar in Led Zeppelin, and other points when the harp turns animalistic, a wounded canine bellowing at the elements.

It's a sound that reaches into the bereaved harp that opens "I Pity the Poor Immigrant." Like the cowboy and the politician, the gangster is an American archetype who makes up his own laws, who lives a double life, and whose motives are always suspect. But more than westerns, gangster flicks work on our collective fantasies about corruption and vice, and how enjoyable it must be to openly flaunt the law, even if it doesn't pay (the worst gangster films are moralistic). Unlike his nondescript but enigmatic cowboys, Dylan's gangster is a pathetic, pitiable ingrate, and Dylan sings about him with a soft-hued empathy—it's a weary putdown done up as a medium-tempo waltz. Void of situation or even a time frame, the song is as much about the narrator's heavy heart as about the ethnic resentments that lead to separate codes of justice: "I pity the poor immigrant . . . Who fills his mouth with laughing / And who builds his town with blood." This is a lithe con job compared with the false heroism Dylan will ascribe "Joey," a glacially slow song about mobster Joey Gallo, whom he learned about through Jacques Levy, his collaborator on *Desire*. The figure in "I Pity the Poor Immigrant" is not without dignity, but he's corrupt beyond repair, and his attitude shapes his fate.

**At once pretentious** and transparent, the songs on *John Wesley Harding* inhabit an unselfconscious zone of feeling that few other Dylan numbers share. In their struggle to articulate feelings that bypass the mind, they get to you in the same way that Warren

Beatty exploits his beguiling lack of acting technique, or Robert Altman makes his infatuation with suggestion both part of the story and its method.

Despite its manifest idiosyncrasies, *John Wesley Harding* becomes another layaway plan for singers. Jimi Hendrix's "All Along the Watchtower" remains a hissing oracle; he made it sound like the grand, tragic foreboding of his generation—the apocalyptic prophecies played out at the Chicago Democratic National Convention, the Hell's Angels' murder at Altamont. Joan Baez's "I Pity the Poor Immigrant" is her best Dylan cover, and Maria Muldaur's coquettish "I'll Be Your Baby Tonight" makes "Midnight at the Oasis" sound like puppy love. "I Am a Lonesome Hobo" is waiting for Tom Waits, and Bonnie Raitt should sing "Down Along the Cove."

You'd think such a sketchy, miniaturist style would depend on distinctions, but these songs avoid even hints about what these characters look like, never mind their motives. "The Ballad of Frankie Lee and Judas Priest" works out to be a joke because of its length: Dylan could have condensed this absurd action-episode and still avoided as much as he does in its anticlimax: "Don't go mistaking paradise / For that home across the road." Dylan's "clue" in the liner-notes yarn isn't really necessary: "Mr. Dylan has come out with a new record," the first king says to Frank. "This record of course features none but his own songs and we understand that you're the key." Only "Frankie Lee and Judas Priest" goes on for more than three verses (it has eleven), and it's one of the first funny numbers about death he writes after "Ramblin, Gamblin, Willie." For Dylan, an entire record of three-verse songs is radical, a reverse tactic in how to leave things unsaid. Instead of being imposingly evasive by being verbose, he's being imposingly evasive by clamming up.

Even Dylan's singing retreats into a dry, remote, at times ethereal detachment, a style marked by control and extreme self-consciousness that is new to Dylan's palette of irony and duplicity. He gives these songs a pallid surface that only makes their depths more bizarre; it's the inverse of his glossy, commercial veneer on *Nashville Skyline* (which has an ironic glint all its own). His singing further qualifies the way we hear things: it's as though the songs' narrators are in the saddle, and Dylan the singer is the bemused onlooker to the oddly familiar events that unfold—he casts himself as one more dazed listener. Without the sparks of involved mnemonic whimsy that drove his earlier rock, the tone of this music takes on a wry stoicism. And with his harmonica playing lead guitar once again, he takes some of the best harp solos of his life (especially in "Drifter's Escape," "I Am a Lonesome Hobo," and "I Pity the Poor Immigrant").

As if to reassure the listener (never a Dylan trait), he goes out with two unabashedly romantic appeals, "Down Along the Cove" and "I'll Be Your Baby Tonight," which look toward *Nashville Skyline*—and wouldn't sound out of place there. But what's more interesting is how these songs strip away even more pretension than the *Basement Tapes* sessions, are even more deliberately two-dimensional, unambiguous. "Goin' to Acapulco" isn't a bawdy song about a trip to the bawdy house; there's an undertone of despair that provides a motive for the escape. Nothing on *John Wesley Harding* has that much overt irony. There's more of an understated grasp of how the world overwhelms people, and a stripped-bare songwriting skill that hoodwinks you into believing that these songs could mean more than what they imply— which is more of a caveat than any singer-songwriter's overtly "naked" tour of troubles.

These songs aren't for escape or distraction, as some of the madcap *Blonde* songs clearly are: they're emotional pictures of philosophical ideas; they hone the country vein of song as metaphysics, as a way of groping for certainties because it may be the only place where you can be sure of anything. In one sense the record is a way of renouncing his "rock star" past, burying the incessant touring and fast living that led up to his motorcycle crisis, a physical event that charged up a new spiritual awareness.

## retro man

Most of these songs aren't about romance but about salvation, and even the last two romances are set up as salvation's salvation, the earthly kudos that wards off spiritual quandaries. "Down Along the Cove" and "I'll Be Your Baby Tonight" are mellower and less confused than even his great seductions like "Just Like a Woman" or "She Belongs to Me." Their very simplicity underscores the relief these songs call out for, the mood that prevails against the idea that surface is all, that life is but a joke.

## Nashville Skyline
Released: May 1969

**John Wesley Harding** demands a lot of its listeners; *Nashville Skyline* goes down easy. And yet there's something imperious about Dylan's ease with this country jaunt, in his ability to kick back and whip off instant country standards. Country turns out to be the biggest part of Dylan's musical personality he's kept hidden from his audience, even if he was always sure to mention Hank Williams as an influence (and cover Roy Acuff's "Freight Train Blues" on his debut). Leave it to Dylan to pull another reverse on his audience: make a comeback record whose songs define enigma, and then turn around and tip his hat as a Nashville crooner, paying his musical respects to apple pie.

Rock's back-to-the-country movement wouldn't have left the ground if it weren't for Gram Parsons, a Georgia songwriter who joined up with the Byrds in 1967. "We set out to hire a piano player and good God! It's George Jones in a sequin suit," said Roger McGuinn (Sid Griffin, p. 12). A long-haired gentleman caller with a rebel-yell soul, Gram Parsons helped perform the ironic feat of retooling country music as outsider chic for the counterculture of the late sixties and early seventies. Conceptually, Parsons modeled himself after Mick Jagger to become country's first bad boy. Long before Willie Nelson and Waylon Jennings and Hank Williams, Jr., began glamorizing their "outlaw" moves, Parsons embodied a redneck's worst fears come true: longhairs who up and turned the fatalistic beauty of country music into a new kind of subversiveness.

With all his bands (the Byrds, the International Submarine Band, the Flying Burrito Brothers), Parsons developed an irreproachably gorgeous style that managed to make Nashville purists uncomfortable—and that was the point. With the Byrds in 1968, he made *Sweetheart of the Rodeo*, which countrified Dylan's "You Ain't Goin' Nowhere" and "Nothing Was Delivered," whipped Woody Guthrie's "Pretty Boy Floyd" into a bluegrass squall, and featured Parsons's love letter to South Carolina, "Hickory Wind." With Parsons, the Byrds made an unprecedented appearance at Nashville's sacred Grand Ole Opry. The next year Parsons left the Byrds (he wouldn't play South Africa) and formed the Flying Burrito Brothers with Byrds bassist Chris Hillman. The Flying Burrito Brothers' *Gilded Palace of Sin* closed with Hillman and Parsons's casual gospel satire, "Hippie Boy," which Dylan was wild about: "Boy, I love them . . . the Flying Burrito Brothers, unh-huh. I've always known Chris, you know, from when he was in the Byrds. And he's always been a fine musician. Their records knocked me out. [*laughs*] That poor little hippie boy on his way to town . . . [*laughs*]" (*Rolling Stone Interviews, Volume II*, p. 301).

Parsons's confessional tenor accented the fatalism beneath the surface of country music's simplicities, the well of dread and fear that poured from sentiments that couldn't sound more plainspoken on first listening. He made ordinary phrases coast on layered meanings ("It's time we stopped pretending things are real" in "How Much I've Lied" and "The sun comes up without her, it just doesn't know she's gone" in "Brass Buttons"); and his solo albums (*GP* in 1973 and *Grievous Angel* in 1974) contained music making that transcended the boundaries of its style so thoroughly that it left no question of country music's subdued vigor, and its importance to rock 'n' roll. Arrangements were marvels of balance and interplay between players, and Parsons's song choices were as crafty as his songwriting (something Dylan might have paid more attention to). Unfortunately, Parsons died on September 19, 1973, of heart failure at the age of twenty-six, with traces of morphine, cocaine, amphetamine, and alcohol in his blood. In one of pop's more egregious ironies, he was over-shadowed even in his Williams–style exit by the passing the next day of Jim Croce.

Dylan, of course, was moving in a similar direction on his *Basement Tapes* sessions and *John Wesley Harding*. And like Parsons, Dylan sang the enemy's song much too well to be caged by its charms. He was impressed with Parsons's ability to fuel country with counterculture mystique and reorient the rock au-dience's awareness of Dylan idols like Johnny Cash and George Jones, and of country session players (Parsons used guitarist James Burton and drummer Ronnie Tutt from Elvis Presley's seventies band). For *Nashville Skyline*, Dylan hired back drum-mer Kenny Buttrey from *Harding* and brought in Charlie Mc-Coy, Pete Drake, Norman Blake, Charlie Daniels, and Bob Wilson.

Dylan's country isn't as dark or as layered as Parsons's, even if "Lay, Lady, Lay" went on to become one of Dylan's most sensual singles (originally written for the *Midnight Cowboy* soundtrack, it became his first top ten hit since "Rainy Day Women #12 & 35" in 1966). He's singing with genteel poise in his smooth new vocal persona, but he's also still Dylan, having fun with this country turn but not letting it define him. "There's not too much of a change in my singing style," Dylan told Jann Wenner, "but I'll tell you something which is true . . . I stopped smoking. When I stopped smoking, my voice changed . . . so drastically, I couldn't believe it myself. That's true. I tell you, you stop smoking those cigarettes [*laughter*] . . . and you'll be able to sing like Caruso" (*Rolling Stone Interviews, Volume I*, p. 283).

Beginning with a duet with Johnny Cash on "Girl from the North Country" (which slows to a halt with some awkward line-trading), *Nashville Skyline* has a lighter touch than the tragic foreboding that Parsons was so good at evoking. This air of sweetness pokes gentle fun at itself with "Nashville Skyline Rag," "Peggy Day," and the soft-shoe "Country Pie," three session coffee-breaks that breeze by without the faintest tension. The record's shapeliness comes from the way romantic moods shift between celebrations ("To Be Alone with You," which Dylan wrote for Jerry Lee Lewis, and "Tonight I'll Be Staying Here with You," the record's closer), entreaties ("Lay, Lady, Lay," "Tell Me That It Isn't True"), and morning-afterthoughts ("I Threw It All Away," "One More Night").

Three of these are seminal, as naturally plucked from the air as "Blowin' in the Wind" or Carl Perkins's "Sure to Fall." Loping along with dreamy pedal steel and clip-clop wood blocks, "Lay, Lady, Lay" sets a gently hypnotic guitar progression in motion, and Dylan has fun with the country convention of cliché by refashioning one from the bottom of the barrel ("You *can* have your cake and eat it too"). "Tell Me That It Isn't True" is the voice of a suspicious man who promises himself he'll take his woman's word for her fidelity, all the time denying the "rumors all over town" that she's "been seen with some other man." Dylan gives it the forced sincerity of someone who can't help deceiving himself, and the song catches a quiet terror. Instead of railing against the elements ("Love Is Just a Four-Letter Word") or his ex-lover's common effrontery ("I Don't Believe You"), "I Threw It All Away" is a glimmer of honesty from a person who has taken love for granted, squandered its rewards, and lived to sing about it. (Best covers: Yo La Tengo, on *President Yo La Tengo*, and Elvis Costello, from his live acoustic tour in 1984.)

• • •

**In Dylan's first** network television appearance since "The Ed Sullivan Show" in 1963, he performs "Living the Blues" and "I Threw It All Away" on "The Johnny Cash Show" on June 7, 1969. Just after completing *Nashville Skyline* in February, he and Cash recorded a complete album worth of material together in New York, which has never been released. With a strange, modulating-key arrangement of Dylan's own "One Too Many Mornings," the record is an unfinished review of shared favorites, including Cash's "I Still Miss Someone," Carl Perkins's "Matchbox," Arthur "Big Boy" Crudup's "That's Alright, Mama," the gospel "Just a Closer Walk with Thee," and an unlaced rehearsal of "Careless Love," with each singer aiming at rhymes ("You can pass by my window pane," Cash sings, "—that don't rhyme with nothin'—But you won't get passed by forty-five *again* . . ."). One more production session and they might have completed a record.

On Cash's program, Dylan looks as uncomfortable and out of place as a circus vendor who wakes up inside the lion's cage. With his faint beard and nervous, offstage glances, he's all sheepish embarrassment, and his suit jacket can't hide his boyish demeanor. After singing his own numbers, Dylan joins Cash for a duet: "Girl from the North Country," halting on *Nashville Skyline*, dissolves mercifully into laughter. And later in the show, Cash and his wife, June (in late-sixties sequins), sing a comically upbeat version of Dylan's "It Ain't Me, Babe," doing the shimmy between verses. (The show, Cash's first, also featured guest star Joni Mitchell, who sang "Both Sides Now" and duetted with Cash on "I Still Miss Someone," a song Gram Parsons sang with his International Submarine Band, and Sandy Denny sang with the Fairport Convention.)

Dylan's country personality brought him as far outside the mainstream of rock as any style could (until *Self-Portrait*). As the hippies descended on his backyard in Woodstock, New York,

## hard rain

that summer of 1969, Dylan was the absent guest at the counterculture's biggest party, a figure who loomed over the pro-
ceedings even more than the Beatles and the Stones. (The Band
appeared on its own.) Instead, Dylan headed for an appearance
at the Isle of Wight, for an uneven but revealing set of rock with
the Band, some of which shows up on *Self-Portrait*. But Dylan
knew that his country period represented an unselfconscious
plateau, especially compared with what it followed. As he told
Jann Wenner at the time:

> These are the type of songs that I always felt like writing
> when I've been alone to do so. The songs reflect more of
> the inner me than the songs of the past. They're more to my
> base than, say, *John Wesley Harding*. There I felt everyone
> expected me to be a poet so that's what I tried to be. But
> the smallest line in this new album [*Nashville Skyline*]
> means more to me than some of the songs on any of the
> previous albums I've made. I admire the spirit to the mu-
> sic. It's got a good spirit. Like a good door, a good house,
> a good car, a good road, a good girl. I feel like writing a
> whole lot more of them too. (*In His Own Words*, p. 90)

# 6: sign on the window

> *Self-Portrait* was a bunch of tracks that we'd done all
> the time I'd gone to Nashville. . . . To open up we'd
> go on and do what we were going to do. And then
> there was a lot of other stuff that was just on the shelf.
> But I was being bootlegged at the time and a lot of
> stuff that was worse was appearing on bootleg records.
>
> —**Dylan in 1986**,
> *Biograph* liner notes

## Self-Portrait
Released: June 1970

## Dylan
Released: December 1973

**Given the manipulative** games he played with his audience, the
idea of a self-portrait from a chameleon like Dylan raised expectations after *Nashville Skyline* (which has aged into a gentle star
turn). But Dylan's concept of a self-portrait wasn't to compose
original songs around autobiographical themes. Instead, his second double album was a musical construct so outsized and his-
torically sweeping that even Dylan got lost inside of it—he didn't
storm this epic platform, he just let the platform become the
entire show. Digging into American pioneer legend ("Copper
Kettle," "Days of '49"), tipping his hat to contemporaries (Gordon Lightfoot's "Early Morning Rain," Paul Simon's "The Boxer"), and leaning back into a couple of his old hits and standbys
as though they belonged to somebody else (live versions of "Like
a Rolling Stone," "She Belongs to Me"), Dylan's autograph cam-

ouflaged its author as much as any of his hit-and-run poses; it's a concept that leaked cynicism through the indifferent performances Dylan turned in. If Dylan was trying to be straightforward and sincere, his singing gave up the game: without a trace of irony, these performances came off flat, halfhearted. And if he was trying to pull another elaborate joke on his audience, the idea boomeranged back on his idea of modesty—except for "Quinn the Eskimo" and perhaps "Minstrel Boy," it's hard to take much pleasure in this music.

*Self-Portrait* received numerous overheated pans when it was released, which makes it Dylan's most trashed record, even though some of it fares better than an armload of his work from the 1980s and 1990s. On *John Wesley Harding* and *Nashville Skyline,* he tailored acoustic-rock and country-and-western departures to his outsider image—they weren't reactionary moves so much as nonchalant masterstrokes that fed off the strengths of *Bringing It All Back Home, Highway 61 Revisited,* and *Blonde on Blonde,* and tapped rock undercurrents that few had bothered to investigate as fully. *Harding* and *Skyline* shared common subtexts—America's idea of itself, rock's idea of itself past youth, and an imagined history of where those themes might meet—but their surfaces were beginning to shift. Moving from abstractions to crooners might have made more sense if the destination was something besides half-witted pulp.

With its frivolous, sleepy-time tone (whatever else it may be, "All the Tired Horses" is a red flag), *Self-Portrait* struck Dylan's audience as a retreat, an abdication that threw his legendary status into high relief. Nashville could be abided as a kind of reverse-subversive gesture, as a king dabbling in his more conservative eccentricities. But along with the killings at Altamont and Kent State and the breakup of the Beatles (with *Let It Be*), *Self-Portrait* must have sounded like another dashed illusion of sixties utopianism. Of the major rock icons, only the Rolling Stones still dealt in the con game of corruption and vice as entertainment, laced with country-and-western lament, with

# hard rain

*Beggars Banquet* (1968), *Let It Bleed* (1969), *Sticky Fingers* (1971), and finally *Exile on Main Street* (1972)—all loaded chambers. The Stones' orbit took them towards their peak just behind the others.

With no outward political fruits for the counterculture's half-decade of self-expression, the Band's musical utopia began to work as panacea. The Band's debut was a hallmark of rock revisionism and the dawn of roots consciousness—what the Beatles aimed for with *Get Back* (which became *Let It Be*) was relayed on *Music from Big Pink* (1968) and *The Band* (1969). A shadow universe of history sprang out of these records, an America that had little to do with the fear, betrayed faith, and urban violence that was erupting after 1968's riots, assassinations, and the ongoing war in Vietnam. The vaudevillian theatrics of acid and psychedelic rock signaled the fading of the music's potential for direct protest into rock as escape. By keeping mischievously furtive, Dylan avoided getting lumped in with the escapism (he despised the hippies); but *Self-Portrait* sounded absolutely lost.

Even the Beatles' *Let It Be* was aced by John Lennon's first solo project, *Plastic Ono Band*, a sixties rite of exorcism that found more to say about bourgeois myths ("Working Class Hero") and the paranoia of starting over in middle age ("Isolation," "Well Well Well") than Dylan yet had. Against Lennon, Dylan's pretentiously titled double disc sounded like a hazy, rearview account of rock tributaries, and not just because of the female backup singers and applied strings. Even Dylan's reaction to critics smacked of defensiveness: "A lot worse stuff was appearing on bootleg records." It was, "so to speak, my own bootleg record," he remarked to Robert Shelton (p. 418). When Columbia finally did release a more "authentic" bootleg product (the outtakes from *Self-Portrait*, called simply *Dylan*, to avenge his leap to the Asylum label in 1973), his limp renditions of Joni Mitchell's "Big Yellow Taxi," J. J. Walker's "Mr. Bojangles," and two Elvis Presley hits, "Can't Help Falling in Love" and "A Fool Such as I," only make the real bootlegs more desirable. (To clinch the irony, "A Fool Such as I" reached number fifty-five, making it the first and only Dylan cover of a song identified with Elvis Presley to reach the charts.)

A third to a half of *Self-Portrait* is a civilized country record buried amid poor song choices of other people's material, lapses in arrangements, and ambivalent singing. And even on the stand-out number, Dylan's peculiar touch has lost its resonance. Instead of operating as a symbol designed to illuminate contemporary myths, rock's past becomes less metaphorical: "Copper Kettle" is an ingenious Appalachian zygote for rock attitudes, the hidden source of *John Wesley Harding*'s shadows. The song captures an idyllic backwoods existence, where moonshine is equated not only with good times but with tax resistance. Appalachian farmers who struggled to make their living off the land would routinely siphon off a percentage of their corn and brew whiskey, hiding the stash from the feds to keep from being saddled with the whiskey tax of 1791. During a PBS special about the roots of Appalachian folk music, archivist Alan Lomax asked a fiddler named Tommy Jarrell about moonshiners. Jarrell told him:

> That land was so doggone poor, had to do something to make a little money. They had to make whiskey on the side to buy what they needed. . . . My granddaddy made apple brandy, but he had to block part of his to make any money. It took four bushels of apples to make one gallon of brandy. At twelve and a half cents a bushel for them apples, that was forty-eight cents it cost him besides the work. He had to pay a dollar-ten tax on the gallon. So we had to blockade it to make any money, slip it out . . . had to moonshine it, had to hide it out. When the gaugers came around, sent word they was comin', hid whiskey and brandy out in the woods, they didn't want them to give a count of it. Had to, to make any money.

It was, Lomax explains, guerrilla warfare between the tax col-lectors and the moonshiners until Prohibition. "We haven't paid no whiskey tax since 1792," Dylan sings, with the conviction that circumventing the law on this matter was tantamount to finding inner peace. If *Self-Portrait* had nothing but "Copper Kettle"'s on it, it would be a step in the right direction. By itself it sounds accidental, as if something from these sessions finally stuck.

All of the blame isn't Dylan's. Producer Bob Johnston's arrangements don't sail. The backup singers often sound synthetic; what's missing isn't pitch or spatial placement but *blend*. When Dylan dares a duet with himself (an intriguing pretext) on Paul Simon's "The Boxer," the result isn't anything like a songwriter looking at himself through another songwriter's reflection; it's like a caricature trapped in a house of mirrors.

One of the things *Self-Portrait* gets right about Dylan is his august inconsistency. A spotless production of C. A. Null's "I Forgot More Than You'll Ever Know" sounds like a *Nashville Skyline* outtake that gets propped up by high pedal steel and piano (on the left). "Days of '49," a traditional mining song that Dylan takes credit for with "revised melody and new music," starts out well, and floods into a fine vocal refrain. But it begins to sag around the time he sings,

> There was Poker Bill, one of the boys
> Who was always in a game
> Whether he lost or whether he won,
> To him it was always the same . . .
> In a game with death,
> He lost his breath in the days of '49 . . .

"Oh, my goodness," Dylan says as the next refrain unravels—it never returns to the brave stand it takes in the first stanza. (Didn't he want just one more chance at the song?) Dylan's arrangement of "In Search of Little Sadie" contorts the traditional verse (also known as "Badman's Blunder" and "Badman's Ballad") into a free-roaming exercise in modulation, each verse winding up in a new key, Dylan's voice skidding into shaky landings on new tonal ground: "Remember you blowed little Sadie down _____." (The unnecessary repeat of the same indigenous song, "Little Sadie," plays it unnecessarily safe.) It's a creaky "Surf's Up" for fugitives.

"Living the Blues" must be what Dylan was trying to do with his record—to interweave originals that would be indistinguishable in tone and feel from the seminal classics he was broaching. Even the female singers sound like they're having fun. But for Dylan to take credit for "Alberta" (numbers 1 and 2), Elmore James's "It Hurts Me Too," and "Belle Isle" is disrespectful at best, deceitful at worst. "That *Self-Portrait* is characterized by borrowing, lifting, and plagiarism simply means Bob will get a little more bread and thousands of kids will get a phony view of their own history," Greil Marcus wrote in his *Rolling Stone* diatribe. Perhaps because Elvis Presley recorded it, Dylan's "Blue Moon" may win points for ambition, but Doug Kershaw's tacky fiddle cadenza comes unhitched from the song's ending like a caboose that comes unhooked from its train. Think of it as an outtake from *Dylan*.

The Nashville tracks are uneven too, but they contain the standouts. The singing on "Take Me as I Am" rivals the pedal steel playing for understated despair—it almost emerges as the record's theme song, or at least as the kind of thing Dylan wants to vent to his audience (and critics) and finds easier to say through someone else's words ("Why must you always try to make me over?"). And "Take a Message to Mary" gets by on sincerity where the other songs could use a little conviction. Stacking the country numbers together with a sprinkling of older emblems ("Copper Kettle") might have made for a sturdy *Nashville Skyline, Volume 2*, but that might have worked only as a stall tactic. Dylan as an unabashed Grand Ole Opry country act—someone who does country as vocation as well as craft—is as trying an image as Elvis Presley doing the hula rock.

You can tell the vocals are out of whack when the instrumentals shine: although "Woogie Boogie" doesn't catch a breeze until the sax solo, about halfway through, it's not as taxing as, say, Dylan's queasy take of Gordon Lightfoot's "Early Morning Rain." ("Wigwam" is such a bromide it almost broke Top 40.)

The cop-out way of making sense of all this inconsistency is to say that Dylan was sincerely trying to seek out a mass-market sound, his own version of a pulpish novel that would draw on American fable as it expanded his audience. But there isn't any other juncture of his career where he can be accused of pandering so to his listeners; and with *Nashville Skyline* just the kind of curveball that gave youth culture pause, he'd already succeeded at tapping the country market, complete with crossover hit ("Lay, Lady, Lay"). *Self-Portrait* wasn't driven by consistency. What it portended most ominously was Dylan's own faltering sense of taste and scattered judgment. Listening to it now, even when his voice breaks through, you don't get the sense that he understands the difference.

**The Isle of Wight** set Dylan turned in with the Band off the coast of England (the week after the Woodstock festival in New York) served as the boilerplate for his live shows for the next half-decade, and the first clue that Dylan regarded his 1965–66 rock records as hosts to his most prized material. But both the Band and the personality of these songs were altered by the new character in Dylan's voice, a leisurely control that replaced urgency with repose, as though his country persona could easily be put to work in material that once made him a musical arsonist. The concert was intended for a live album, since the 1966 stage material had entered myth but was still judged too scrappy (or perhaps too inflammatory) for commercial release. Of the songs on the set list ("She Belongs to Me," "I Threw It All Away," "Maggie's Farm," "Mountain Thyme," "It Ain't Me, Babe," "To Ramona," "Mr. Tambourine Man," "I Dreamed I Saw St. Augustine," "Lay, Lady, Lay," "Highway 61 Revisited," "One Too Many Mornings," "I Pity the Poor Immigrant," "Like a Rolling

## sign on the window

Stone," "I'll Be Your Baby Tonight," "Quinn the Eskimo," "Minstrel Boy," "Rainy Day Women #12 & 35"), Dylan selected "Rolling Stone," "Quinn," "Minstrel Boy," and "She Belongs to Me" for *Self-Portrait*.

"Like a Rolling Stone" isn't the tonic *Self-Portrait* needs, and this version will never hold its own alongside the 1966 live English version or the *Before the Flood* finale of 1974. But inside the last verse (Dylan skips verse three, and forgets his own lyrics in the second), Garth Hudson's organ singes the top of the Band's sound and makes everyone else simmer beneath Dylan's half-remembered vocal. The Band seems muted, bass-heavy, and some of the power is lost in the quality of the live tape—but none of the intent. Focus on Dylan's voice and you'll hear a man trying to ease into a song that once humiliated class comforts; crank up the Band, and you'll hear overdrive that does everything but smother the singer. Likewise when Robertson wrestles down his own feedback in his guitar solo to "The Mighty Quinn." The best dialogue comes in "Minstrel Boy," where the players fight their way up to the refrains with Dylan and let the music fill in the wrinkles.

**There are crimes** worse than indifference, and in Dylan's case they work out to be a disgust for his situation that he vents on both his songs and his listeners. At several points during his long career (*Self-Portrait, Live at Budokan, Saved, Empire Burlesque, Down in the Groove*) this air of self-loathing is hard to miss beneath all the surface ambivalence—the lifeless singing, the aimless solos, the rambling cut-offs. Dylan doesn't have the same ease with himself that Elvis Presley did, when he threw away a lifetime of talent on-screen and onstage in Las Vegas, just to watch the crowd shudder in awe at the sheer effrontery of it—after all, as Marcus points out, it takes a King to renounce his crown. If *Self-Portrait* was Dylan's way of attempting a "straight" record that would ascribe him historic "legitimacy," and toy with assumptions about the hippies' oracle, it fell short of, say, the way Hank Williams turned sentimentality into another kind of disdain for the world. Without an ax to grind, Dylan managed what once seemed impossible: he sounded at a loss for ideas. Because some fine music came to the rescue, *Self-Portrait* didn't sound prophetically self-descriptive until his born-again gospel music (with *Slow Train Coming* in 1978), which became overbearing and grim.

After releasing *Self-Portrait*, Dylan welcomed George Harrison to his home in Woodstock, and together they collaborated on two songs that survive as demos: "Everytime Somebody Comes to Town" (which found a home on *The Bootleg Series*) and "I'd Have You Anytime." The second number appeared on Harrison's solo debut, *All Things Must Pass*, later that year—another double album that attempted a bloated self-definition with the help of overambitious production (via Phil Spector) and overambitious length (two versions of "Isn't It a Pity," an extra third disc of leaden jamming). It doesn't do Dylan any good to note that even Harrison's frail vocals, swamped by strings, female choruses, and Spector's baroque sense of mass, outdistanced what Dylan threw away on *Self-Portrait*.

*Self-Portrait* is not the sound of an inscrutable counterculture prophet doing a show-biz turn; it's the sound of a domesticated rebel who, having taken refuge in the certainties of country, burrows further into the falsities such certainties can induce: the reflex towards acceptance that succumbs to the urge to please.

## New Morning
Released: October 1970

## Bob Dylan's Greatest Hits, Volume 2
Released: November 1971

## The Concert for Bangla Desh
Released: December 1971

## Pat Garrett and Billy the Kid
Released: July 1973

**Dylan may never** live down his identity as the sixties' singing soothsayer. But what many people forget is that he was also the best conduit for the breakdown of sixties values, beginning with *John Wesley Harding*'s return to rural sentiments, and the creeping disillusionment with rock culture's power to sustain its own myths ("Idiot Wind" on *Blood on the Tracks*). That Dylan responded to his critics at all is perhaps the one puzzling motivation behind his second (after *John Wesley Harding*) "comeback" record; that he responded euphemistically goes without saying. With a nonchalant pastoral calm, *New Morning* sets the tone for his next several records: middle-aged quixotisms, attitudes that dig obscure niches into romance, daily life, and an idealized rural mind-set as they flirt with religion, philosophy, and the countercultural twilight they spring from. It's a family man's set that renders as much serendipity in its outlook as it does caution. Dylan's impulse to continue creating finds a theme that was running through *Self-Portrait* like a fault line: ambivalence.

For Dylan, modesty counts as a skillful turn, and several of these songs roll by as preordained standards without the least bit of pretension: even the kittenish Australian singer Olivia

## hard rain

Newton-John records the soft-core "If Not for You," which first appears as a lithe, acoustic-rock mirage on Harrison's *All Things Must Pass*. Along with the title track, a wry take on the easygoing country life that takes after "You Ain't Goin' Nowhere," it seeks out a strain of sentimental affection that doesn't grate (it makes "Early Morning Rain" sound like drizzle). Of course, Dylan's return to a vocal intensity gives these songs subtle undercurrents that other singers don't reach for. When he veers towards his harmonica solo in "If Not For You" (". . . and you know it's true"), he gives you the sense that to try to read this song ironically—as a lover trying to convince himself of his feelings, like the overbearing groom in "Wedding Song"—is to miss out on the unforced sincerity he hits here. The track glides on feelings that aren't articulated—only a very complex and abiding love could inspire this kind of unaffected flattery, levied with such rich shades of shared experience. Dylan's funneled delivery enriches these deliberately uncomplicated lyrics ("Anyway it just wouldn't ring true . . .").

These aren't songs that orbit arguments; they're exchanges between lovers who can guess each other's thoughts before speaking. In "The Man in Me," Dylan surrenders to the person he sees when his lover looks through him—it's acceptance writ humbly. He's not trying to impress this lover, so the title hook resonates enough to carry things. Dylan has pared down his language so much it must have given fits to zealots like Al Weberman (it's as if Dylan deliberately set out to put such clowns out of business, and still conjure intricate, three-dimensional songs). "Take a woman like you to get through / To the man in me" is so direct in its expression of the unflinching cues of intimacy, you forgive him the occasional forced rhyme.

Not all of the romances are direct—he gets his sniggers in. "Winterlude" is a tongue-in-cheek send-up of pop romancing, a waltz that has fun with domestic clichés ("Winterlude, let's go down to the chapel / Then come back and cook up a meal"). Obscure verities on parade, it depends on the spray of good feeling he leaves behind in the vocal to make the connection—a few of these jocularities (the gone-to-hell-and-forgotten "One More Weekend") don't lighten up a record's tone so much as round out its feel for experience.

The key episodic tableau here is "Sign on the Window," which achieves in microcosm what *New Morning* skirts in broad strokes: the dissolution of the counterculture, and the transient sweep of postadolescence. Like *Blood on the Tracks*, his tour-de-force treatment of this theme (decaying romance as a symbol of a fading epoch), "Sign on the Window" works as a precarious fable of the mood swings this record's liaisons summon up.

The first verse neatly encapsulates a search for love, satisfaction, encroaching chains, and the final breach (". . .'Three's a Crowd,' " sung twice). This is terse impressionism that evades narrative in favor of shorthand imagery, and it shoehorns the listener into a sense of the swiftly approaching predicament the singer feels. Verse two gets some distance from the situation: a lover has chased the California dream with a new boyfriend, and another friend's warning rings in his ear. The sense of isolation in this song is compounded by the arrangement: verses sung alone at the piano, interludes with drums, bass, and backup singers nudging things along.

But then, hiking the song up a couple of keys, Dylan turns in a bridge that outclasses the rest of the song, and puts the solitude across with such a strong vocal presence that it stands out as the best stretch of singing on the record: "Sure gonna be wet tonight on Main Street . . . / Hope that it don't sleet." There's nothing to those words—a borrowed rain image, an irregular three-line pattern that gets compensated for by some repeated piano chords. But what it gives up goes to the core of what the song is trying to express: the impending breakdown and withdrawal that extends from the inferences of the first verse, the bereft mood of the second, into the broader cultural allusions that get stirred up in the reference to "Main Street."

This is the context that *Self-Portrait* pretended didn't

exist—the encroaching fear and crisis of hope that settled in on the counterculture as Nixon escalated the war in Cambodia and the nation looked the other way from the disgrace of Kent State. Since Dylan was a leading symbol of the antiestablishment consciousness that triggered mass bohemia in the mid-sixties, his charting of the failure of this consciousness to sustain itself in political terms rings especially bleak. But *New Morning*'s expression of confusion and dismay went down a lot easier than *Self-Portrait*'s denial and diffidence.

This is one of the best examples of how Dylan's voice fills in the gaps the lyrics leave deliberately open. Beginning hesitantly, the last verse of "Sign on the Window" builds towards its repeated last line not as a forced projection of false hope but as simple, matter-of-fact acceptance of middle-age sentiment. Coming from rock's number-one outlaw, a subversive whose strangeness the masses could identify with, these words make sense as the logical extension of the down-home comforts he visits on *Nashville Skyline* and *Self-Portrait*. But more than that, they offer a way of redefining one's values that doesn't mean copping out or giving up. The antithesis of the family man, at thirty a father of four, begins broaching homeliness without irony—and still convinces you not to hear it as strict autobiography.

**Dylan doesn't abandon** his yen for riddles; they just assume earthier tones and play off subtler yucks. "Day of the Locusts" snubs academia, angling off the ceremony in which Dylan receives his honorary Doctorate of Music from Princeton on June 9, 1970. "The man standin' next to me, his head was exploding / Well, I was prayin' the pieces wouldn't fall on me." Like the Nathanael West novel whose title the song appropriates, it's another outsider anthem that exposes the hollowness of "respectable" culture; instead of roasting Mr. Jones in cap and gown, Dylan keeps his mouth shut and surveys a distance he feels between these fawning highbrows and his emotional radar:

## sign on the window

**I glanced into the chamber where the judges were talking,**
**Darkness was everywhere, it smelled like a tomb.**

The way the band tugs verses into refrains might be called laid-back rock—firm grip with a straight face, minus the singer-songwriter pout. Given Dylan's well-charted denouncement of academia, it's hard to say which is more comic: that he shows up for the Princeton honor, or that by extension he equates academic balderdash with the crass underworld of West's Hollywood. It's almost as if Dylan went through with the farce of getting his honorary doctorate just so he could write a song about it—there isn't an undergraduate alive who can't identify with the song's cool sense of how going through the motions of getting a degree gives way to release, lighting out for the territory of life.

Where cast-off academia makes for smug rock, his passes at religion coax genre experiments. "If Dogs Run Free" is a spoken ditty laced together by female scatting and snide, scampish piano. Nobody else could read the lines "My mind weaves a symphony and tapestry of rhyme" and sound this ambivalently cavalier about the conceit—its echoes a beat poet's coffeehouse reading. And the record's gospel intermission, "Three Angels," is such a clean parody you're tempted to buy into its facetious lyric, which vilifies the homeless by way of the cold civility of city life ("Three fellas crawlin' on their way back to work / Nobody stops to ask why"). (He does this better in his R&B saunter, "Watching the River Flow.") "Father of Night" is more puzzling, especially considering its placement as the finale to all this flirtation with weighty issues, and the calm but sober detachment Dylan adopts with renewed ambiguity. He's always been able to lampoon style-as-content ("Sign on the Cross") without completely giving himself over to the simplicities such satires normally exact from their targets. Read the lyrics out loud and believers might be tempted to take him at his word; listen to his delivery and you're constantly thrown off guard as to whether he's invoking a higher spirit or laughing along with it, cuing his listeners into how farce can turn itself over into another form of respect. It's a line Randy Newman casts aside for sheer disdain in "God (That's Why I Love Mankind)," and one Dylan walks without wavering.

This comic treatment of spirits and oracles reeks of obsession, which is why even his better putdowns (God as supreme negotiator in "Dear Landlord," God as reluctant traffic cop in "Father of Night") hinge on devout assumptions, and trace a path towards his own spiritual (and musical) crisis when he tackles gospel. In "Went to See the Gypsy," the singer seeks out his fortune at a big hotel, but gets interrupted, and when he returns to the hotel at dawn, the gypsy has split with the dancing girl who recommended him so highly. It's been said that the dancing girl's testimonial is Dylan's sly reference to Elvis Presley's Las Vegas appearances. Presley's selling out didn't mean he couldn't still make his music matter, this reading goes, whatever stage he put it on. But that's a little overdrawn for a song that plays it safe and goes out with a shrug ("So I watched that sun come rising / From that little Minnesota town"). Dylan interpreters always seem to have some problem with the idea that a song isn't meant to be about something larger—they seem to think that Dylan's sense of symbolism and twisted cliché isn't pleasure enough as open-ended ambiguity.

Perhaps *New Morning* gets away with all its ambiguities because, as Michael Gray explains it away, it "doesn't offer us the same complacent countryman persona: it queries it. The happy-family-man comes under a delicate but unwavering scrutiny; and so does the whole post-'67 hip ethic of retreating to the country" (pp. 284–94). There's a loose positioning here that allows Dylan to go from sincerity to self-doubt without sounding schizophrenic; and since only a couple of the songs here are guitar-based, his piano playing emerges as yet another hidden streak of expressiveness. Only a few of his great tracks are built around his piano playing ("Ballad of a Thin Man," "I'll Keep It with Mine,"

"Dear Landlord"); this is his only record that makes piano rock a corner of his writing style.

There aren't any major statements on *New Morning*, except perhaps that now Dylan knows how to relax and admit confusion without sounding bored. But feeling out where the next major themes might appear becomes a subject all its own—it's as if Dylan can't help registering his audience's inertia, its self-doubts, and the directionless attitudes that persist once its fantasies are dashed.

**Dylan's surprise appearance** at George Harrison's Concert for Bangla Desh on August 1, 1971, his first live American appearance since the Guthrie memorial show three years earlier, was a comeback reminiscent of Presley's 1968 television special. Dylan made the shock factor work for him (he was iffy about appearing right up until Harrison announced him), but his five songs shot through what everyone had been assuming about his live powers since his glory days with the Hawks. In less than half an hour of singing, he managed to atone for *Self-Portrait*. The set didn't relive past glories, but brought old songs' sustaining relevance into an uncertain new present and established his significance as far greater than that of any of these ex-Beatles. As in the Isle of Wight set, he drew on mid-sixties achievements instead of current work (not a *New Morning* song among them). But what gave these songs their bite was the imminence Dylan brought to them—the most recent title was at least six years old, but Dylan rendered them anything but nostalgic. With Leon Russell on bass, George Harrison on electric lead, and Ringo Starr on tambourine, the set stood out as the best thing these shows had to offer, upstaging even Billy Preston (whose hits would give Harrison spotlight trouble during his 1974 Dark Horse tour).

The Bangla Desh take of "It Takes a Lot to Laugh, It Takes a Train to Cry" gives it new status as a quiet classic, perhaps his best straight love-blues; and the way he sings "I wanna be your

lover, baby, I don't wanna be your boss _____," stretching out
the last vowel, forcing the others to follow him, he hits emotions
even he probably didn't plan on—fatigue, determination, release. (Leon Russell had just recorded the song, along with "A
Hard Rain's A-Gonna Fall," on his *Leon Russell and the Shelter
People*, the CD version of which includes three outtakes of Dylan songs: "It's All Over Now, Baby Blue," "Love Minus Zero /
No Limit," and "She Belongs to Me.") "Just Like a Woman"
takes the set home with a flush of benevolence that shoots
through the formality of the original (with its careful organ-guitar
interludes), and you begin to hear the way Dylan can make these
relationship songs address his audience. "Please don't let on that
ya knew me when / I was hungry and it was your world" has
completely different subtexts of personal history in it than when
he first sang those lines. "Blowin' in the Wind" has a perfunctory
feel to it, as though Dylan dare not omit his sixties torch song;
but both "A Hard Rain's A-Gonna Fall" and "Mr. Tambourine
Man" remain unerringly contemporary, not songs of a past epoch
so much as beacons of idealism that are destined not only to
define their historical context but to outlive it. To a New York
audience that was both stunned and rapt at his unannounced
appearance, hearing these love songs made so vividly into career
confessionals only made the element of nostalgia that much more
secondary. (The afternoon show substituted "Love Minus Zero /
No Limit" for "Mr. Tambourine Man.")

**The charge leveled** most often at Dylan by those for whom his
singing didn't ring any bells, and who thought his songwriting
sounded more clever than wise, was his contempt for modern
studio sound. Long after multitrack recordings became staple
procedure, Dylan stuck with one-take live sessions. His single in
June of 1971 featured him alone at the piano, singing a mournful
love song called "Spanish Is the Loving Tongue." Because of the
delay between records (and the long-since-abandoned credo that

a major rock star churn out one record per annum), Dylan had a large hand in assembling his second *Greatest Hits* package (his first, from April 1967, was a stopgap measure during his sabbatical). Dylan took it upon himself to lay down some tracks that were already receiving wide attention on bootlegs: "Tomorrow Is a Long Time" was taken from a 1963 Town Hall concert. He sat down with old folkie chum Happy Traum for three acoustic songs ("You Ain't Goin' Nowhere," "I Shall Be Released," and "Down in the Flood,") dashed off with feeling but nowhere near the same serendipitous fancy they have on the Basement Tapes. The rest of the collection, after the newly recorded single "Watching the River Flow," wedges in "Stuck Inside of Mobile with the Memphis Blues Again" from *Blonde on Blonde* (never even remotely a hit), hypes *Nashville Skyline* (its hit, "Lay, Lady, Lay," "Tonight I'll Be Staying Here with You," which went to number fifty, and *Harding*'s "I'll Be Your Baby," in place of "I Threw It All Away," which peaked at number eighty-five), and atones for it with "Mighty Quinn (Quinn the Eskimo)," the Manfred Mann smash.

That's why Leon Russell was brought in to produce "When I Paint My Masterpiece" (on September 24, 1971): to assemble some players who could follow Dylan's haywire vocal cues as they hewed to more professional studio standards in terms of arrangements. Russell had masterminded the Mad Dogs and Englishmen tour with Joe Cocker and had popularized the swamp-gospel style that proved white singers could sing songs like "Let's Go Get Stoned" and not sound ridiculous. He put this same tack to work on Dylan (and made you wish Cocker had tackled something more bluesy than "Girl from the North Country" with his Mad Dogs).

"When I Paint My Masterpiece" is one of the few Dylan songs that incorporates a key change for the last verse, a stock device used to intensify emotion, usually when a song needs a boost. This hilarious parable about the disorienting comedy of rock touring is first recorded by the Band for *Cahoots* (1971) and is now a Grateful Dead staple. Dylan goes through its paces here without a trace of irony, as though stumbling onto an old favorite in the middle of a session—it might as well be about the delight of a hick singing in front of some slick city boys, rather than a hipster escaping a press feeding. "Oh, the hours I've spent inside the Coliseum / Dodging lions and wastin' time" may be the most modest dismissal of his disdain for press conferences he ever makes.

The last verse's "pulling muscles" image is British slang for getting some tail (Chris Difford and Glenn Tilbrook built a song around this conceit for Squeeze called "Pulling Mussels [from a Shell]"). Russell pulls off a first for Dylan—that key change before that last verse—and almost gets away without it sounding like a cliché. The other track Russell supervises becomes a single, "Watching the River Flow," a natty time-killer that treads water (it could be Huck on his raft) in the same way that *New Morning* scrutinizes Dylan's audience's uncertainties.


**After the Bangla Desh** show and a single ("George Jackson," his weakest protest song, released in November), Dylan spent the rest of 1971 and most of 1972 finishing off *Greatest Hits, Volume 2* and working on friends' projects: backing up a record for Allen Ginsberg (*Holy Soul / Jelly Roll*); a single for Steve Goodman ("Somebody Else's Troubles" and "Election Year Rag," under the name Robert Milkwood Thomas); and sessions for Doug Sahm and Roger McGuinn. In early 1972 he worked on the set of Sam Peckinpah's *Pat Garrett and Billy the Kid* in Mexico and Los Angeles. Dylan leapt to take part in the counterculture's big-screen shot at a rock 'n' roll western, and agreed to score the film and play the small role of "Alias." But his presence in the movie is a washout—even Kris Kristofferson upstages him. "I was just one of Peckinpah's pawns," he told Robert Shelton. "There wasn't any dimension to my part and I was uncomfortable in this nonrole . . ." (p. 426). The project yields only one memorable song, the overrated "Knockin' on Heaven's Door," a lyric about death's imminence that Dylan wrote in homage to Slim Pickens's memorable death scene—the movie's one great moment.

That summer, he went to Muscle Shoals, Alabama, to produce a record for Barry Goldberg. Goldberg had played piano at the famous 1965 Newport electric set and was a member of Mike Bloomfield's Electric Flag. Dylan plays percussion on "It's Not the Spotlight" and sang on "Stormy Weather Cowboy," "Silver Moon," "Minstrel Show," and "Big City Woman." He also showed up on *Broadside Reunion, Volume 6,* singing "Train A-Travelin'," "Emmett Till," "Donald White," and "Dreadful Day" as Blind Boy Grunt. In November of 1973, he returned to form in the studio with some friends he hadn't played with since the Isle of Wight.

# 7: napoleon in rags

You don't have to hear what Bob Dylan's saying, you
just have to hear the way he says it.
   —**John Lennon** in
      *Rolling Stone*, 1970

**Planet Waves**
Released: January 1974

**That Dylan formed** few lasting partnerships with his session players after 1968 says as much about his retreat mode as it does
about the material he was putting on tape. His method of drawing spontaneous sounds out of seasoned Nashville types was
risky—at first listening with the tape rolling, Dylan songs must
have been something to get lost in. When he did play live—at
the Isle of Wight Festival by way of snubbing Woodstock, and
the Bangla Desh concert, by way of upstaging his friend George
Harrison—he either called on his brothers-in-arms from the pi-
oneering tour of 1966, the Band, or relaxed and went out acoustic (and made sure Leon Russell either produced or played bass).

   According to Dylan lore, the emotional reception at the
Bangla Desh concert whetted his appetite for more touring; but
it's hard to figure how two shows of a five-song set could lure
anybody into six weeks of hockey rinks. His ambition must have
been building up beforehand, and he must have known the studio gigs would satisfy only so much of his talent's appetite. He
made a big deal out of staying a step ahead of his listeners; but
unlike the Beatles, Dylan never found holing up in the studio his
idea of giving his songs life—he needed his audience as much as
they needed him.

## hard rain

And by late 1973, the Band's career was in a sorry stall after *Cahoots* and a live set, *Rock of Ages* (1972), that, although charged and in places brilliant, was more a summary than a vision. *Moondog Matinee* (1973), a priceless intermission of songs made famous by Sam Cooke, Elvis Presley, and Bobby "Blue" Bland, was the parallel album the Beatles had in them when they began *Get Back*—to the Band's lasting credit, their *Matinee* only made the Beatles unfinished oldies project beside the point. The Band were the logical players for Dylan to call—a fallback that promised to be more than a safe bet. That they made some of their best music together ever during the proto–rock reunion spectacle is only half of the irony. That they made you forget all about show-biz reunion truisms goes more to the point.

To get the tour off the ground—and work up some new material—they holed up in the studio for three days in November 1973, to cut a record. *Planet Waves* was criticized for its rough, unfinished tone (as though other Dylan records were varnished), but they hit the road as if the lukewarm reviews had missed the point. This music is casual to the point of missed cues, dropped rhythmic kicks, and Garth Hudson's organ overhangs, left on after cutoffs instead of overdubbed (after his roughhouse solo in "Tough Mama," the best song here, it's like Hudson doesn't want the music to end).

As Dylan's breakneck recording disposition goes, *Planet Waves* ranks among his most slipshod efforts, even if it's not among his toughest (in *Rolling Stone*, Jon Landau complained of hearing the buttons of Dylan's shirt click against his guitar in "Wedding Song"). But Dylan's one-take dictum throws up a lot more than most bands erase in the process of polishing up arrangements: if there's not as much to mine in these 1973 songs as there is in his 1965 or 1966 output, there's still plenty to chew on when Dylan delivers a line like "You know who you are and where you've been," in "Tough Mama." You can hear the Band react to that self-referencing irony, and it pushes the song open in the past-lover shorthand that follows, a cryptogram for the players' own road stories.

The *Planet Waves* mood is frumpy, an afternoon scrimmage against tunes that weren't written to break a band in, and they wear these songs like loose garments. For the hockey rinks, they even outfitted the stage with a couch. It's as close to the privacy of the Basement Tapes as they would ever approach again; you wonder why they considered those earlier tracks unfinished by comparison. The fact that "Forever Young," a song Dylan wrote for his kids, finds a different tone in two distinct versions only underlines how certain Dylan songs gain from flexibility; that the song works both as a slow prayer and a middle-aged jig affirms its theme of inexplicable change.

The domestic themes on *Planet Waves* are easier to swallow than the tripe on *Self-Portrait*, in part because Dylan gets performances that are more serious-minded (even when he's being funny), and there's enough doubt swimming around in the sound to keep you on your guard about just how sure he is of his certainties. The simple pleasures get caught by the undertow of death ("Dirge"), suicide ("Going, Going, Gone," a song that doesn't toy around with the idea), and the brick wall that love collides with when possessiveness curdles into obsession (the overstated contradictions of "Wedding Song"). As a totality, this album is more satisfying than *Nashville Skyline* or *New Morning* with their settled-in homilies, because it's rounded out with more than one shade of romance; subterfuge, suspicion, self-hate ("Dirge," "Tough Mama"), and memory ("Something There Is About You") counter lighthearted celebration ("On a Night Like This").

**The Band's windup** pitch to "Going, Going, Gone" is a wonder of pinpoint ensemble playing: Robertson makes his guitar entrance choke as if a noose had suddenly tightened around its neck, and you get the feeling these guys could shadow Dylan in their sleep.

## hard rain

By the end of the first verse, their shaping of the song, and feel for Dylan's ambiguities, is so perfectly attuned to the bottomed-out quality of Dylan's mood that Robertson's guitar sounds like it's scratching the itch in Dylan's throat—it's a suicide note that gives up far more than what it tries to express. The bridge has one of those lines that's easy to mishear: the way Dylan sings "Grandma said 'Boy, go and follow your heart' " is slurred; it could be heard as "*don't* follow your heart," a warning. What might be a little bit of kindness from a sincere matriarch can turn into a stretch of sarcasm from a cynical person who regrets her romantic folly. Again, it's as though Dylan wants the ambiguity to trouble, give you pause about the "All that's gold doesn't shine" cliché he hasn't bothered to snarl.

Robertson's guitar suffocates the singer even more in "Dirge," a set piece with Dylan on piano and Robertson buzzing overhead, this time on acoustic. The sound is brittle, spooked; and the lyric traces suspicions and misgivings about the mood of the early seventies that *New Morning* kept at bay: the loneliness, the fiberglass surface of materialism, the debts of star isolation.

John Herdman points out the equivocal meanings sent off by the lines "I hate myself for lovin' you, but I should get over that": "Does he mean that he should get over loving her, or get over hating himself for loving her? And does 'should' mean 'ought to' or 'probably will'?" (p. 38). There are other Dylan songs where the vented anger works as a veil to the singer's self-incrimination—"Positively 4th Street," "Don't Think Twice"—and "Dirge" takes its place as a romance that doubles as a crack at the zeitgeist. It's almost like the singer of "Dirge" is warming up to the density of despair in "Going, Going, Gone," that the forced faith of the lesser devotions ("Hazel," and "Wedding Song") has already snapped.

**Cornered by clichéd** romantic handles that link verses two and three with verses four and five ("Dark Beauty," "Sweet Goddess"), "Tough Mama" is the track that exemplifies the best playing on *Planet Waves*, and a pitch of writing that shows Dylan can still challenge himself. Hudson's organ strings everything else together; he could be this band's unacknowledged leader. The last verse's sacrificial lamb follows up on the suggestions of fate in "Dirge."

The last verse is a screed to his audience: Dylan may be back with his old band, but he's not going back to offering himself up as a human tabula rasa to the masses, a sixties piñata-doll martyr. Besides the obvious "Forever Young," the most widely quoted lines of this album when it first appeared were from "Wedding Song": "It's never been my duty to remake the world at large, / Nor is it my intention to sound the battle charge"—a point-blank refusal that steps on ironies he would have breathed fire into ten years earlier. That last refrain of "Tough Mama" has more grit to it, more of the shifty tough-guy stance that found its voice in "It Ain't Me, Babe" and "My Back Pages." The sixties are over, and as late as 1974, the seventies are still unknown territory—where will it all lead? His recognition has cost him his appetite, which says more about ambivalence towards an uncertain future than most of his other crafty dodges. "Can I blow a little smoke on you?" He has to ask?

When these new love songs aren't being ironic by way of overstatement—the voice of a lover trying to convince himself of his own passions—they're hitting a streak of affection by accident that his country numbers managed through genre studies. Where some of those Nashville tracks found a satisfying emotional pace in their own preoccupation with style, "Hazel" rains down with pleasure; "Something There Is About You" is a foil for Hudson's organ. It's like a duet between Dylan's fond remembrances and Hudson's abilities to make long-forgotten truths echo with possibility. And there's even some thorny self-doubt peeking through the devotions: "I could say that I'd be faithful, I could say it in one sweet, easy breath / But to you that would be cruelty and to me it surely would be death." Those are words that don't sound out of place on a record with "Dirge" and "Going, Going, Gone"—the confession of a self-deceiver who refuses to rope his lover in. "You Angel You" and "Never Say Goodbye" aren't as strong as side one's romances—even Dylan could hear that: in the *Biograph* liner notes, he says the words sound like "dummy lyrics."

**Dylan has never** been guilty of the kind of cheap wrap-up a lot of bands use as an excuse for summations when closing side two. He more often downplays entrances and exits, or openly parodies them ("Desolation Row"). "Wedding Song" is an overwrought failure (on a par with "Sara," from *Desire*), which comes unglued because it remains oblivious to its own overstatement, the degree to which the singer pledges himself into a self-contradicting rut. It's an echo of the grand sweep he could summon in his earlier romantic mosques—the bleary fixation of "Visions of Johanna" or the confounding eulogy that is "Just Like a Woman." What rings false about "Wedding Song" is its seeming unawareness of its own clichés—he doesn't make anything of these tired proclamations, and it seems to matter even less how it all stacks up. Verses are interchangeable, and the song simply ebbs instead of growing organically towards some pitch of feeling. It doesn't take a Dylan to write lines like this, but it speaks even more poorly of Dylan that he throws away the song's concluding couplet and sings it like he does every other line here—as though this lover's refusal might only prompt him to turn around and sing the same lyric to somebody else. Imagine this number on *Blood on the Tracks* and you get an idea of how commonplace the writing is; that it doesn't completely deflate *Planet Waves* speaks for the vitality most of the other tracks sustain.

The most banal way to read Dylan songs is to link them up with his life, as though he had no greater ambition than to record his autobiography—this is the injustice his lesser profilers fall into. He's obviously greater than this; his songs inhabit personas, and he shifts characters so often on the larger stage of rock stardom that it's clear he enjoys toying with "Dylan." But the larger biographical realm he roams in—as the voice of his times—is relevant in the uncanny manner he registers his audience's tics and emotional quivers. It doesn't seem like such a paradox that his records between 1968 and 1972 are either abstractions (*John Wesley Harding*) or meditations on indifference and directionless motion (*New Morning*). "Wedding Song" upsets this comeback with the Band even more than a couple of tossed-off romances, "You Angel You" and "Never Say Goodbye," which may mean only that when Dylan gets serious and slow at the same time, he can't pull off the same intensity as he used to. It could also mean he had as many self-doubts about his comeback as he did about his songwriting.

> And I knew that I was glad to be loose from that
> sentimental and dreamy trash, and gladder to be edg-
> ing on my way along here singing with the people,
> singing something with fight and guts and belly laughs
> and power and dynamite to it.
> —**Woody Guthrie**,
>  *Bound for Glory*

## Before the Flood
Released: June 1974

**If the Dylan/Band** tour of 1974 was greased by a pushover press, a delirious coast-to-coast crowd, and a grand synchronousness of ambition between players that sounded like no previous tour, it all made for an even better concert album. Besides slamming the door on the sixties (which by early 1974 were in the final stages of twilight: the troops were returning from Southeast Asia, Nixon would soon resign, Saigon would soon fall), *Before the Flood* slammed the door on all assumptions about how live records could work. These weren't tidy run-throughs punched up by a crowd's adrenaline, which fed a band's jitters (and tempos), energy compensating for adroitness. This is the nostalgia album that beat the oldies trap, a tour of sixties landmarks that made a glance backward seem entirely contemporary. Instead of making sense of this music's history, these echoes came to bear on the pop present they interrupted. Not only that, the music has legs: its pop antipathy and disdain for manners sounds just as relevant some eighteen years after its release. You can hear the bitterness in Dylan's voice as he howls out these classics—the bitterness of feeling obligated to sing numbers to please the crowd—and hear him finding energy in that; hear him realizing mid-song, around the time he gets to the words "I'll only let you down" in "It Ain't Me, Babe," that his gall suits the lyric exactly—and then pushing through even that. (And Dylan wonders why listeners so covet his bootlegs.) Singing like this extends what we can expect from our performers when they sing their familiar work. Defining an epoch is relatively easy, Dylan seems to be saying; living it down is the hard part.

Eyebrows cocked above his hipster shades, Dylan marched onstage with a deadpan scowl and delivered songs with an equivocal menace. It was never clear whether he felt he had to sing these songs for the fans who would be disappointed without them, or based his selection on what he felt stood up best over time; he left that up to this listeners. Certainly, most of this record's selections were tour staples, but the range of songs he and the Band performed covered even vaster territory; it could have easily filled three records without diffusing the impact (left off the record's initial lineup were "Ballad of Hollis Brown" and the Band's "King Harvest").

## napoleon in rags

The shows kicked off with the *nah-nah-nah* guitar taunt of "Most Likely You Go Your Way and I'll Go Mine," which quickly became a way of saying farewell as well as hello. (For the first show in Chicago, Dylan opened with "Hero Blues," an old song from 1963, rewritten for the occasion.) On the Band's studio records, they reclined into their music and seduced their listeners into doing the same. Their live sound was more chaotic, but there was still a warmth to the frenzy.

"Most Likely . . ." trots along to Helm's shuffling drums: he lashes his snare like he was cracking a whip across the song's neck. Robertson's guitar spars with Manuel's riffraff piano; Hudson's synthesizer swells flutter around everything else like a tattered flag pitched at the summit of some romantic battle. At the center stands Dylan, a strangely oblivious anchor to the drama surrounding him. His voice is frayed, drenched in feeling, and he defines the sound as he redefines the song: "You say my kisses aren't like his / Yeah, well, I'm not gonna tell you why that is." When he sang this number back on *Blonde on Blonde*, Dylan took a debauched pleasure in dressing his lover down—the joy of the song was in its killer instinct, its decadent, knife-twisting smirk. Here, Dylan isn't playing around anymore; he knows the accusations reflect back on him—he's no better for falling for her lies than she is for taking up with someone else. What cakewalked as deadpan irony back in 1966 now fairly seethes—it's a song less about the comedy of a fallout than the ravages.

All of these 1974 performances are driven in part by anger, and a self-doubt that becomes a kind of self-respect—a strength that comes from staring down self-debilitating flaws. The original version of "Lay, Lady, Lay" was gentle to the point of gentility; with the Band, he cuts into it with sharp, biting attacks— "mowing down his old songs like a truck," as Christgau says. This is a platform for Robertson's guitar, answering Dylan's every line, as though Dylan's fever needs constant dousing. But even so, Hudson's scene-stealing subtext outlines the arrangement with different keyboard textures for each verse. "It Ain't Me,

## hard rain

Babe" starts out as a quaint two-step, jump-charged by Dylan's opening yowl ("Go away!"), but it opens up into a broiling refrain. Dylan blasts his own vocal style—stretching out words ("do-how-hown"), chopping up vowels ("HA-HA-HEART"), trampling lines underfoot ("A lover for your life—but what more?," a spin on the original ". . . an' nothin' more"). A lesser singer would collapse into self-parody (as Dylan later will); this is singing motored by the resolve of a phoenix.

In early Dylan, the fuming was an end in itself; here, the indignation brings release. You can hear it in the over-the-top rhapsody of "Rainy Day Women #12 & 35," completely rewritten on the spot, or in the resigned farewell of "Knockin' on Heaven's Door," with the whole band lending their voices for the refrain. Dylan's vocals come out like a resentful eulogy of lost hopes, and got more than a few listeners associating the song with the mass graveyard of Vietnam: "Mama, put my guns in the ground / I can't *shoot* them anymo-wer."

After a superb entrance that clinches Dylan's choppy opening piano chords, "Ballad of a Thin Man" closes the opening half, in colors that are more resigned and controlled than his liontamer antics of 1966: he doesn't sound so pissed off by the hounds of journalists back on his trail (in fact, he gives some of his first straightforward interviews during this period); he simply sounds tired that nothing much has changed. Danko's bass flies up and down the song's spine: he shoots high, stoops low, falls back into the groove, then leaps again during refrains to juice Dylan's voice; Hudson lets fly some synthesized wah-wah catcalls. The transition from bridge back into verse ("tax-deductible organizay-*shuns*") begins to suggest the peaks of 1966: there isn't any structure to speak of in these few bars; the song hangs suspended on the tenuous faith that everyone will land together—only the fall is so ripping nobody gives a hang, so they shoot right past the landing into the final verse, accenting the climax by blitzing it.

One of the Band's defining strengths is the way they alternate lead vocalists, and the way these exchanges play up the idea of collaboration. Danko might be the Band's most endearing singer; Helm has heart and then some (and not just in his voice); Manuel could be a sentimental weeper. With Helm's Arkansas modesty, "Up on Cripple Creek" (their first, and high—number twenty-five—Top 40 hit, from 1969; the other was their cover of Marvin Gaye's "Don't Do It" in 1972) settles into a funky credo. Danko plays the lanky kid brother who rises to a song's energy level if only to show that the Band can't leave him behind. In "Endless Highway," you can hear how much he depends on the others, and there's a sibling charm in the ambition he summons just to keep up. In "Stage Fright," he plays out the tale of a man who gets caught by the spotlight and finishes the show only to find, like a hard pro, he wants to "start all over again." And in "When You Awake," he even saddles up to his grandfather's advice about the soul ("You will believe your only soul / You were born with to grow old and never know . . ."). In moments like these, Danko becomes the Band's symbolic Ringo: the everyman the audience identifies with. ("It Makes No Difference" shows another side of Danko: anxious, tormented, enraptured.) These connections only become stronger when these voices join together, or alternate verses in "The Shape I'm In," or mounting the ladder refrain in "The Weight" ("and . . . and . . . and _____ / You put the load right on me"), which works as a vocal metaphor for the musical traditions the Band shoulders.

**The second half** of 1974's shows began when Dylan took the stage alone with an acoustic guitar and rewrote the book on multidimensional self-reliance. The acoustic set caught on *Before the Flood* matches what he does with the Band for energy, and reminds you all over again how electric Dylan's presence was before he plugged in at Newport. In these tracks, you begin to hear how Dylan turns these romances into larger metaphors for his fans and for everybody's relationship with the fading sixties spirit. When he sings "I gave her my heart but she wanted my soul" in "Don't Think Twice, It's All Right" the sentiment steps around time and ropes in new meanings: mulling over how raw and betrayed he feels by an emotional child's persistent detachment, Dylan superimposes a layer of an aging god's perplexities in confronting his audience once again. His stance is defiant towards cheers; the harmonica solo sounds like a siren that just won't turn off. The spirit of "Just Like a Woman" is a bit scarred compared with the Bangla Desh take, but the audience metaphors are unmistakable: in the line "But she breaks just like a little girl," the lover who puts up a good front but collapses into vulnerability becomes a keep-the-faith audience that practices hero worship. Raving about Dylan used to connote concern for contemporary issues; by 1974, it had turned into another kind of ritual. The last verse takes this idea to the scalding point; the line "Please don't let on that you knew me when . . ." is a tacit suspension of what has passed between Dylan and his listeners that almost counts as a renunciation—a letting go, if not a denial, of everything that once brought them together: shared ambitions, shared political values, shared pleasure in how much humor and subversiveness can count in growing up.

These themes come together in "It's Alright, Ma (I'm Only Bleeding)," which Dylan delivers with such strength it sends you back to the original in wonder that it could be improved upon (he skips verses ten to twelve, and you don't even miss them). This rendition seems to grow in the moment of the performance, a torrent against phoniness, deceit, and the curse of auspicious beginnings that only Dylan could get away with and not sound like a schoolmarm. The loneliest moment in the song—and the album—comes when he cries, out of both desire and impotence: "I got nothin', Ma, to live up to!" The line about LBJ ("Even the president of the United States / Sometimes must have / To stand naked") comes back to haunt Richard Nixon, and the crowd eats it up—tour manager Bill Graham even worked out a red-white-and-blue stage light to hype the moment.

These acoustic selections offer up only a taste of what Dylan chose to sing during his solo sets—a smattering of bootlegs covers the rest. One of the best live sets appears on *Love Songs for America*, recorded at the Boston Garden on January 14, 1974. *Bob Dylan on the Road, 1974–75* features acoustic-only numbers: "I Don't Believe You," "She Belongs to Me," "It's All Over Now, Baby Blue," "Nobody 'Cept You" (a *Planet Waves* outtake), "Love Minus Zero / No Limit," "Simple Twist of Fate," "Hard Rain," "Desolation Row," "Wedding Song," and a hard, vicious reading of "Visions of Johanna." Other songs in his solo set included "Blowin' in the Wind," "Gates of Eden," "Girl from the North Country," "The Lonesome Death of Hattie Carroll," "Mama, You Been on My Mind," "The Times They Are A-Changin'," and "To Ramona." With the Band, sets included "As I Went Out One Morning," "Forever Young," "I Don't Believe You," "It Takes a Lot to Laugh, It Takes a Train to Cry," "Just Like Tom Thumb's Blues," "Leopard-Skin Pill-Box Hat," "Maggie's Farm," "Something There Is About You," and "Tough Mama." The Band also pulled out "Holy Cow," "Life's Carnival," "Long Black Veil," the Four Tops' "Loving You Is Sweeter Than Ever," "Rag Mama Rag," Bobby Bland's "Share Your Love," "Wheel's on Fire," and "When You Awake."

**There are several** essays to be written about "Like a Rolling Stone," because there are several different songs to consider even if they all draw on the same words. What Dylan does to it on tour in 1966 is fairly straightforward: he takes aim at a disgruntled fan, laces each verse with a bit more bile, and darts ahead of the band's runaway train. It's a moment in Dylan's career when everything comes into focus, even though it speaks through blurry bootleg sound: a year after the song hit number two, the live rendition drew from a noise and vitality that the Rolling Stones would chase for the next half-decade, and it united Dylan's ambition and message into a single streak of provoked irascibility.

**225**

## hard rain

At the Isle of Wight festival, he makes this outsider anthem something more like an outsider's apology; as a country yarn, "Like a Rolling Stone" doesn't truck in humiliation, it finds a degree of compassion. Perhaps Dylan, like everybody else, was undone by the exhilarating advocacy Hendrix found lurking in the song—and the humor: "At Napoleon in rags and all that [*coy pause*] *sweet* talk that he used . . ." When Dylan returned to it in 1974, this was the only song that could close shows, and when the house lights lit up after the bookend "Most Likely . . ." nothing could follow "Rolling Stone." Perhaps the most startling aspect of the *Before the Flood* version is the tonnage the Band finds in the song by simply backing into it. Dylan plays a few opening chords alone—you can almost see him sauntering about onstage, wagging his head, preoccupied with himself—and after some guitar licks from Robertson and some wispy organ from Hudson, the others glide in on top until suddenly every piston is pumping. It isn't until the end of the first line that the song catches charge.

There's a whine to Dylan's voice here that betrays the nine years that have passed since he sprang his counterculture credo on the world. There's a lifetime in those nine years, and it explodes from his delivery in ways that automatically draw his audience in as coconspirators in what the song is all about. "Like a Rolling Stone" has grown into a celebration, though of what and at what cost is difficult to say. As in a lot of the arena-crowd singalongs that define the seventies, the hockey rink masses of America would become one at the end of the evening, joining every word, transporting themselves through this missive of class revolt into a communal rant of transcended miseries. You can't say that halfway into the 1970s, Dylan was exactly the vanguard anymore; but with nobody savvy (or prolific) enough to take his place (yet), the song seems to work just as well as a diatribe on lost hopes, a clenched fist to clouding ideals and aging hipsterism gone to seed. "Would you like to [*long pause*] make a dee-uhl_____!" he sings, as subtly as a convict who's strapped to the chair asking the governor for a stay of execution. It's a performance that's as mysterious and involving as anything Dylan has ever done, and it easily outranks all future versions of this song he feels compelled to keep in stock. Director Martin Scorsese uses this version for his *New York Stories* segment, "Life Lessons," in which Nick Nolte plays an aging, obsessed painter. With Helm's rapid-fire snare fills during refrains, and Hudson's rainbow organ lines, the song opens up into new realms of feeling, things even Dylan was only discovering as he sang it on this, the last night of the tour. (In light of this, "Blowin' in the Wind" comes as a letdown—an electrified touch-up of his best-known song that deflates everything "Rolling Stone" built up and then surpassed. It's as if Stevie Wonder followed up the hot funk of "Superstition" with "You Are the Sunshine of My Life.") As barbed and penetrating as "Rolling Stone" still is, there is a strain of idealism wrung from anger in this performance that turns this sixties canon into a joint farewell, a hero's return sung to an audience that leaps with him into the uncertainty of where such songs can lead.

# back in the rain

I took the tune to church, took it holy roller, shot in a few split notes, oozed in a fake one, come down barrel house, hit off a good old cross-country lonesome note or two, trying to get that old guitar to help me, to talk with me, talk for me, and say what I was thinking, just this one time. . . .

—**Woody Guthrie**,
*Bound for Glory*

## Blood on the Tracks
Released: January 1975

**As manipulative as** Dylan is with abstractions, his records don't rest on vagaries, as Joan Baez suggests in her mawkish memoir "Diamonds and Rust." It's the way his readings of those vagaries tempt listeners into hearing possibilities—his ambiguities are always something better than a cop-out, even when he's putting you on. He must have sensed this on tour; you can hear him revel in the way his vocal attacks claw away all pretense of nostalgia in "It Ain't Me, Babe," a song that in any other singer's world might have been passed over for being ten years old. His audience's thirst for what they could still hear in performances like this only goaded their author, and that's the kind of performing experience that can send a singer to new expressive altitudes, and a writer back to his element.

After his triumphant winter 1974 tour with the Band (twenty-one cities in forty-two days), Dylan mixed the *Before the Flood* live tapes, and sang "North Country Blues," the single "Spanish Is the Loving Tongue," and a singalong "Blowin' in the

## hard rain

Wind" at a benefit with Arlo Guthrie in New York on May 9. In September he laid down tracks at Columbia's Studio A in New York, with Eric Weissberg and his band, Deliverance: Tony Braun, Paul Griffin, and steel guitarist Buddy Cage. But while vacationing at the home of his brother, David, outside Minneapolis over the holidays, Dylan became disenchanted with the way these tracks held up, so he phoned Columbia Records on the eve of the album's release to halt pressings. At his brother's urging, Dylan returned to Minneapolis and booked time with local players. Recording continued on December 27 and 30 at the Sound 80 studio with bassist Bill Peterson, guitarists Ken Odegard and Chris Weber, drummer Bill Berg, and keyboardist Greg Inhoffer. Four of the ten final tracks came from the New York sessions ("Meet Me in the Morning," "Shelter from the Storm," "You're Gonna Make Me Lonesome When You Go," "Buckets of Rain"); six from Minneapolis ("Tangled Up in Blue," "You're a Big Girl Now," "Simple Twist of Fate," "Idiot Wind," "If You See Her, Say Hello," "Lily, Rosemary and the Jack of Hearts"). The result mapped Dylan's restored creative powers, his gift for serendipity (and when to rerecord), and still ranks with any music he would ever make.

This confidence rebounds off the tenor of the songs, which are stoked by fragility and loss. *Blood on the Tracks* takes the ambivalence and unfocused air of *Self-Portrait* and *New Morning* as a starting point and turns those moods into images of emptiness and lack of purpose, the flip side of flake-power euphoria that was always chafing at the surface of the sixties. (One of the album's signature lines comes in "You're a Big Girl Now": "What a shame if all we've shared can't last.") If the Band's jaunty rumble on *Before the Flood* makes you forget abut the comparatively stiff rhythms that mark Dylan's early rock (the Band seems to be the only ensemble that can make Dylan danceable), Dylan's return to folk inhabits a different universe of feeling than the cocky autonomy of *Another Side of Bob Dylan*. Even the ire of "Idiot Wind" stems from the intimacy of the surrounding songs—it's a face-off, all right, but it projects more than the fusillade of insecurity that goads "Positively 4th Street." Nixon's resignation in August 1974 snuffs out the sixties' twilight, and the timing of *Blood on the Tracks* is as crucial as the timing of "Like a Rolling Stone" nearly ten years earlier. It's as though the era is fated for *Blood on the Tracks,* even though the music's undertow does more than sum up the fate of the era. In the reluctant acceptance of "If You See Her, Say Hello" or the wee-hour blues of "Meet Me in the Morning," Dylan opens a vein of the sixties that finds middle age something of an anomaly to youth culture, and the triumph isn't that he has the poet's inclination to shake down the passing youth that everybody else was only too willing to deny, but that he has the poet's courage to embrace it, and turn what had been denial into hard-won wisdom. The record sustains the image of a cherished face whose visage fades long before the infatuation.

Dylan gets away with being sentimental about the sixties largely because he spent so much of that decade renouncing sentimentalism. Working out his metaphors of lost love, he strikes a melancholy tone that few could articulate without drowning in their own self-pity. Given the pile of clichés these songs employ, the strength flows from Dylan's emotionally barbed vocals, and his ability to summon these charred memories as a way of reconnecting with his audience. Turning these intimate trials into public metaphors is what separates Dylan and Joni Mitchell—who symbolize something greater than figures unburdening their problems on the world—from the relatively two-dimensional mode of the singer-songwriter clique that epitomizes everything self-serving about the "me" decade (acts like Carole King and James Taylor). A pox on the self-referencing rut that by 1975 is the industry's bread and butter (with the Eagles weenie-roasting James Dean, and Linda Ronstadt deflowering Motown), the aging-troubadour tension on *Blood on the Tracks* plays off Dylan's early folkie persona and nests in his oracular vocals and lonesome whistle harmonica solos. *Blood on*

## hard rain

*the Tracks* maps the haunted romance of the sixties, which would cast a pall on the seventies, which wouldn't come unstuck until punk. And even then, because it owed a lot of its rage and open contempt for civility to Dylan, punk blitzed past the soul-searching and denounced the burden of sixties ideals altogether.

*Blood on the Tracks* single-handedly re-establishes Dylan's stature in the rock world as the kind of genius who can refashion all the tired folk clichés into a masterstroke of self-definition—both for himself and for an audience that hears themselves once again as he reads between their lifelines. This is the first folk record that counts as rock, just as *Freewheelin'* is the first rock LP that counts as folk. No folk album would be complete without a two-step like "Lily, Rosemary and the Jack of Hearts"; no rock record is worth its weight in vehemence without a circling buzzard like "Idiot Wind." And with a leading man like the elusive "Jack of Hearts," Dylan is playing on his own mythical imagery: these songs are the lament of a cowboy moving on from territory that has watched him come of age.

Song in, song out, there's really only one lover driving these feelings—either various intimacies punching the same emotional buttons, or one lover throughout a life visiting the singer in different disguises. The narrators of these romances sound like the same person, and Dylan makes these songs sound like visitations to a character the same way the singer is visited by cyclical heartache in "Tangled Up in Blue." In "If You See Her, Say Hello," he turns the listener into a reliable distraction from his obsession (as he did in "Girl from the North Country"). In "You're Gonna Make Me Lonesome When You Go," he bids farewell by way of owning up to how much he needs love—quite a leap from "Don't Think Twice." By closing with the resigning-ironic "Buckets of Rain," he acknowledges how even a deluge of affection can make a person indescribably restless ("Everything about you is bringing me Misery"). In "You're a Big Girl Now," he has an imaginary conversation with a lover who has grown more than he has. Some of this song has the desperate, longing quality of the overstatements on *Planet Waves'* "Wedding Song" ("I can change, I swear"). The vocal squeeze Dylan gives to the "oh"s between lines floods the song with missed chances, and it becomes a musical hook all its own, especially on the line "I'm going out of my mind, oh _____ . . ." In the New York version on *Biograph,* he gets a hushed intensity by singing the same phrases through pursed lips.

The stories on *Blood on the Tracks* don't define an odyssey so much as inhabit one. In catching this tone, Dylan captures the seventies at least as well as he ever did the sixties. This lost Eden would subsume even lumbering heavy-metal acts like Led Zeppelin, who wound up sounding like bloated asterisks to acid rock's heyday (mighty asterisks, to be sure, but still asterisks). In 1976, the Democrats would get their due from Watergate, and many would interpret this as the final White House victory for the antiwar demonstrations, the rightful culmination of a decade-long civil rights consciousness. But a good year before Jimmy Carter's name became national news, "Idiot Wind" foretold the seeping fear and anomie that Carter would go on to dub "malaise," and sent the truest believers careening towards easy answers—cocaine, est, and in Dylan's case, born-again Christianity.

**Among the few** extended works in rock that could be called tragic (Van Morrison's *Astral Weeks,* John Lennon's *Plastic Ono Band*), *Blood on the Tracks* dwells in a tragic mood that doesn't elude the popular audience. Dylan comes down somewhere between Robert Johnson's abject rage at the world (a rage that betrays a profound love) and Woody Guthrie's undaunted chipperness (an uppity pluck that finds hope amid oppressive conditions). What the sixties hadn't come to terms with yet was the relative privilege its youth culture enjoyed compared with the nomadic poverty of singers like Johnson and Guthrie. The continental sweep of "Tangled Up in Blue" takes this for granted as well: Dylan isn't singing about homeless people who drift because they have to; he's singing about people on the run from situations—and themselves—by choice. This makes the situations they encounter all the more self-destructive, and more tragic.

In the first verse of "Tangled Up in Blue," the singer stands hitchhiking on the side of a road in the rain, thinking about his dues. By the end of the second verse, he's driven with his lover to the West Coast and abandoned the relationship along with the car. From there, the song is a tableau of encounters that conveys an atmosphere of detachment from both his lover and the people they knew together.

The way Dylan sings the words "she *never* es*caped* my *mind*," somewhere between a squeal and a wounded dog's bay, lifts the whole abandoned-car episode from cliché. And there's something sly about how Dylan chooses the word "grew," instead of what might be expected—"flew"—for the singer's impulse to escape. "Grew" implies, if only for an instant, that his journey is headed towards a linear conclusion, something the song subverts on every possible level. But the tag line pulls the meaning back in—the singer's growth has only become more ironic, and the pangs for his ex-lover travel as constant an orbit as the song's title. Dylan uses this device on several songs from these sessions: giving a key concluding phrase a different spin as every verse rolls around, so that by the time the song is over, he's gotten as much mileage as he can from such resonating phrases as "Simple Twist of Fate," "You're a Big Girl Now," and, in the best example of this trick, "Up to Me."

The singer encounters the mystery woman first in a topless place, where she greets him with a sly understatement ("Don't I know your name?"—later, she goes so far as to say "You look like the silent type," which is another way of Dylan poking fun at his own long-windedness). But by verse six, the singer has moved in "with *them*," and the triangle disintegrates: "He started into dealing with slaves," which throws the scenario back perhaps a century, or at least into a symbolic netherworld (drug dealing, hustling) that is meant as a corruption of values. The characters never resolve anything—he feels something die inside him; she freezes up; they're victims of their own distractions.

In the *Biograph* notes Dylan dubs a later version of this song, on 1984's *Real Live*, the "finished" work: "On *Real Live* it's more like it should have been. I was never really happy with it. I guess I was just trying to make it like a painting where you can see the different parts but then you also see the whole of it." But the changes on the *Real Live* rewrite don't amount to as much of a new song as Dylan would have you think—there are fewer twists in verb tenses, and more unredeemed clichés. When his lover greets him at the "Blindin' Light" bar, where she works, she doesn't say, "Don't I know your name?"—she says, "What's that you got up your sleeve?" Overall, the vocal performance is far less affecting when Dylan is alone with his guitar. And the *Real Live* version omits the central scene where the lover takes the singer home and presents him with a book of thirteenth-century Italian poems.

By this point on the *Blood on the Tracks* version, the band has been gaining on the song in the same way the players do on "Like a Rolling Stone," and you can hear how the words begin to carry them, how Dylan's reading of the lyric insinuates musical touches no formal arrangement could approach. And this sense of the musicians connecting up with the music they're making— their realization of the scope of the song as they perform it— lends "Tangled Up in Blue" a far more compelling quality than Dylan gives it alone on *Real Live*.

In the past, Dylan's anger and disillusion were thin veils for the kind of insecurity that a towering wit passed off as a power trip. He could be fearless and still compassionate in exposing his lover's flaws ("Just Like a Woman," "Love Minus Zero / No Limit"), but more often he took spray paint to the scene of the crime and splattered graffiti all over someone who done him wrong (the irresistible one-liners he gets off in "Most Likely You Go Your Way and I'll Go Mine" or "Leopard-Skin Pill-box Hat"). The voice on *Blood on the Tracks* couldn't be further from this kind of romantic larceny; and whether you hear Dylan exposing himself or not, the narrators of these songs have long since forgotten about keeping face. Part of what's tragic about this tone is Dylan's ability to find the dignity in hearts as confused and self-abased as the ones he essays here. Whatever the circumstances, these characters seem nobler, more promising than the situations they put themselves in.

The deliberately jumbled tenses and temporal references in "Tangled Up in Blue" give it an aftertaste of disorientation. You're never sure how many lovers the narrator is addressing: whether his journeys chase the redhead in the first stanza—the slightest verse with the most clichés—or whether the odyssey is a series of encounters with different women who set off the same yearning. Aside from being a return to folk roots, this is an adventurous return to narrative that replaces abstractions with prismatic memories. Even when he arrives at the present tense in the last verse ("So now I'm goin' back again"), you're not sure whether he's singing in the present or simply remembering a moment when he got his feet back on the ground. The final verse finds him hitting the road again, with a vague resolution to stay true to himself, and not turn into a mathematician, a carpenter's wife, or any kind of society stooge. What the song leaves elegantly unstated is that simply by chasing this illusory romance ("So now I'm goin' back again / I got to get to her somehow"), this figure has become a slave to the road, chained to the chase.

**When he's on** his mark, Dylan does to bold clichés what a worn razor does to tissue paper. In "You're a Big Girl Now," he gives two successive lines such different emotional hues they could be stitched from different songs: "Love is so simple, to quote a phrase / You've known it all the time, I'm learnin' it these days." His inflection underlines the distinction between what she knows and what he's catching up to, and carries a resentment against the insight. At first he demolishes the axiom; then he half-admits to it ironically by offhandedly renouncing it as just "a phrase"; finally he succumbs to it. Part of Dylan's charm has always been how he gets away with cliché, either by subverting it to his own ends or by upending it to expose its internal logic, as Christopher Ricks points out in the quickened tense change of "I see better days and I do better things" from "I Shall Be Free" (*The Force of Poetry*, pp. 366–67). In "Simple Twist of Fate" the narrator wakes up after a magical one-night stand, sits in an empty room, and wonders if the woman he paid for the night before is thinking about him at all.

It's not just the way Dylan's vocal—plaintive, resigned, brooding—redeems such a stock situation (he even has the tart drop money into a blind man's cup—quite a touch!); it's the way he makes the singer's experience into something larger than just a contemplation of a brief, unsettling encounter. Like Otis Redding, who brings time to a standstill in "Sittin' on the Dock of the Bay," where the "loneliness won't leave me alone," Dylan gets inside his young initiate so well that he makes his plight inhabit the same ebb and swell of timelessness. Half of this conceit is built upon the sex roles being reversed—it's a man's openly deflated machismo—but that's a pop cliché all by itself. It's the sense of loneliness the lover feels *before* the woman leaves him that gives off such a strong sense of desolation: "She looked at him and he felt a spark tingle to his bones / 'Twas then he felt alone and wished that he'd gone straight." This betrays a hunger for connection so profound that even connection won't relieve it—by letting himself fall for this fling, he's admitting he'd rather be alone than feel anything. It's the sound of a man who knows he's trapped inside a dime-store novel and falls for the hooker despite himself.

**Tragedy gets a bad rap,** especially from pulp-culture stereotypes, where sensibilities tend toward the bite-sized. Dylan's farewell to the sixties wouldn't ring true if he didn't capture the sense of fun and danger that defined it, and he always puts his satirical instincts to work best through farcical heroics that are as impressive for their sustained length as for anything else. "Lily, Rosemary and the Jack of Hearts" is an intricately evasive allegory about romantic facades that hide criminal motives, and the way one character's business triggers a series of recriminations from people he doesn't even know. Jack is the quintessential mysterious stranger who barely has to lift a finger to set the town on its ear—he works as a dandy simile for Dylan. The Jack of Hearts is more than just a pretty face—he's such a ladies' man that his gang puts him to work as a decoy while they perform their heist. This buck is so distracting that nobody suspects his pals are in the next room dismantling the safe. And the music trots along at such a steady clip you can lose the story's thread and still get off on the pace of events.

Lily the showgirl carries on with Rosemary's husband, Big Jim, and this public triangle is the town's yardstick of Jim's wealth and prestige. But a young stud like Jack trumps Jim's opulence with a knowing smirk. Jack buys the house drinks, upstages the town's two-timing swell, narrowly escapes calamity with Lily on his lap, and blows out of town with the loot before anybody has a chance to figure out who he is. One night he simply appears— the next day he's a legend.

Jack takes the room with the same sweep with which Lily takes the stage, but Dylan insinuates a deft maneuver of action between the time the lights go down and when Jack visits Lily in her dressing room after the show. She has spotted him from the stage, perhaps even flirted with him in front of Big Jim, and she welcomes her ex-lover with the line "Has your luck run out? . . . Well, I guess you must have known it would someday." What the listener knows (but the characters don't) is the way Jack is exploiting his own good looks (and luck) to distract the audience from the heist: a public visitation to the well-known mistress of the local diamond-mine owner is bound to cause a stir. Sure enough, after a verse that Dylan leaves unsung (reprinted in *Lyrics: 1962–1985*), just as Jack embraces Lily, Big Jim and Rosemary storm the room: Jim with an unexpectedly unloaded gun (it clicks instead of fires), Rosemary with a knife in the back of her cheating husband. Rosemary's motive is apparently to kill her husband in the act of defending his mistress's "honor," but her eyes give up her feelings for Jack. The next day, Big Jim is laid into the ground, and Rosemary is up on the gallows platform. In the final verse, Lily, the showgirl with one too many agendas, rinses the dye from her hair and wonders if Jack will ever pull another job at her expense.

As Herdman points out, Rosemary was ripe for revenge; the Jack of Hearts was only an appearance of opportunity. And the Jack of Hearts is enigmatic largely because we get to know him through how the others respond to his presence: Lily's feigned cool, Big Jim's insecurity, Rosemary's self-hate and jealousy (she's weary of being Big Jim's wife, but as Big Jim's revolver clicks, she understands all of a sudden why Lily would cheat on Jim).

Unlike a lot of Dylan's antinarratives ("Stuck Inside of Mobile with the Memphis Blues Again," "Sad-Eyed Lady of the Lowlands"), "Lily, Rosemary and the Jack of Hearts" stacks up in a conventional manner that manages to mock linear concerns. You don't have to wade through the plot twists in order to take pleasure from the thoughts passing through these characters' minds. As is his specialty, Dylan delivers the song with a poker face, and everything moves at a good clip. Only after you sort out all the mixed motives and dangling expectations do you realize that Dylan has been tipping his hand the whole time: Rosemary "lookin' to do just one good deed before she died" sets up a larger irony: she kills for love as a way of killing herself (she'd even tried suicide)—she wants to take Big Jim along with her. Lily is one of those showgirls who, in Herdman's perfect description, have a little too much experience, and the Jack of Hearts neatly fixes her offstage dilemma. And in what could have been

## hard rain

a shaggy-dog anticlimax—the scene where Big Jim's revolver clicks instead of fires—Dylan juices the tension by understatement. "You couldn't say surprised" is too sly a phrase for someone who gets stabbed by his wife the moment his gun goes shy.

The success of what Dylan sometimes throws away as elaborate emptiness is the way this farce turns out to be an apt mirror of sixties veneers. Everyone is so engaged with the romantic intrigue Jack sets in motion that they pay no attention to the drilling in the wall.

**All the romantic** bereavement revolves around two songs that work like hubs to the other songs' narratives. Side one's "Idiot Wind" is an emotional soapbox as fearsome and cutting as any of the cutlery that flies in Edward Albee's *Who's Afraid of Virginia Woolf?* Side two's "Shelter from the Storm" is the flip side of all the fuming—it's a meditation on the depths of "Idiot Wind," tempered by the soft despair of "If You See Her, Say Hello."

In a marriage marinated in dread, lovers hang on to each other by honing their contempt (he won't even touch her *books*). In "Idiot Wind," it's no coincidence that Dylan leads with a joke about the press, which was always his way of talking about his public persona, and the out-of-control anxiety he felt over his own image. Somebody's been planting stories about him, he sings, and the slander makes him look like he shot a rich man's wife and married her for the money. The kicker is, so what if he's lucky?

This war starts out as farce but quickly turns into drained exasperation—Dylan's lover is no friendlier to the truth than the journalists and sycophants that make demands on his persona: "Even you, yesterday you had to ask me where it was at / I couldn't believe after all these years you didn't know me any better than that." As the song veers into the first refrain, he caps that line off with the profoundest insult—a sarcastically sung "sweet lady" that drips with malice. It's such a clear analog to everyone's soured romance with the sixties (which took a long time to go away), it makes you wonder why he bothered to follow it up with the last-gasp bohemian excursion of his Rolling Thunder Revue. Still, it's somehow fitting that the trapdoor hiding in Dylan's sensitivity on *Blood on the Tracks* is a return to the non-narrative routine that heaps abuse on a lover (and audience, a gaggle of critics) in the spirit of "Leopard-Skin Pill-Box Hat." As he swerves in and out of past personas by playing the wronged heir, the beleaguered husband, the misunderstood bard, and the western outlaw, his stabs burn and fester ("One day you'll be in the ditch, flies buzzin' around your eyes, / Blood on your saddle"—a cop from a Tex Ritter song). There are patches of raw, unalloyed rage that measure up to any of his sixties broadsides, and verse five's digressions touch on the folly of success, and how the heated rhetoric of sixties utopianism begins to ring quaint.

By itself, "Idiot Wind" would have made a damning conclusion to this song set, turned the tragic journey that began with "Tangled Up in Blue" into a finality too hopeless for tragedy, and too pat for the loose ends these characters are forced to carry. "Shelter from the Storm" is the more apt conclusion; and near the end of side two, it accepts bitterness and solitude as a necessary price for buying into love's illusions, the inward scorn that repays innocence. " 'Twas in another lifetime, one of toil and blood," he begins, casting an old-world net over one of his more contemporary fables of betrayal and estrangement. You have to call Dylan on the way he romanticizes this female right off the map ("Try imagining a place where it's always safe and warm"); but the naif he plays singing those words is an irresistible archetype—nobody makes it through the era unscathed, and the blood on these tracks is everybody's. Anybody who'd been stalked like a crocodile would have to fall for that kind of salvation, even contract a lethal dose. The futility of overstatement makes the images stack up like comic gags; but Dylan delivers every line with an overbearing hush, and what might have been a disaster song about a weakling's comeuppance is rendered as a

parable about the fragility of faith, and the necessity of belief
when nothingness and doom are everything. He even allows
himself the melodramatic excess of wishing he could turn back
the clock, as if to point out that some weaklings deserve sympathy. The relationship never has a chance in this song: in verse
five she comes to him almost as an apparition, by verse six,
there's a wall between them. The mood makes up for the drama
here, and "Shelter from the Storm" scabs over the festering
wounds of "Idiot Wind."

**What the characters** chase on this record, and what many of them
know they can't have, is a myth that outweighs even the songwriter. The larger theme at work here is how Dylan is exorcising
some of his own myth's excesses by writing about them. In crys-
tallizing what sixties culture believed about itself, he's relieving
himself of the mantle that was at work in his music since "My
Back Pages." And that's what makes the record a signal sixties
accomplishment, one that defines the seventies as pure after-
math. Over the next three years, Dylan himself would act out
the last vestiges of the communal ideal by reuniting with Village
folkies and taking a caravan of players on an old-fashioned tour,
not trying to relive the spirit so much as to demonstrate that it
was still alive out there for anyone willing to breathe life into it.
The central image of the Rolling Thunder Revue isn't Dylan and
Allen Ginsberg visiting Jack Kerouac's grave; it's Dylan and
Baez, their breath hanging in the air in front of the mike they
share, duetting on oldies as though they might inhabit the same
cherished atmosphere as Guthrie's "This Land Is Your Land."
Dylan was still giving Baez—and his audience—the ride of their
lives, and he could still summon the sixties' ethos at will.

Perhaps there's ironic justice to the fact that a song as good
as "Up to Me" got left off this record (it sounds like a melodic
rough draft of "Shelter from the Storm"). It shows why Dylan
was probably right to chuck the New York tracks for the Min-

neapolis band, not only because with new players the songs get
a refreshingly naive surface that rubs up against their world-
weary outlook, but because Dylan's singing in New York is so
soft it sounds swallowed—a whole record of that couldn't have
carried the same load. Another nonnarrative that traces a narrative mold, "Up to Me" resembles a coat rack on which he hangs
one-liners ("Oh, the only decent thing I did when I worked as
postal clerk / Was to haul your picture down off the wall near the
cage where I used to work"). The song trots out the usual
suspects—aimless characters, shady situations in irresistibly
named places ("the Thunderbird Café"). It's another buried treasure that becomes a sublime cover, on Roger McGuinn's *Cardiff
Rose* (1976). And its armload of self-referencing touches operate
as blueprints for *Blood on the Tracks'* major themes of obsession,
denial, and melancholy humor. "Up to Me" works as both the
engine of feeling underlying the album and one of the sliest
self-references Dylan ever gets up the nerve to sing:

> **How my lone guitar played sweet for you that old-
> time melody.**
> **And the harmonica around my neck, I blew it for you,
> free, . . .**
> **You know it was up to me.**

# 9:  idiot wind

I walked ten years from town to town on big hot blistered feet singing and trying to learn how to sing my folk songs. And now you tell me I didn't do no work to win my little place. You say it was all handed me on a silver stick.

   —**Woody Guthrie**,
      *Pastures of Plenty*

A strong recurring feeling I get from watching Dylan perform is the sense of him playing for Big Stakes. He says he's "just a musician," and in his boots he needs that kind of protection from intellectual probes, which are a constant threat to any artist. Even so, the repercussions of his art don't have to be answered by him at all. They fall on us as questions and that's where they belong.

   —**Sam Shepard**,
      *Rolling Thunder Logbook*

## Desire
Released: January 1976

**The thing that** pierces so deeply in "Idiot Wind" is the way Dylan himself gets caught in the cultural vortex he details. As much as the song is about a long-failing relationship that extends to a critique of its times, he more than insinuates that the rot he's singing about is part of the air everybody breathes. And he thought living down a myth was hard.

There are plenty of Dylan followers who will defend his

career straight up through his muted appearances with the Grateful Dead in 1988 and beyond; but even the most ardent fans will admit that just the question of Dylan coming under such repeated attacks is enough to separate his work into two stretches: that which comes before *Blood on the Tracks* and that which comes after. Under this scrutiny, *Desire* should be the crowbar album—at least that would make it easier to find out which camp you fall in. But the record doesn't seem to make strengths out of its weaknesses, the way *New Morning* chews on its own ambivalence. *Desire*'s best moments work out to be the unambitious ones: the charm of "Mozambique" (even though the country plunged into civil war shortly after the song became its tourist jingle), the semi-Tex-Mex dance cues of "Romance in Durango," the certain Mexican doom that awaits in "One More Cup of Coffee," and the disaster-movie parody that finds more to say than you'd expect in "Black Diamond Bay."

"George Jackson," Dylan's 1971 single, might have faded as forgettable (even though it broke Top 40) if Dylan had left the protest theme alone. Instead, he comes back with "Hurricane," his habeas corpus for the jailed middleweight contender Rubin Carter, which might be subtitled "Ballad of a Black Man Done Wrong." Wordy and repetitious, the song recounts Carter's side of his arrest for triple murder in Paterson, New Jersey, in 1966. Dylan doesn't just admire Carter's tenacity (Mohammed Ali had been championing his release for years before Dylan played lightning rod); it's like he sees himself in Carter's professional attitude:

> **Rubin could take a man out with just one punch**
> **But he never did like to talk about it all that much**
> **"It's my job," he'd say, "and I do it for pay,**
> **But when I'm done I'd just as soon be on my way . . ."**

But there doesn't seem to be much to Carter's fantasies, and he's the kind of subject that seems less an inspiration to Dylan than a prop.

## idiot wind

There aren't any inspired leaps going on here—none of the savvy commentary on the divide-and-conquer power plays that Dylan uncovers in "Only a Pawn in Their Game"—and this only makes "Hurricane" sound at best warmed-over, and at worst, disingenuous. He nailed this theme as long ago as "The Lonesome Death of Hattie Carroll," and with far more torque. (Partly as a result of the publicity and funds raised by the song and two benefits Dylan's Rolling Thunder Revue played—one at Madison Square Garden, one at the Houston Astrodome—Carter's original trial was thrown out by the New Jersey Supreme Court for lack of evidence. A new trial found Carter and an accomplice, John Artis, guilty again; the witness who had previously confessed to conspiring with the police for an early verdict recanted his confession. On February 9, 1979, Carter was sentenced to two consecutive life terms; he was released on parole in November 1985.)

As a companion to Dylan's gangster snow-job, "Joey"—even slower and more labored—his return to social protest couldn't have been more disappointing. Joey Gallo was a well-documented New York mobster whom Robert Kennedy once dubbed Public Enemy Number One; he was gunned down on April 7, 1972, as he celebrated his forty-third birthday in Little Italy. Part of what intrigued Dylan was Gallo's reputation as a sixties inmate who supposedly steeled himself into an Attica intellectual, reading Nietzsche and Wilhelm Reich (prisoners who happen to read books, like John Wesley Hardin[g], are automatically heroes to Dylan). Imprisoned for extortion in 1962, Gallo was released in 1970 and began ingratiating himself with show-biz types, who quickly canonized him in a display of what Lester Bangs called "mobster chic." Among the entertainment faction to get to know Gallo was Dylan's collaborator for *Desire*, Broadway musician and director Jacques Levy. Levy got Dylan interested in Gallo as a song subject, and the two of them met with actor Jerry Orbach and his wife, Marta, for their reminiscences about the convicted extortionist. Apparently, that's all the

247

research Dylan bothered to do: Orbach had played the Gallo figure in the film of Jimmy Breslin's book *The Gang That Couldn't Shoot Straight,* which was based on the Gallo family's legendary incompetence.

In answering Dylan's groaning "What made them want to come and blow you away?" at the end of each tiresome refrain, Bangs wrote in a *Village Voice* article (March 8, 1976),

> There are several theories in answer to that question. The most prevalent was that, since most people took it for granted that Joey was behind the shooting of Joe Colombo almost a year before, there was an open contract out on Gallo by the Colombo family, meaning that Joey had effectively committed suicide in having Colombo shot. Two other theories advanced by investigators extremely close to the case have Gallo once again trying to muscle in on territory occupied by other, more powerful mob factions. In one case, he could have told two thugs to crack a safe for $55,000 in Ferrara's Pastry Shop in Little Italy, a landmark frequented by Vinnie Aloi, at that time a very powerful capo in the New York mafia. This would certainly have been the straw that broke the camel's back in regards to the mob bosses' patience with Gallo's hustles. . . .

Dylan's defense of Gallo seems to rest on the tired theme that justice is corrupt, and that since he was nice to children and never carried a gun, he must have been innocent. But without doing much legwork, Bangs consults Gallo's biographer, Donald Goddard, to discover that Gallo not only beat his wife and abused his children but was a well-known racist and had taken part in a brutal gang rape of a young boy while in prison. It's enough to make Dylan's romanticization of the outlaw not just arrogant but contemptible.

## idiot wind

• • •

**There's plenty of singing** here that ranks with what you'd expect from Dylan, and on the heels of "Tangled Up in Blue," the romances fare much better than what he tries to pass off as judicial activism. "Isis" is a cross between his grand ersatz-epics of the sixties and the heavy mythological obsessions that will bog down his movie *Renaldo and Clara*. With its piano-rock cadence and Scarlet Rivera's swashbuckling fiddle, it has a better sense of drama than its counterparts, "Oh, Sister" and his last-ditch plea to his wife, "Sara."

"Isis" tells the story of a young groom who marries his bride before he learns the value of loyalty. After leaving his wife, he sets out on an odyssey with a man he meets in a Laundromat, who turns out to be a bounty hunter. Heading north, they come to the pyramids, where his partner dies. But the tomb is empty, and the groom feels he's been cheated. He buries the guide and heads back to Isis. In shorthand, the story reads like one of Dylan's lesser wild tales—man learns about the love of a woman via the deception of another man. But Dylan pulls more from the thirteen verses than the song's monochromatic format might suggest—it works out to be a parable about an empty quest for riches that resigns itself to the quest for human contact.

Love's higher plane is spun out in "Oh, Sister" as well, and it's the first time Dylan invokes God as a method of wooing a woman. Flanked by Emmylou Harris, Dylan turns four verses into a lengthy discourse on the fragility of love (although not as well as Gram Parsons does with the same duet partner in Boudleaux Bryant's "Love Hurts" on *Grievous Angel*).

"Sara" is such an ambitious tribute, it sounds like it grew out of the line "I can change, I swear" from "You're a Big Girl Now." It's not just the only song Dylan ever steps out of his myth to sing directly to a real person; it's a fevered cry of loss posing as sincere devotion. Coming from a female singer-songwriter, so maniacal a don't-leave-me number would probably garner cries of overdependency. It's a wonder that Dylan feels that he needs to bring his personal life into music here—he's managed so well without going public that a confession like this only feeds tabloid appetites: he remembers writing "Sad-Eyed Lady of the Low-lands" for her while taking the cure in the Chelsea Hotel.

A shaky farewell to a long romance, built on reminiscence, "Sara" plays off images of the ocean and the beach, where Dylan watched his children play. In "Oh, Sister," "time is an ocean that stops at the shore," and at the end of "Sara," "the beach is deserted except for some kelp / And a piece of an old ship that lies on the shore." That "kelp" is the Dylan touch, and it gives his maudlin pleading away as a bit of solipsism—he's equating his marriage-on-the-rocks to a piece of smelly refuse.

Not everybody's good at rejection, but *Blood on the Tracks* did a better job of mourning a romance than "Sara" will ever do. Like "Oh, Sister," it's too much a part of Dylan's infatuation with womankind—anybody would be disappointed with somebody who didn't always want him unconditionally. Like the desperation that coats *Street Legal*, its loss curdles into selfishness, and it gives backhanded credence to all those crackpot autobiographical theories about Dylan's artistic slippage. When asked if he resented questions about his personal life, Elvis Costello told *Rolling Stone* (June 1, 1989, p. 68):

> It's voyeurism, you know? For years and years, Bob Dylan wrote all these great songs, then he wrote that song "Sara," and people assumed "Sara" was Sara, his wife. But does it matter? It never diminished any of his other songs that we didn't know who he was speaking about—except for those garbage-pail diggers that insisted on finding out who it was. Who *cares*? If someone like Bob Dylan or myself wanted to put that detail in, we would've written an extra verse saying, "And what I really wanted to say is that so-and-so woman I split with is a bitch that I really hate / This is her name and address / And if you want to, go and burn down her house."

## idiot wind

*Desire* didn't get released until January of 1976, but Dylan played most of these songs onstage with Rolling Thunder, and played "Hurricane," "Oh, Sister," and "Simple Twist of Fate" for a television special in honor of the man who signed him, Columbia Records' John Hammond, on September 10, 1975. He also released a single, "Rita Mae," a jaunty blues, which Jerry Lee Lewis later recorded on *Jerry Lee Lewis* (1979). And he sat in on Bette Midler's sessions for "Buckets of Rain" on her *Songs for the New Depression.*

### Renaldo and Clara
Filmed: October–December 1975
Released: January 1978

### Hard Rain
Released: September 1976

### The Last Waltz
Released: April 1978

**Beginning with a** slow, pressing rendition of "When I Paint My Masterpiece," which Dylan sings from behind his plastic Dylan mask, *Renaldo and Clara* tries to capture the spirit of the last-ditch counterculture blowout that was the Rolling Thunder Revue. Ever since *Eat the Document,* Dylan wanted to step outside his songwriting medium and create something truly original in another form. His "novel," *Tarantula,* is a case of an early book contract gone awry when he began to realize how hard it would be to build and sustain a narrative (he finally turns it in during his sabbatical in 1967, just to get the publishers off his back). Halfway through the four tedious hours of *Renaldo and Clara*, you realize that the Rolling Thunder jaunt was as much an excuse to collect footage for his screen "masterpiece" as it was to reunite with his Greenwich Village crowd. Some of Dylan's songs may work well off visual sequences, but his cinematic sense on celluloid is a mess—it makes *Eat the Document*'s single hour look like a model of coherency.

You'd think a concert film of one of Dylan's most highly revered tours would make for charged viewing, and the film has its moments: Joan Baez doing the frug to Roger McGuinn's "Eight Miles High" guitar jam; a brief excerpt of bassist Rob Stoner barreling through "Catfish" (a *Desire* outtake about the baseball pitcher Jim Hunter). But besides the film being choppy, Dylan manages to reduce the entire outing to a pretext for his peculiar obsession with dressing his wife and Joan Baez up like whores, staging numbingly clichéd domestic spats between Ronee Blakley and guitarist Steven Soles, and cutting back and forth between the "action" and different thematic episodes. Greenwich folkie David (Cohen) Blue's pinball monologue, Allen Ginsberg's recitation to an elderly women's mah-jongg convention, and a woman named "Momma" singing to Baez and reading Ginsberg's palm don't provide any interesting commentary or context on the music we see onstage; and Dylan's own perpetual close-ups only make the attention given to other performers seem like rank tokenism.

The Rolling Thunder cast grew out of a summer evening's jam at the Other End in Greenwich Village, when Dylan was coaxed onstage by his *Don't Look Back* cohort Bob Neuwirth. Uncharacteristically (to say the least), Dylan leapt at the idea of getting his friends on the road, and the project was launched as a grand revival of the familial spirit that had inspired the Almanacs, the folk troupe that Pete Seeger and Woody Guthrie toured with during the Roosevelt administration. Along the way, Dylan hired Sam Shepard to come out from California and help write movie scenes for an accompanying film project. The idea was to hit towns unannounced, distribute leaflets, and play small halls and keep prices low—and since the Bicentennial was on the horizon, they opened in Plymouth, Massachusetts, on October 30, 1975. So why does Dylan edit the movie with the decidedly undemocratic technique of hacking up other people's songs? At one point, we see Ramblin' Jack Elliott finish a song and introduce Guthrie's "Pretty Boy Floyd," only to jump to yet another aimless cut of Dylan walking—no song. When Dylan does let a performer have a full song, he sabotages the setup. Ronee Blakley gets to sing "Need a New Sun Rising" (the one song that seems dated), but only after getting chewed out by Soles for spending too much time putting on her makeup and making everybody wait. (She fares better as a pampered country celebrity in Robert Altman's *Nashville*.) Often riveting onstage, Dylan is lights-off remote when he's not singing. He's the unresponsive elusive-man, making like his reality is too flipped out to ever be explained, never mind answered to.

Having your camera crew face down security guards and follow you as you enter the CBS Building in Manhattan (the "Black Rock"), take the elevator up to the corporate nerve-center, and meet company kingpin Walter Yetnikoff to discuss the rush-release plan for the "Hurricane" single may make for semiamusing footage of how out-of-place you look at your own record company, but it has nothing to do with social protest. It's an insincere wash on how Dylan wants to project concern for civil rights justice to his audience. But even that sequence looks noble compared to the man-on-the-street shots he includes at the beginning of the movie's second half, intercut with excerpts from Rubin Carter's press conference in jail. Dylan plops a camera crew down outside the Apollo Theatre in Harlem and has his interviewer ask folks if they've ever heard of Carter's plight. He gets exactly what you'd expect: people talking about what they've read in the news; angry, unformed outbursts; a woman who gets into her evangelical routine. Dylan doesn't just let it go at that—he zooms in on these subjects, freeze-frames them after they've said something utterly innocent ("Is this going to be on TV?" one kid asks enthusiastically), and keeps fiddling with the volume knob on the music. You want to say his heart is in the right place, but after watching this sequence you come away feeling like you've been patronized, too.

In his songs, Dylan makes outré references ring like inside jokes between himself and the listener as a way of drawing you in—he's intelligent, all right, but his curveballs can be transparent. *Renaldo and Clara* scans like a fledgling art-student movie that people tolerate only because they're afraid to admit they don't "get it." Dylan spent all of 1977 holed up editing footage with Howard Alk, who also helped him confuse the 1966 stage footage to *Eat the Document,* to produce a film that aspires to the dubious distinction of being "understood" only by Dylan himself and *Rolling Stone* scribe Jonathan Cott. "Using his physical image and name as the raw material of the film," Cott writes, "Bob Dylan—like the Renaissance kings of masque and spectacle— moves daringly and ambiguously between fiction, representation, identification and participation."

"So Bob Dylan may or may not be in the film," Cott asks him in 1978.

"Exactly," Dylan responds.

"But Bob Dylan *made* the film," Cott counters.

"Bob Dylan didn't make it. *I* made it," says Dylan (*Dylan* p. 158).

On his good nights, Dylan was drawing music out of these players that would have made even the Band sit up and listen. The snatches of concert footage we get—mostly from Boston, Providence, and Montreal in November 1975—are tantalizing, even though the Revue overrates itself. The key problem is drummer Howie Wyeth, whose untuned tom-toms made *Desire* sound hollow. Bandleader Rob Stoner is a marvel of a bassist; and with avid support like David Mansfield on fiddle and mandolin, T-Bone Burnett, veteran hipster crank Bobby Neuwirth, Steven

Soles, and guitarist Mick Ronson (the British glam rocker, late of David Bowie's band, who turned everybody on to stage makeup, including cowboy Ramblin' Jack), there's plenty of interplay to take in. And Dylan knows how to steer a song—his vocal coercion chisels some grit into the sound.

Some of the tour's most dramatic moments are not here: Dylan and Baez would often open the second half duetting in the dark on "Blowin' in the Wind," and although there are some duet passages here, Dylan seems to prefer having Baez camp it up as a floozy (dropping lines like "I think I may have gone out with someone who you were seeing" to her madam, Dylan's wife, Sara). And it's not just his support whom he shortchanges; he has his cameras so tightly focused on his face when he sings "Tangled Up in Blue" near the end that the song actually seems to compress in scope—his eyes are often shaded by his perpetual wide-brimmed white hat.

A better take on Rolling Thunder is the offhand journal of Sam Shepard (who also appears in a scene with Sara), called the *Rolling Thunder Logbook*. (Larry Sloman's *On the Road with Bob Dylan* tries to cop the Tom Wolfe technique of turning the backstage story into a plot with the journalist as beleaguered hero, only he doesn't have Wolfe's stylistic panache, and his movie scenes in the deli come off like the bowling-alley bull session that recurs on *National Lampoon's Radio Dinner*.) In Shepard's book, the future Pulitzer playwright is frank about the chaos involved in shooting a movie with no script, especially by novices who fancy themselves artistes, on the road with shows every night, and no feel for how to play off of a camera. (Dylan hires two professional actors, Harry Dean Stanton and Helena Kallianiotes—the hitchhiker from *Five Easy Pieces*—and wastes them.) Scenes are improvised on the spot, and the movie never shakes its amateurish, half-baked foundations. It's like a *Magical Mystery Tour* for the seventies, only it's trying to be about how the sixties live on.

In the movie's howler, the entire troupe gathers at a riverbed for Ginsberg's benediction of mantras, and with Barnett, Ronson, and Soles digressing into doo-wop, the group chants away at the spirits as Dylan wanders down to the water with a bottle of wine in one hand, a trumpet in the other. The best Dylan and Ginsberg can do when they visit Jack Kerouac's grave site is to muse on what other graves they've seen. Dylan says he's been to Victor Hugo's; Ginsberg claims he left a copy of *Howl* on Baudelaire's stone. It's like they're back in high school comparing notes on how many books they've read. "I want to be buried in an unmarked grave," Dylan says somberly. ("Of course," wrote Pauline Kael in her *New Yorker* review. "That's why he's made a four-hour movie about himself and his pilgrimage.")

Shepard's book is worthwhile for its incidental qualities—he gives you an idea of what it felt like to be suddenly called from California to hit the road for six weeks with a band of gypsies that were literally reviving the sixties folk ideal for an audience that couldn't believe its own good fortune. He doesn't bother to explain how Dylan came upon the lanky Texan, T-Bone Burnett, who's the most unselfconsciously comic presence in the film and turns out to be a major discovery. "He has a peculiar quality of craziness about him," Shepard writes.

> He's the only one on the tour I'm not sure has relative control over his violent dark side. He's not scary, he's just crazy. . . . He does a full 180-degree pivot on the heel of his Tony Lama cowboy boots, bends from the waist, and jabs his chin in my neck. I don't move. I'm listening to what he has to say, even though it feels like I'm being mugged on the Lower East Side. His Texas drawl cuts into my ear bones. "I'm so proud of the fucker [Dylan]. The first superstar. He's given me reason to live. I only want to be shot about ten times a day now." He pivots again, and disappears into the dark. (p. 58)

Along with whiz kid Mansfield and Soles, Burnett goes on to form the Alpha Band for three sturdy records on Arista (*The*

## idiot wind

*Alpha Band, Spark in the Dark,* and *Statue Makers of Holly-wood*) before launching his own solo career in the eighties: his *Truth Decay* and *Trap Door* show how much catchy obliquity he soaked up from Dylan. The Alpha Band revolves around its members' born-again-Christian persuasions, and they were said to have influenced Dylan in this direction. Later, Burnett becomes an important producer for Los Lobos, as well as for Elvis Costello's watershed *King of America* and his own country sleeper, *T-Bone Burnett* (on which he sings a Neuwirth song, "Annabelle Lee").

Robert Shelton reports that Dylan names the project after hearing thunder roll across the sky one day, and "appeared pleased when someone told him that to American Indians, rolling thunder means speaking truth. Along the way, a Cherokee medicine man named Rolling Thunder joined the troupe . . ." (p. 452). This biographer is generous not to remind Dylan that Rolling Thunder was also one of Lyndon Johnson's code names for a bombing mission in Vietnam.

Of the bootlegs that capture these shows, the November 21, 1975 Boston date makes you wish Dylan had stuck to making a concert movie: these are rugged and inspired reworkings of many Dylan standards—he even talks casually to the audience (now a thing of the past). After "Masterpiece," a duet with Neuwirth, he lights into a biting electric version of "It Ain't Me, Babe," and then a thoroughly convincing rock take of "The Lonesome Death of Hattie Carroll" (which Shepard likes to call "Williams and Zinger"), "It Takes a Lot to Laugh, It Takes a Train to Cry," "Romance in Durango," and an "Isis" that makes the *Desire* take sound like a greeting card. With Baez, he offers "The Times They Are A-Changin'," the new song "Never Let Me Go," "I Dreamed I Saw St. Augustine," "I Shall Be Released," "Wild Mountain Thyme," "Blowin' in the Wind," "The Water Is Wide," "Mama, You Been on My Mind," and "Dark as a Dungeon." By himself, he does "I Don't Believe You," "Tangled Up in Blue" (which is beginning to undergo lyrical surgery), "Mr.

Tambourine Man," "It's All Over Now, Baby Blue," "Love Minus Zero / No Limit," and "Simple Twist of Fate." He takes the band through "Oh, Sister," "Hurricane," "One More Cup of Coffee," "Sara," "Just Like a Woman," "Knockin' on Heaven's Door," and Woody Guthrie's "This Land Is Your Land," a revival from the old Newport Folk Festival sing-alongs.

**The Rolling Thunder** tour had two legs: after a long holiday break, the troupe regathered for another five weeks of dates in the South and Southwest. One of these dates (May 23, at Hughes Stadium in Fort Collins, Colorado) was filmed for a one-hour television special that aired in September, and was released as a live album called *Hard Rain*. Unfortunately, the range and intensity of this material are nearly as pointed here as they are in the concert scenes in the movie; and although the band has been playing together longer, the charm has gone out of their exchanges. On camera, Dylan's intensity is one-dimensional: you begin to hear his late-career repulsion, a grimacing-leer delivery that seems affronted at the task of getting through the song.

The pervasive close-ups become oppressive ("Not since the final frames of *Queen Christina*, when the camera enshrined Greta Garbo in silent spellbound reverence, has any face been so obsequiously honored," wrote James Wolcott in *The Village Voice*, September 27, 1976). And even when he's sometimes able to put his contempt to good use (especially in the closing "Idiot Wind"), the nonsellout crowd and inclement weather seem to have pricked Dylan's ego. This "One Too Many Mornings" will never benefit from comparisons with his scalding 1966 treatment with the Hawks; but he does pull a new resentment from the song here (he alters the closing lines: "I've no right to be here / And you've no right to stay"), and its arrangement transcends the melodramatic silences he insists on in "Maggie's Farm," an abbreviated "Stuck Inside of Mobile with the Memphis Blues Again," "Oh, Sister," "Lay, Lady, Lay," and "I Threw

## idiot wind

It All Away" (in which he sings the second verse-ending for the first, repeats the title line as part of a new arrangement, and fakes his way through the second verse mumbling sounds that rhyme with "coo-coo"). The flock of guitars that nests in "Shelter from the Storm" could be the album's saving grace—done up with Mick Ronson's guitar-hero flights, Dylan storms the number and gives the song a completely different angle on the cost of forgiveness. You're forced to wonder how many different places these songs might have gone if they hadn't been hampered by Wyeth's drumming: whatever he's playing on "Maggie's Farm," it isn't a two-four beat that the players can sit back in; he's pushing instead of cushioning, and it distracts from all the tension squirting from Dylan's voice. Robert Christgau complains that these folkies' "idea of rock and roll is rock and roll clichés," but the other problem is that they don't know when to scale things down. "You're a Big Girl Now" doesn't gain anything from the full-throttle surge they give it; it just sounds overblown.


**When the Band** called together their friends for a good-bye blowout in San Francisco on Thanksgiving Day of 1974, they were enacting a ritual farewell to the era in much the same way Dylan had done on *Blood on the Tracks*. But *The Last Waltz*, the film of the event that Martin Scorsese directed, though full of prime performances, has a self-conscious air that would have made Dylan's melancholy ring hollow. The musicians' commentary and Robbie Robertson's preening get in the way of the film's better moments: Muddy Waters smiling down the audience, Van Morrison calling down like thunder in "Caravan," Emmylou Harris duetting on "Evangeline," Levon Helm singing "Ophelia." By the time the camera pans down on Bob Dylan, his huge, feathered white hat acquires a talismanic aura that competes with his grimace. He gives them a warm and sweaty "Forever Young" that segues into "Baby, Let Me Follow You Down" before leading rock's all-stars in "I Shall Be Released." "Hazel," "I Don't

Believe You," and another version of "Baby, Let Me Follow You Down" wound up on the editing-room floor. (Only "Hazel" is missing from the soundtrack album.)

"The road was our school," Robertson tells Scorsese at the end. "It gave us a sense of survival, it taught us all we know. There's not much left that we can really take from the road. We've had our share of . . . Or maybe it's just superstitious. . . ."

"Superstitious in what way?" Scorsese asks.

"No, you can press your luck, the road has taken a lot of great ones—Hank Williams, Buddy Holly, Otis Redding, Janis, Jimi Hendrix, Elvis . . . It's a goddamn impossible way of life."

"It is, isn't it?"

"No question about it."

# 10: temporary like achilles

His career had followed a mythic pattern of journey from poverty and obscurity, of mortal struggle, and of victory and return. His hero's frame was transformed by a revolution in the printing of news and the appetite for news, and he became a celebrity—in Daniel Boorstin's definition, "a person who is known for his well-knownness."

 —**Justin Kaplan** on Mark Twain,
  *Mr. Clemens and Mark Twain*

Joe Strummer is a fake. That only puts him in there with Dylan and Jagger and Townshend and most of the other great rock writers, because almost all of them in one way or another were fakes. Townshend had a middle-class education. Lou Reed went to Syracuse University before matriculating to the sidewalks of New York. Dylan faked his whole career; the only difference was that he used to be good at it and now he sucks.

 —**Lester Bangs**,
  "The Clash," *Psychotic Reactions and Carburetor Dung*

Goodbye, Bob. You looked happy on Farm Aid. I thought maybe I shouldn't write all this stuff about you, but as it turns out, it's really about me anyway, isn't it? It won't affect you. The death of Elvis affected you. I didn't relate to that, either.

 —**Joan Baez**,
  *And a Voice to Sing With*


**It's a truism** that artists are always the last ones to understand their strengths. After 1978, Dylan turns this dictum into an overbearing credo. To true believers, Dylan has never gone into decline, he's simply turned from an original into an unyielding, misunderstood cur, and you have to catch a lot of his concerts to stay convinced that he can generate anything like the old magic. He's been on the road virtually nonstop for well over a decade, and in that period he has not released a single album that measures up to *Blood on the Tracks*, or acquired enough of a live reputation to support the counterargument that off-record he still delivers.

The measure of Dylan's slide lies in his singing. Even if his writing had remained consistent, the way he begins to whine his songs, nobody would want to sit through them. He's no longer the mythic channel of an audience that has grown from a broad-based culture of youth into fragmentary markets that feed the corporatization of rock, and the instances of Dylan cutting deep are infrequent, surrounded by long stretches of indifference. Where he once squeezed juice from his words and breathed relevance into songs that never seemed to age, his stage set has since slipped into a series of boilerplate standards. Sometimes it's news when he rearranges sets. More often, he's likely to lob a choice cover into the mix (Ricky Nelson's "Lonesome Town" in memory of Nelson's death, for example). The more he sings, the more he tends to clip his words as if there were nothing there to commit himself to, and he sets a new standard for a performer's full-frontal arrogance with an audience: sometimes he spends entire evenings ignoring his listeners, as if called by some higher distraction they aren't privy to. He turns his back, he mumbles, he sleepwalks. And over the years, Dylan has grown even more remote from his various bands than from his songs.

The other yardstick of Dylan's wane is his failing sense of humor, which evaporates after the wry glint of "Buckets of Rain" and "Lily, Rosemary and the Jack of Hearts." Records are visited by the occasional hell-bent farce ("Brownsville Girl" on *Knocked Out Loaded*), but out-and-out gags are nonexistent. It isn't until the Traveling Wilburys projects that his comic persona reappears, and then it seems like a happy by-product of an oppressed star's burden being lifted through the camaraderie of superstar friends (George Harrison, Tom Petty, Roy Orbison, and the Electric Light Orchestra's Jeff Lynne). "Tweeter and the Monkey Man" tweaks Springsteen's underworld of highways, fast cars, and sour deals and parodies Dylan's own wheel-spinning plots that work as platforms for his gear-grinding deliveries. It's such a shot of insouciance that it makes you realize how thick and solemn the rest of his latter-day solo efforts are. Even when his records sound good—like the Daniel Lanois–produced *Oh Mercy* (1989)—they tend to lag from their own self-righteousness ("Disease of Conceit").

**After spending 1977 holed up** in his editing booth cutting *Renaldo and Clara*, Dylan emerged a divorcé, slapped a record together, and hit the road with his suitcase of sixties material completely revamped. By retaining some of the Rolling Thunder faithful (David Mansfield, Stephen Soles, and for the *Budokan* album, Rob Stoner), it first appeared as though Dylan were jumping back into what he did best: performing. But *Street Legal* (1978) contained some unflattering inconsistencies—blurry sound, halfhearted arrangements, and misplaced passion. He sang the line "Can you cook and sew, make flowers grow / Do you understand my pain?" in "Is Your Love in Vain" without embarrassment, and gave his feminist critics ammunition to add to the tabloids' allegations of wife-beating surrounding his divorce (never mind his obliviousness to the song title's copped Robert Johnson conceit). His lyrical sensibility dwindled: would the moon "shine bloody and pink" if there weren't "No Time to Think"? "Where Are You Tonight? (Journey Through Dark Heat)" was so fervent with obsession that he never bothered to let on what makes his lover so desirable. His road album *Bob Dylan at Budokan* (1978) fared even worse. It's more than just the spectacle of Dylan cashing in on Cheap Trick's freak hit from Japan, *Live at Budokan* (with the cartoon-metal cover of Fats

## temporary like achilles

Domino's "Ain't That a Shame"); Dylan's mix-'n'-match arrangements seemed as out of touch as his sequins (a reggae arrangement that deflates "Don't Think Twice, It's All Right," an
underwhelming rewrite of "Going, Going, Gone"). The pedes-
trian reading of Dylan's plight went that his separation from
Sara, such a source of strength and inspiration (witness *Desire*'s
"Sara"), had brought on a creative collapse, and that his resto-
ration, as always, was imminent. Hope against hope, his audience couldn't help wondering if he had simply taken a wrong
exit, à la *Self-Portrait*, and wouldn't come roaring back just as
reassuringly.

But Dylan's private life has always been the least interesting aspect of his creative work—even he knows "Ballad in Plain
D" was a mistake. The drop his writing takes after 1978 is more
acutely disappointing because Dylan himself seems the least
aware of it, the most estranged from his muse. After *Street Legal*
and *Budokan*, his Rolling Thunder cronies fall off, and his hired
guns (impeccable musicians like keyboardist William "Smitty"
Smith, who later played for David Lindley's El Rayo-X) turn into
robots and do his bidding without much motivation. Dylan begins to sound oblivious to his surroundings, as though some new
stage threads and eye makeup take the place of interacting with
his players. Part of what carries even *Bob Dylan at Budokan* to
the faithful is the idea that Dylan is at least transforming himself,
and that can't be bad, even if he is taking some wrong turns. He
has taken wrong turns before; he will bounce back. Going country, after all, was an anathema to the hippies. If only going gospel
hadn't meant going evangelical.

**Dylan's loss of faith** in his ability to transform his circumstances
and imbue each situation with some inimitable spin tipped the
scale of the seventies against him as his students formed a line.
Randy Newman cut through all the early seventies' preening
with *Sail Away* (1972), a seductive number about the slave trade

that was as piercing in its understatement as the Rolling Stones' slave-ship brawl, "Brown Sugar," was pronounced. He reinvented the pop conundrum with 1977's "Short People," an anti-bigot cakewalk that reversed rock's positivism-via-negativism strategy to become offensive to more than just the Archie Bunker intolerants it lampooned. A brilliant reversal. Newman went on to compose some truly icky Hollywood scores (Barry Levinson's *The Natural* and *Avalon*), like his uncles, Alfred and Lionel.

British glam-rocker David Bowie used a lot of Dylan techniques to look forward rather than backward. Flaunting the new outrageousness—cross-dressing, effeminate makeup, overt bisexuality—Bowie got Dylan's media hustle down solid. Over-rated as a wordsmith, Bowie nonetheless understood plenty about theatrics, and for all his gentility and actor's sense of detachment, he could throw himself into a song, and developed as a singer. He wasn't just an enigma; he was an enigma with a thousand faces. His first mark was with an acoustic number, "Space Oddity," which brought some psychological meat to a subject that Harry Nilsson treated as camp ("Spaceman") and Elton John treated as a homesick postcard ("Rocket Man," an updated "I'll Be Seeing You"). Dylan invented the shoes that Bowie could walk in without ever following Dylan's path: on Broadway in *The Elephant Man*, and in film roles like Pontius Pilate in Martin Scorsese's *The Last Temptation of Christ*, Bowie understood that his media could be shaped to his pop personae, wherever those characters might take him. In 1972's *Hunky Dory*, Bowie offered explicit tribute: "Song for Bob Dylan" began the same sheepish way Dylan's "Song to Woody" had ("Hear this Bob Zimmerman / I wrote a song for you . . ."). It went on to laud the way Dylan put "pointed ladies," in their place: "But a couple of songs from your old scrapbook / Could send her home again." If Bowie never wrote a song that would measure up to Dylan, he jumped from style to style so aggressively he sometimes seemed like the force of nature he was always trying to be—a "Thin White Duke" who could make "plastic soul," an obstetrician of punk who penned "All the Young Dudes" for Mott the Hoople. Hemmed in only by the pop conventions he deemed himself worthy of, Bowie was a human style in constant search of a context.

Except for country, Van Morrison has traveled many of Dylan's stylistic paths as well, but he knows better how to transcend lesser material by singing holes through it. The sheer heated reverence and mutability of Van Morrison's voice—a soulster's latticework cut with an Irishman's burr—has outclassed more than twenty-five years' worth of backup bands, material, and uneven stage work. Like Dylan, he's had a string of songs that still drive Adult Contemporary Radio formats (from 1967's "Brown-Eyed Girl" to 1991's "Hymns to the Silence"), and the eighties saw him tour religious themes with unabating sincerity. His fans gladly abide his religious imagery and philosophical airs to be transported by his earthy mysticism. Many chart his early-seventies greatness (*Moondance,* 1970; *His Band and Streetchoir,* 1970; *Tupelo Honey,* 1971; *St. Dominic's Preview,* 1972; and a live effort, *It's Too Late to Stop Now,* 1974) as his glory days, which ebb after 1979's *Into the Music.* But even when he's bathed in the lush, romantic strings of *Avalon Sunset* (1989), the result is a fetching romantic downpour that turns his vision of the idealized woman into an extension of his idealized Irish homeland. And who else could make a pacifying, born-again duet with a lightweight like Cliff Richard so gently inoffensive ("Whenever God Shines His Light")? Morrison can find repose in fleet tempos, and turn genre moves into extraordinary orbits of emotion. His work with the Chieftains (on 1987's *Irish Heartbeat*) is as soulful a take on traditional Irish music as one can imagine. With "I'll Tell Me Ma," he showed how a sense of humor can keep a stylistic experiment alive.

**By contrast, gospel has never** been more stringent and pious than it is when it issues from Dylan's throat. His three born-again records suggest a musical chameleon who's trying on styles the way he might try on personalities to get out of a slump. With his voice going thin, he doesn't bounce off alternate meanings of lines so much as laser-fry them with the full force of his condescension. *Slow Train Coming* (1979), the first, featured Mark Knopfler dodging Dylan's pinched rasp with his fluid, ticklish guitar parlance. Knopfler's band, Dire Straits, had been thrust into the spotlight via Knopfler's Dylanesque vocals on "Sultans of Swing" in 1978. But even with some of Dylan's stronger vocal moments ("I Believe in You"), the record sounded as much like the debut of a hot young guitar sessionist as it did a day job for its songs' author. For a conversion album, Dylan could have done worse than to record at Muscle Shoals, and his gospel production team of Jerry Wexler (Aretha Franklin) and the keyboardist Barry Beckett carve a crisp, focused attack of sound (which may be why "Gotta Serve Somebody" garnered Dylan his first Grammy award—for Best Gospel Recording). He wasn't shy about his newfound faith: he went on "Saturday Night Live" to sing "Gotta Serve Somebody," "I Believe in You," and "When You Gonna Wake Up" in October 1979, and hecklers at concerts were answered by lectures from the stage. But except for the broken stretches of "I Believe in You," a vigilant romantic testimony, Dylan's vocals don't play off of Knopfler's terse darts of feeling, and only on "Do Right to Me Baby (Do Unto Others)" a moral cakewalk, and "Man Gave Names to All the Animals," a trip to the zoo, does Dylan sound like his brand of Christianity has a gentle side. The title song remains a credible foray into ominous R&B revivalism, but "Gotta Serve Somebody" is so paternalistic to the Dylan faithful that John Lennon, alone at his piano in the Dakota, makes a demo of an answer song, "Serve Yourself" (never released, it aired on Westwood One's "Lost Lennon Tapes" more than ten years later):

> **Say you've found Jesus, he's the only one**
> **Say you've found Buddha, he's a lot of fun**

## temporary like achilles

> Say you've found Mohammed
> Found Krishna, he's the light of the day
> Something's missing in this god-almighty world,
> It's your mother
> Hear me callin, Ma? M-O-T-H-E-R . . .

Nineteen eighty's *Saved* has a lot of the same problems, even though the same producers have loosened up the sound, and Dylan adds Clydie King, Regina Havis, and Mona Lisa Young for call-and-response backup vocals. Red Hayes and Jack Rhodes's "A Satisfied Mind" (best known to folkies via Ian and Sylvia on Vanguard's *Play One More*) starts out with some promising vocal glides, and sets up the title cut's uppity piano stomp with some chemistry that makes you notice how much Dylan has been listening to his gospel support. But the lyrics are unremarkable, the kind of garden-variety faith that you'd think Dylan would rise above ("By His truth I can be upright / By His strength I do endure"). "Solid Rock" is a credible overdrive shuffle; and "In the Garden" with its unearthly harmonic plan takes its place in the Dylan canon as a standard—he performs it well past his gospel phase. But it's hard to hear this record as much more than spiritual jingoism: if you don't agree with his new direction, Dylan seems to be saying, you don't count.

With *Shot of Love* (1981), produced by Chuck Plotkin and Dylan, he finally hits a middle ground for music that satisfies both his born-again audience and listeners who would just as soon leave Jesus out of it. The players are a mix of studio veterans and guest stars (Ringo Starr, Danny Kortchmar, Ron Wood); and the added female singers, Carolyn Dennis and Madelyn Quebec, don't sound as out of place. It's not a uniform effort, but the stronger songs here make you see what he was after all along. "Heart of Mine" is a jaunty self-rebuke that atones for its clichés ("If you can't do the time, don't do the crime") with some Tex-Mex melodic tricks; "Property of Jesus" dresses the Dylan put-down up as religion ("You got something better / You've got a heart of stone"); "The Groom's Still Waiting at the Altar" (added after the release) is a generous return to slow-burning defiance that restores not only the lust to Dylan's heart, but the power to his voice. The way he sings "Got the message this morning, the one that was sent to me / About the madness of becomin' what one was never meant to be" can make you believe all over again that he understands the dilemma of his career. Seeing as the song was first left off the record, and got attention only after it was discovered as the B side of the "Heart of Mine" single, that belief is perhaps wishing for too much.

You can see why Dylan would identify with Lenny Bruce, the subversive Jewish comic who was put on trial for obscenity, and died the perennial junkie's death, decadent and glamorous, ahead of his time in 1966. But while "Lenny Bruce" is anchored in the resolute cadences of piano gospel, as a tribute it does little more than turn this prescient counterculture genius into a dime-store martyr. "He was the brother that you never had" doesn't sum up Bruce's image (Billy Carter might as well be the brother you never had), and the song slights the finer points of Bruce's comedy. "Never robbed any churches nor cut off any babies' head." Needless to say, plenty of other people are not guilty of those same crimes, and praise by omission has never been the highest form of flattery. Apparently, to expect an original insight about Lenny Bruce from Bob Dylan has become a form of fanatic self-delusion. Dylan actually drops a line in about riding with Bruce in a taxi, like he wants to impress us—his one great brush with a comedian whose bits challenge Dylan's snooty misan-thropy. It's the kind of cheap moralistic tribute that were it targeted at Dylan would make him cringe.

Fading with the accepting twilight of "Every Grain of Sand," *Shot of Love* goes home with a prayer that inhabits the same intuitive zone as "Blowin' in the Wind"—you'd swear it was a hymn passed down through the ages. As Milo Miles wrote, "This is the one Dylan song in ten years on which the raggedness—or expertise—of the back-up band is irrelevant. It

## temporary like achilles

is also the only Dylan song in at least that long in which he examines a pop-culture paradox (that legendary stars in particular have to believe in ideals greater than themselves) more eloquently than any other performer has." And it doesn't go unnoticed: Bruce Springsteen cites the tune when he inducts Dylan into the Rock 'n' Roll Hall of Fame in New York on Janury 20, 1988.

**During the eighties,** Dylan's postgospel career is marked by the controlled but seething rock of *Infidels* (1983), and the obligatory star benefits, from his *We Are the World* squawk to *Sun City* (both 1985) to the Traveling Wilburys' title-song contribution to *Nobody's Child* (1990). *Infidels* is the set most Dylan admirers hold up in defense of his current work, and it's one case where the streamlined production doesn't seem to work against the rugged authority he can still command as a singer. The backup players team Mark Knopfler with reggae's Sly Dunbar and Robbie Shakespeare. "Jokerman" is a squinting slur at the Reagan presidency and phony televangelists (as is "Man of Peace"); "Neighborhood Bully" is a cranky, double-edged defense of Israel; and "Union Sundown" is a diatribe about capitalism chasing cheap labor in foreign countries ("I can see the day coming when even your home garden / Is gonna be against the law").

But the standout is "I and I," which updates the Dylan mythos. Even though it substitutes self-pity for the other songs' pessimism, you can't ignore it as a Dylan spyglass:

> **Someone else is speakin' with my mouth, but I'm listening only to my heart.**
> **I've made shoes for everyone, even you, while I still go barefoot.**

Dylan's relationship with himself has always been at the heart of his best work—the way the man who was born Robert Zimmer-

man communes with the songs, odyssey, and mystique of Bob
Dylan. But "I and I" is perhaps the only song to take this subject
on as an artistic issue. That he comes up a shade self-pitying (he
still goes barefoot) is reconciled only by the fact that he's made
the subject songworthy this late in his career. In other words,
without giving up very much of his true self, he conveys the
distance he feels between his inner identity and the public face
he wears. "I and I" is a fiercer song than "Up to Me," and it
seems to cut truer to the tension that weighs on Dylan with age.

His live set from this period, captured on the tedious *Real
Live* (1984), worked in two of the better *Infidels* songs: "License
to Kill" and "I and I." (The *Infidels* song least worthy of defending is "Sweetheart Like You," which exacerbates the sexist streak
held over from *Street Legal*.) During a listless turn with Keith
Richards and Ron Wood as one of the closing acts of the Live Aid
benefit in Philadelphia on July 13, 1985 ("Hollis Brown," "When
the Ship Comes In," and "Blowin' in the Wind"), Dylan mum-
bled something about the plight of the American farmer. It was
a mumble that became a benefit cause all its own: within two
months, Willie Nelson had organized a two-night stand of Farm
Aid at Memorial Stadium in Champaign, Illinois, with Dylan as
one of its key performers (backed by Tom Petty and the Heartbreakers, he delivered "Trust Yourself," "Lucky Old Sun,"
"Maggie's Farm," and "I Trust It Like That," and added "Clean-
Cut Kid" and "Shake" on the second night).

Later that fall, the five-record three-CD set of *Biograph*
came out, intended to stem the continuing flow of bootleg material that had been plaguing Dylan and his record company
since the sixties. Among the first of the superstar-career boxed
sets, *Biograph* boosted Dylan's stock immensely and fueled his
legend even as his eighties records guzzled it up.

As a corporate public-image campaign, *Biograph* is the kind
of outsized gesture that can lure you into feeling thankful that
Columbia Records finally unleashed gems like "Percy's Song"
and "I'll Keep It with Mine," when what they did was cave in to

consumer demand so voracious it made no sense to sit on these tracks any longer. With eighteen previously unreleased tracks, *Biograph* certainly offered a more generous inducement than most future boxed sets would—1990's Led Zeppelin box threw in only four rarities. But *Biograph*'s layout is hit-or-miss—there aren't any thematic arcs between songs, and the lack of chronology does nothing to shed light on Dylan's development.

Far from being a panacea to collectors' appetites for unpublished material, *Biograph* functioned more like an ad for what had not yet been released; and when the M. Witmark & Sons publishing demos and 1966 live material emerged on *Ten of Swords,* it was obvious how the audience had been shortchanged. A ten-record bootleg that dwarfed *Biograph* in terms of previously unavailable material, *Ten of Swords* collected demos and outtakes from 1961 to 1966 and mapped Dylan's epochal years. It provided a musical diary that *Biograph* barely hinted at, and made Columbia's entire handling of his catalogue look tainted with greed and unnecessary reserve—it made you wonder what else they still had in their vaults.

**After Farm Aid,** Dylan kept on Tom Petty and the Heartbreakers for a tour of Australia and the Far East. This was the same kind of serendipitous turn that made a lot of Dylan's sixties' records emblems of good faith and the fruits of communalism. The arrangement yielded a white-hot single, "Band of the Hand," for the movie of the same title, which only begged the question as to why the rest of their work together sounded so marginal.

Directed by Paul Michael Glaser, *Band of the Hand* is a hack morality tale about Joe (Stephen Lang), a Vietnam-vet social worker who trains a pack of hard juvenile felony cases to survive in the Florida Everglades. After getting these ethnically and socioeconomically prefabricated groups in touch with their "self-esteem" (it's one of the picture's buzzwords), he brings them back to the jungle of Miami's inner city and declares war on drugs. Dylan's song—the best rock he had produced in ten years—bookends the film, and he sings it hard over the opening sequence, where the young criminals get arrested:

> **Out in these streets the fools rule, there's no freedom or self-respect**
> **A knife's point or a trip to the joint is about all you can expect**

Save yourself the heartache of watching how the film turns what are passable words into bumper stickers for street life. As the re-habilitated youths take over their new headquarters, there's a scene where they paint their squatters' house with bright colors to bring it dignity. Naturally, they break up a fight between blacks and Hispanics and hand out brushes, working Tom Sawyer's whitewash charm on coke addicts with Uzis. That one of Dylan's best performances in years works to pump up the sentiments of such vigilante pulp is enough to taint previous on-the-lam thrills like "Tombstone Blues"—it turns Dylan's live-outside-the-law smarts into a reverse parody of itself.

*Hard to Handle*, a video from a February 1986 date with the Heartbreakers in Sydney, Australia, shows how lifeless Dy-lan's stage persona had become. Dylan could look misplaced with the Band and it only seemed to feed the tensions that were already at play in the music—his aloofness had the aroma of hip. But with the Heartbreakers, Dylan comes off like an aging des-pot, running these young pros through his paces as if drilling them in rock pedantry. On a good night, the band could fill in his vocal gaps as only this experienced, tight-fisted ensemble could. But Petty's top hat is a throwback comic touch (Dylan used to wear one), and it only accents Dylan's fathomless grimace. This band obviously learns plenty from Dylan's outré panache (the follow-up, *"Let Me Up, I've Had Enough"* and Tom Petty's 1989 solo album, *Full Moon Fever*, are clear improvements on 1985's

**temporary like achilles**

*Southern Accents*, Petty's glorification of the rebel yell). Dylan simply trudges forward, abstracted.

Eventually, everything Dylan had once made seem providential began to work against him. After his Heartbreakers gigs, he churned out *Knocked Out Loaded* (1986), which included a decent Heartbreakers song he cowrote with Petty, "Got My Mind Made Up," and "Brownsville Girl," a Sam Shepard collaboration about Dylan's unlikely identification with Gregory Peck, which aimed at the high-camp sallies of his heyday. "Brownsville Girl" is notable for its line "She said even the swap meets around here are getting corrupt," which diehards clung to as an example of his wit lying in wait. But in Kris Kristofferson's "They Killed Him," Dylan fronts a sound mass that would make Phil Spector blush and hauls out the overblown fraudulence of a children's choir. An American tour with the Heartbreakers followed.

That fall, the film *Hearts of Fire* is released, with Dylan in his first big-screen acting role (Alias in *Pat Garrett and Billy the Kid* wasn't really a role at all). The *Hearts of Fire* soundtrack album includes Dylan's cover of John Hiatt's "The Usual," where he applies his ham-fisted eighties singing style to a contemporary songwriter and comes up respectful. But the movie, produced in Britain, rehashes *A Star Is Born* Hollywood platitudes. Dylan plays Billy Parker, a rock has-been who now works the oldies circuit "like a freak in a circus," and whose enthusiasm for music is rekindled by a plucky young songwriter (the doe-eyed Fiona). Directed by Richard Marquand (*Return of the Jedi, Jagged Edge*), the movie is such a washout that it never gets released in America (it's available on video). You get the feeling that Dylan takes the role just so he can voice his burned-out scorn for the way pop treats aging stars: "It's a trap," he tells young Fiona. "The better you are, the bigger the trap." But he also participates in the movie's "larger" agenda—it's really about the way the thin air of superstardom breeds contempt in rock stars for the fans, who do nothing but annoy them for autographs or mob them in public places. In one scene, Dylan trashes a hotel room in disgust because the music business is so corrupt it affronts his dignity. (Oh, so that's why rock stars have the right to toss color TVs from windows.) In the climactic scene Fiona's rock-star producer-lover, the plucky songwriter, confronts a deranged fan in his dressing room after a show. Forget the fact that the fan is blind; she aims a pistol at the rock star, and just as he's about to grab the gun from her, she holds it to her head and kills herself instead. You'd think the fan-as-enemy theme gets played out enough in real life (witness the 1988 *People* magazine cover of John Lennon's murderer). The film doesn't even draw on his better eighties material (he does "Had a Dream About You Baby" from *Down in the Groove* and "When the Night Comes Falling from the Sky" from *Empire Burlesque*). Dylan's subscription to the movie's attitude cloaks his image in superstar self-pity.

The following year (1987), Dylan hooked up for seven dates with the Grateful Dead (released as *Dylan and the Dead,* 1988). None of this had any of the excited overtones of musicians gearing up for a collaboration they all had longed for over the years—it simply seemed like another chance for Dylan to hit the road. You can almost trade Dylan's singing with the Heartbreakers and his singing with the Dead and come up with the same affectless results: he doesn't work off these musicians, he simply drags them around during intros and cutoffs, and sounds pained and fretful, as if he wonders why nobody can seem to connect with him in his private netherworld. Word of bad vibes between the bard and the Dead's Jerry Garcia were legion. "He's not really a musician, he's a performer," Garcia told the *Golden Road* newsletter in the spring of 1989.

> You really have to pay attention to him to avoid making mistakes, insofar as he's doing what he's doing and everybody else is trying to play the song. If you don't do what he's doing, you're doing something wrong. [*Laughs*] In that sense, he de facto becomes the leader of the band . . .

INTERVIEWER: But it's not fair to say that he's insensitive to what's around him, is it?

GARCIA: Yeah it is! [*Laughs*] He's insensitive. Insensitive is probably the wrong word . . . He's funny. He has a chameleon-like quality. He goes along with what he hears, so it's not as though we're fighting with him. It's nothing like that. He makes an effort to fit into what he hears. But he doesn't have a conception about two things that are very important in music: starting and ending a song. [*Laughs*] Really. The middle of the song is great; the beginning and ending are *nowhere*.

The *Dylan and the Dead* album is poor for more reasons than Dylan's vocal hootch. The song selection is far from what Deadheads could expect as fair reward for listening to the Dead work up their classic readings of Dylan numbers over the years. "Joey" manages to be slower than on *Desire*—a twilight zone of bad taste. Once again, the better stretches of this collaboration make the rounds as a bootleg, spliced from a three-hour rehearsal and dubbed "The Front Street Tapes." The material here is notable: an Ian and Sylvia song, "The French Girl," with Jerry Garcia playing pedal steel; "Union Sundown"; "In the Summertime" done calypso; "It's All Over Now, Baby Blue"; "If Not for You"; "When I Paint My Masterpiece"; Garcia singing "Señor"; Dylan singing Buddy Holly's "Oh Boy"; "Tangled Up in Blue," with Garcia and Dylan duetting; a bluegrass take of "John Wesley Harding"; "All I Really Want to Do"; and the Dead's read-through with Paul Simon's "Boy in the Bubble" from *Graceland*.

**After another European tour** with the Heartbreakers in 1988, Dylan released *Down in the Groove*, one more stillborn oddity. Taking on other people's songs can be a valid time killer for inveterate overdogs, and more than a few legends have turned in sets of other writers' songs for satisfying results (David Bowie's *Pin-Ups*, John Lennon's *Rock 'n' Roll*). On *Groove*, Dylan collaborates with the Grateful Dead's lyricist, Robert Hunter, for a one-dimensional single, "Sylvio," and a highly suspicious satire, "The Ugliest Girl in the World." But he also covers a couple of songs that are obviously near to his heart: "Shenandoah" and the Stanley Brothers standard "Rank Strangers to Me." Dylan had covered another song the Stanleys were known for, "Man of Constant Sorrow," on his debut, and doing "Rank Strangers" provides a clue to where a rock star might trace his country roots to gospel, if a bit after the fact. Short and uneven, with "Death Is Not the End" patched in from the *Infidels* sessions, *Down in the Groove* is another stack of butts—and the portions are so small!—but at least Dylan began to let up on his insistence that he perform all his own material even if it was subpar.

Hitting the road with his latest touring unit ("Saturday Night Live" guitarist G. E. Smith, Kenny Aaronson on bass, and Christopher Parker on drums), Dylan chased gigs like he had to, and persisted in onstage embarrassments like forcing Smith to guess where the song would end. Smith, a master player with almost no sense of what lead work entails besides showboating, often gave cutoff signals to the band you could read from the back row.

On some occasions, the fog lifted: at a Neil Young Bridge School benefit in Oakland in December 1988, Dylan appeared with Smith for an acoustic stint. Three dates at Radio City Music Hall the month before had been visited by the usual groundless mediocrity (apparently, the way Dylan strikes you depends on your sympathies, and which date you catch: Jon Pareles hailed the opening show in the *New York Times*). But in California, Dylan came out smiling, swung straight into Jesse Fuller's "San Francisco Bay Blues," and then did Woody Guthrie's "Pretty Boy Floyd" like it was written with him in mind. The difference between the two sets was vast: at Radio City, Dylan affected the leather-clad iconoclast and acted as if his adoring crowd were there to be squinted at; in California, his spirits seemed to soar. The contrast made his legendary inconsistency unchartable.

The next spring, *The Traveling Wilburys, Volume 1* came out, a super-session that had blossomed from informal jams during sessions for Roy Orbison's sterling comeback, *Mystery Girl* (released posthumously in 1989). *Wilburys* is a tidy record, with Jeff Lynne's spotless synthesizer wash; and your first impression is of a lighthearted send-up of fame itself. George Harrison's "Handle with Care" became a hit and drove the album to the top of the charts, making it a favorite not only with Petty's following (and fans even younger), but with the older set who could remember both the Beatles *and* Orbison. The three Dylan entries were revelations to those who didn't know his sixties work: "Congratulations" was a smoldering kiss-off that reaped a dirt-tough meanness out of the candy-coated production; "Dirty Mind" crackled at off-color, Prince-like non sequiturs; and "Tweeter and the Monkey Man" piled on the Springsteen clichés (the Jersey girl, the mansion on the hill, and "You could hear those tires *squeal*"). In its gentle self-mockery, the Wilburys project sent up just how bloated rock superstardom had become, and pre-empted the lofty self-importance of U2's Bono in the U2 film of the same year, *Rattle and Hum*.

This only made *The Traveling Wilburys, Volume 3* more a joke past its prime. Middle-aged and cranky, dropping lines about hitting the golf course and twisting with false teeth, the follow-up was humorous mainly to rockers who fancied adapting rock to the ravages of their age, instead of enlivening it. "She likes to stick her tongue right down my throat," Dylan growled in "My Baby," the single—funny the first time, deadly soon after. What this group found wanting after the death of Roy Orbison seemed irreplaceable; and "You Took My Breath Away," Harrison's tribute, didn't feel worthy of him.

## hard rain

•   •   •

**Dylan's most recent work** only extends all the unevenness of the eighties. With U2 producer Daniel Lanois at the boards, *Oh Mercy* (1989) is steeped in the soft heat of the town it was recorded in, New Orleans, and its single, "Everything Is Broken," has a clumpy, frayed-nerve rattle (the video got plenty of exposure on MTV, though with Dylan looking zoned-out, you wonder why they pushed it). And songs like "Man in a Black Coat" stirred a few critics to life. It was a paradoxical record, finally: you could like it without taking to any of the songs much. And the flaws seemed to grow on you. Fifteen years before, Dylan would have made a leftover-memories number like "Most of the Time" resonate far beyond what a lingering affair can do to a person. Here, he doesn't seem to be singing about his music, his audience, his New Orleans accoutrements, or his new lease on credibility with his Wilburys—he's just singing about another woman who suckered him.

By this point, Dylan takes to the road as a matter of principle—he only sporadically enjoys performing, and he doesn't need the money. But throw enough gigs against the wall and something will inevitably stick. In the fall of 1989, he gave a mammoth live rehearsal at a club called Toad's Place in Connecticut, where the Rolling Stones had first tried out their *Steel Wheels* set. Dylan's performance, broken up by laughter, actual documented verbal communication with his audience, and a hilarious cover (Springsteen's "Dancing in the Dark") once again restored his legend to the times. If he could erupt with this much music and sound this together, there was still hope. Duly reported in fanzines like *Wanted Man*, the gig became a buzzword for the new Dylan tour, and the cultists were happy again. But these perennial comebacks began to wear thin, and nobody has argued very well that any of these "returns" has anything to do with the flair and pluck of Dylan's early career.

Like *Oh Mercy*, which helped vault Lanois into a solo ca-

## temporary like achilles

reer of his own, Dylan's latest solo record, *Under a Red Sky* (1990), does more to secure Don Was's reputation as its season's producer-in-demand than it does to restore Dylan's reputation. He came to Dylan hot off the success of Bonnie Raitt's *Nick of Time*, which snared four Grammies. But Was was getting better Dylan yucks outside the production job: in the film *The Freshman*, Was plays in the lounge band as Bert Parks sings "Maggie's Farm." And producing a record means hanging around until your star turns in some decent vocals.

The idea of a full-fledged Dylan comeback is irresistible, even to those who know better: one of rock criticism's most consistent voices, *The Village Voice*'s Robert Christgau, gets lured into proclaiming "Dylan's Back" in his review of the album ("Dylan Back: World Goes On," *Village Voice*, October 30, 1990). Christgau is enamored of Kenny Aronoff's drumming, which provides a lot of what Dylan was lacking in heft. And in many ways, *Under the Red Sky* is close to what a great Dylan return might sound like if backup was what counted most. Aside from the faceless vocals, the songs seem all juiced up with nowhere to go: "They said it was the land of milk and honey / Now they say it's the land of money / Who'd ever thought they could make that stick?" Wasn't it Dylan in "Man of Peace" and "Union Sundown"?

As might be expected, the new cynicism surrounding Dylan sets off its own backlash: standing up for Dylan (which was benevolent during his born-again phase) became fashionable once again. When the industry had let a suitable length of time pass, and realized that one of America's most influential songwriters was on the verge of turning fifty, they rounded up Jack Nicholson to present Dylan with the Grammy Lifetime Achievement Award. After the obligatory montage of Dylan's career, Dylan and a new band of upstarts kicked into an impenetrable cloud of noise that turned out to be "Masters of War." Given that President Bush was at that time bombing Iraq with more tonnage in six weeks than had been used in the entire Vietnam war,

## hard rain

Dylan's return to his uncompromising antiwar stance seemed welcome.

But where Dylan used to mumble and garble his words in arresting fashion, his Grammy appearance made him look more sullen and remote than usual—even admirers had trouble deciphering which song he was singing. His acceptance speech was halting and unfocused: "My daddy, he didn't leave me too much. You know, he was a very simple man. But what he told me was this . . . he did say, 'Son . . .' . . . [long pause] He said so many things, you know? [laughter] It's possible to become so defiled in this world that your own mother and father will abandon you. And if that happens, God will always believe in your own ability to mend your own ways."

Within weeks, Columbia released *The Bootleg Series, Volumes 1–3 [Rare and Unreleased], 1961–1991,* which induced a whole new flood of press. Compiled largely from the same tapes that were used to assemble *Ten of Swords* six years earlier, *The Bootleg Series* was the largest and most comprehensive response Dylan ever made to the vast bootleg audience he had scorned for thirty years. Naturally, to make the three-CD box set indispensable to collectors, it included several unheard-of rarities: Dylan's pensive, halting version of a song previously available only from Joan Baez ("Farewell Angelina"); a new outtake from the Basement Tapes sessions ("Santa Fe"); a few takes from the New York sessions to *Blood on the Tracks* (including "Call Letter Blues"); and a third disc devoted to work left off of his albums through the 1980s.

With superior sound quality that restored the Hawks on "She's Your Lover Now," to the kind of cosmic alliance of players and material the muffled bootleg sound could only suggest, you couldn't help but embrace *The Bootleg Series* as a long overdue gesture. But given the fact that Dylan had sat on these tracks for so long, a question hung over this release: Why had he suddenly relented to everybody's better judgment about this material? For one thing, by 1991 Dylan needed his audience more than they needed him. His career might still give the occasional rush, but it usually used his sixties' work as a reference point. And no matter how many revisionist critics lined up behind *Under the Red Sky* or *Oh Mercy,* Dylan still needed *The Bootleg Series* or its equivalent to breathe life back into his legend.

The song sequence to *The Bootleg Series* is full of holes for Bobcats to write letters about to fanzines for ages: folks will still want to hear "Dink's Song," and a dozen other early numbers that *Ten of Swords* includes. Even though the average rock fan may delight in hearing Dylan read "Last Thoughts on Woody Guthrie" (from the 1963 Town Hall concert), there can't be many who hear the rough take of "Like a Rolling Stone" (as a shorthand waltz) as anything but a goof. And no matter how much John Bauldie raves in the liner notes about the tenuous ensemble Dylan's musicians reach on "I'll Keep It With Mine," most will prefer the solo version that first appeared on *Biograph*. The most promising thing about *The Bootleg Series* as an idea is that the forthcoming volumes promise to gather the long-awaited Dylan and the Hawks live material from 1966. That will fuel the pro-Dylan backlash even more than it will establish the fabled "Royal Albert Hall" show as one of rock history's greatest events.

The third disc of *The Bootleg Series* is devoted to outtakes from Dylan's latter-day period, beginning with "If You See Her, Say Hello" from *Blood on the Tracks.* There's an unevenness to the third disc that only amplifies how charmed and alluring the first two volumes are. "Every Grain of Sand," perhaps his finest religious song, is offered here in a vocal rehearsal with Jennifer Warnes as a dog barks from outside (it suggests that Dylan has a sense of humor, a side that all but disappeared behind his evangelical scowling). And the alternate take of "When the Night Comes Falling From the Sky" has such an undeniably raunchy attitude (and guitar solo by Miami Steve Van Zandt) you wonder why Dylan stuck with the lifeless take that makes *Empire Burlesque* drift off on side two. It only shows how far Dylan is from being a good judge of his better material: "Series of Dreams" should have been the working title song to *Oh Mercy*, not a leftover pendant.

If the signal Dylan work of the 1980s is *Infidels*, it's also the record with the most heatedly discussed outtake, and Dylan's best stab at the blues. On the surface, "Blind Willie McTell" is about the landscape of the blues, and the figures Dylan pays respects to on his 1962 debut. But it's also about the landscape of pop, and how an aging persona like Dylan might feel as he casts his experienced gaze over the road he's walked. Always skeptical about the quality of his own voice, he didn't release "Blind Willie McTell" at first because he didn't feel his tribute lived up to its sources. The irony here is that his own insecurity about living up to his imagined blues ideal becomes a subject in itself. "Nobody sings the blues like Blind Willie McTell" becomes a way of saying how Dylan feels displaced not just by the industry—his colleagues, his critics, his career, his waning muse—but by the music he calls home.

**Dylan the poet-jester** goes to sleep while "Bob Dylan" the pop-star lumbers through albums and tours, but his influence spreads to every pocket of today's pop. From all the nonsingers who find inspiration in his wildcat deliveries (deadpan talkers like Lou Reed and Leonard Cohen, not to mention rappers), to songwriters who pay respects with genre turns and writing chops (Tom Waits, John Hiatt), Dylan's legacy is hefty. You can even read the career of Madonna as homage to the Dylan school of how to exploit the press, control your material, train your players to read vocal cues, and navigate a hyperconscious series of reversals to the point where your image not only sells albums but enhances them. (Some contend that Madonna inherits Dylan's misapplied mantle of nonsinger—but those ears have never appreciated "Live to Tell.") Largely because of Dylan, any nineties rock (or media) star who is not completely self-aware as an icon—as a *commodity*—is liable to be exploited out of work far sooner than he or she had planned.

It's the roots music that Dylan and the Band sought out in their prime that informs a great deal of latter-day rock, even if critics are skeptical about the roots movement as a whole. Bands as obsessed with the past as Tom Petty and the Heartbreakers and the Bo-Deans sound too retro, too uninventive, and too run-in-place safe to advance the dangerous side of rock's agenda that punk spat out all too well. The critics have a point: the two super-powered writers who produced the eighties' greatest roots rock both predated the trend, and each had already built their stature on nostalgic sounds and attitudes. Bruce Springsteen, who started out a visionary, back-shifted into fifties' car-cruising themes, and veered off into a whole new perspective on middle age as augmented (instead of arrested) adolescence. Neil Young, a Canadian hippie from the sixties, always had a yen for low-rent country calamities, even though his Reagan-apologist attitude seemed to cheapen much of his eighties music. What Springsteen and Young learned from Dylan was how to get an audience on your side, even when you were busy doing stylistic back-flips.

The mission of the eighties roots-rock movement was to leave behind the singer-songwriter hype of "the new Dylan" and invent the modern equivalent of the "Bob Dylan Band," a self-contained group that played American R&B with the same searing intelligence as the sixties master. With his brainy jump on adult emotions, classic sixties Dylan became a model for the new revivalists, who had to confess that rock wasn't just for teenagers anymore. They set out to make rock that restored the ideals of youth (fun, self-discovery) as seen from the horizon of adulthood.

Trading Dylan's kinky surrealisms for more common language, roots rockers settled on a few self-conscious themes (post-adolescent slants on girls, cars, and America) and arrived at nostalgic sounds with postnostalgic outlooks. And roots music wound up holding the mainstream as disco self-destructed, punk went underground, Michael Jackson booted black pop into the commercial stratosphere and Prince kept it in orbit, metal went corporate, rap ruled the streets, the Brits rediscovered soul, Top 40 dance pop descended into drum-synthesizer hell, and the next Elvis Beatles failed to materialize (again).

The other influences most eighties rootsy types cited fell into two camps: the arty self-consciousness of the East Coast's Velvet Underground, who were rootsy by virtue of their limited chord patterns, and the unforced fatalism of the West's Creedence Clearwater Revival, who played garage rock with social overtones. With arrows darting toward the twelve-string shimmer of the Byrds, and lost psychedelic troves like the Chocolate Watch Band, the group that bridged the Creedence/Velvets nexus was R.E.M., especially on their first three records. But R.E.M. proved to be bloated folkies (witness "Wendell Gee") with an overrated sense of humor (witness "It's the End of the World As We Know It [And I Feel Fine]"). And the band's reserve of originality disappeared faster than a pickup gulps gas.

Since punk helped plow the new roots landscape, in form if not attitude, it's natural that one of roots rock's most important acts clawed its way up from punk's ashes. In 1981, X's *Wild Gift* (which is now paired on an essential CD with their first album, *Los Angeles*) fused punk disgust with country and western's lyrical sense of hazard ("The Once Over Twice," "When Our Love Passed Out on the Couch"). And after the brilliant polemics of *More Fun in the New World*, X's John Doe and Exene Cervenka teamed up with fellow L.A. rootsmeister Dave Alvin from the Blasters for a country sideshow dubbed the Knitters. (Overlooked roots keeper: Alvin's *Romeo's Escape*, with his version of "4th of July," X's only hit.)

The other band to kick the movement into high gear, Jason and the Scorchers, hitched a southern boy's ballast to a hotdog guitarist's regalia for *Fervor* (1983), an EP that interfaced country-and-western attitudes with metallic heat. Both X and the Scorchers shared Dylan as an axis: X with their live "Positively 4th Street" done up like an apocalyptic bolero (on the B side of "4th of July"), the Scorchers with "Absolutely Sweet Marie," a joyride worthy of David Lynch, which earned its status as one of the finest Dylan covers ever. On the country side of the tracks, Ricky Skaggs and Randy Travis returned to the Dobro and fiddle Dylan had employed on *Desire* and the Rolling Thunder Revue and got dubbed "new traditionalists." Across the pond, punk-rock veterans the Mekons unveiled themselves as honky-tonk cynics and unearthed "Lost Highway" as a quietly chuckling dirge. The Mekons are still the band most likely to cover Dylan who haven't yet.

The most ironic thing about the whole eighties roots story is how Bruce Springsteen, himself marked as one more "new Dylan" in the early seventies for his visionary song forms, began paring his narratives down toward Chuck Berry–style vernaculars. Springsteen's early records engaged in verbal overkill that took Dylanesque characters and their travails back to the streets of Manhattan and New Jersey. Up through *Born to Run* (1975), Springsteen was busy stuffing songs with detailed street imagery ("Sprung from cages out on Highway 9 / Chrome wheeled, fuel injected / And steppin' out over the line") and building layered arrangements to accommodate up to six and seven song sections. Although it was drenched in pop history, it became such a visionary sound that even Springsteen found he could develop more as a songwriter by scaling back; and with *Darkness on the Edge of Town* (1978), he began pruning his songs and arrangements.

The roots album of his that cast a long shadow over the decade was *The River* (1980), which was received coolly because (a) it was not the Big Statement the bulk of its cruising songs first implied and (b) it yielded "Hungry Heart," the most sentimental yet of his singles (his first top ten). He may have taken the abstract route to songwriting, but the Dylan (not to mention Woody Guthrie) imprint on the desolate rough-rider tales of *Nebraska* (1982) was unmistakable. Apparently, Springsteen

struck a deal with his record company and promised a block-
buster on the heels of *Nebraska*'s predictably unsexy sales. But
by heading for *Nebraska*'s backwoods when he could have
stooped to conquer, Springsteen had also cut a deal with his
listeners, whom he performed to as though they were coconspirators in his raid on rock history. By as early as 1978,
Springsteen's live reputation was even giving the Rolling Stones
headaches.

The follow-up, *Born in the U.S.A.* (1984), did more than
just turn Springsteen into the pop savior he was always meant to
be; it crystallized his audience's will to sustain teenage excite-
ment through adult perspectives. As irreproachable as this idea
was, it didn't attach itself to anything especially topical. (After
all, *Nebraska* was a calculated look at Reaganism's effect on the
underclass.) Even the title track's Vietnam-vet theme ("Born in
the U.S.A.," which contorted itself into a perverse patriotic jingoism) wasn't pegged to any specific incident. By 1984, Hollywood, usually the follower of rock initiative, had been milking
the Vietnam saga for at least six years (*Coming Home, The Deer
Hunter, Apocalypse Now*).

That didn't make *Born in the U.S.A.*'s songs any less glo-
rious, or the album any less penetrating (some of the tracks were
recorded during the *Nebraska* sessions). "Darlington County,"
about a night out with a buddy who winds up "handcuffed to the
bumper of a state trooper's Ford," angled expertly off a triumphant guitar lick and Max Weinberg's caged-hellion drumming.
This was a conservative, nostalgic sound, all right, but the
glances back toward youth ("Glory Days," "My Hometown")
defined a roots attitude that made getting older and dealing with
responsibilities seem part of a larger rock experience that out-
reached pining for the good old days. Dylan's rock never sounded
this controlled, but it chased many of the same symbols.

Springsteen wasn't just a totem for the roots movement;
like Dylan, he was an embarrassment of riches. He wrote "Fire"
for rockabilly singer Robert Gordon (even though the cruise-

control mix by the Pointer Sisters took it to hit radio) and "Because the Night" with Patti Smith, around the same time she covered the Byrds' "So You Wanna Be a Rock 'n' Roll Star." During the early seventies, Springsteen made a point of covering Dylan's "I Want You"; in the eighties, he revived "Chimes of Freedom," which took on new echoes of Nelson Mandela, Bishop Desmond Tutu, and Lech Walesa. (Then, in another reversal, Springsteen turned from social themes to the romantic interiors of *Tunnel of Love* [1988]—his own *Blood on the Tracks*, and then some.)

*Underground* roots rock was soon fashionable: California's Long Riders (whose leader, Sid Griffin, wrote a biography of former Byrd Gram Parsons); Boston's pre-Miller-ad Del Fuegos; and south-of-the-border acts like Los Lobos and the Texas Tornados. Best of all were Minnesota's Replacements, who despite all obstacles, including themselves, turned their raspy, hardcore basement beer jags into spry and scabrous rock with *Let It Be* (1984). "Sixteen Blue" remains a knowing reflection on teen angst, an older brother's consolation. Their cover of Kiss's "Black Diamond" showed that metal cartoons could transcend hard-core target practice. "Unsatisfied" transcended itself. The band's major-label efforts (*Tim, Pleased to Meet Me, Don't Tell a Soul,* and *All Shook Down*) all extend *Let It Be*'s virtues.

**Neil Young makes** the Dylan connection just the way Springsteen does: as a prolific songwriter who remains the best interpreter of his own material. So far, both have been able to combat the rub of longevity, which is part of what works against them among those who begrudge pop monoliths. Neil Young has been around longer, and he claims a more telling connection to punk (Springsteen acts like punk never happened). Young turned in solid solo work right alongside his work with Crosby, Stills and Nash (still his blind spot), with torments like 1969's *Everybody Knows This Is Nowhere*. Johnny Rotten revered steelbrush guitar albums like 1973's *Time Fades Away*; Young returned the compliment with "Hey Hey My My (Into the Black)" from *Rust Never Sleeps* (1979). Young's *Tonight's the Night* (1975) sustained a level of white rage that directly inspired both Rotten and his Sex Pistols and Joe Strummer of the Clash. When Young wasn't dramatizing how a peculiar voice with an acoustic guitar singing songs of oblique allure could still be an effective shtick, his work with the band Crazy Horse made Dylan's whole folkie/rocker battle seem beside the point all over again. It was clear that Young had learned a great deal from Dylan about how taboo subjects could make great rock fodder (killing your baby in "Down by the River," taking on critics in "Ambulance Blues," rock commercialism in "This Note's for You"); but the strange thing was that Dylan didn't play off Young's career, or pick up on how to keep melodies alive (Young's gift) when he ran out of arresting topics.

The eighties were not Young's decade the way the seventies were. He was beleaguered by his children's birth defects and a drug problem he owned up to in "No More" (on 1989's *Freedom*) and then quickly recanted in a *Village Voice* interview. Only *Reactor* (1981), *Life* (1986), and *Ragged Glory* (1990), all with Crazy Horse, peal out with the screech of his best work. However, *Old Ways*, his 1986 country diversion, shows off a strong feel for the style, and "Misfits" remains as successfully off-the-beam as anything he's ever done.

Young's recent *Freedom* (1989), a violent reaction to George Bush's CIA consciousness, is his most pungent, and by turns most accessible, album since *Comes a Time* (which harbored the hit "Lotta love"), and grows more relevant by the day. *Freedom*'s songs are linked by the idea of liberation—romantic quandaries circling around fear of commitment in "Hanging on a Limb," celebrity isolation and the urge to break through in "Wrecking Ball," and a life story that plays out the corruptive influence of rampant capitalism: the exploitative boss in "Crime in the City" casually orders up a *Rolling Stone*, a cheeseburger, and a songwriter to go. "Rockin' in the Free World" is the late-eighties answer song to "Born in the U.S.A.," wailing on the Reagan boom's victims, the street-war vets who have no home to return to. The way Young transmogrifies the Drifters' "On Broadway" with crack-cocaine tremors says more about the effects of Reaganism than Springsteen—or Dylan—has to date. ("War," the Edwin Starr hit the Boss revived for his *Live: 1975–1985* boxed set, is token antiwar sentiment that doesn't mention Grenada, Lebanon, or any of Reagan's bloody debacles—besides, he leaves out the refrain's baritone sax solo, which Clarence Clemons was born to toot.)

On *Ragged Glory* (1990), Young writes an open letter to Dylan in "Days That Used to Be." The melody borrows from "Chimes of Freedom," but the theme links fallen heroes with dashed hopes, and doesn't find much to borrow from in contemporary Dylan. On the live album from his 1991 tour (*Weld*), Young pulls out a spooky electric "Blowin' in the Wind," which fits right in with the horror on the rest of the record.

Young and Springsteen spanned a couple pop generations, but they weren't the only major figures you can't explain without referring to Dylan. Elvis Costello made his debut in 1978, with *My Aim Is True*, which signaled the Dylan influence on new wave (or, all music during the punk era that acknowledged pop history). With his horn-rimmed Buddy Holly specs and misanthropic tilt towards the world (especially women like "Alison"), Costello quickly assumed the mantle of pop's most self-conscious saboteur. His visits to R&B (*Get Happy*, 1981) and country and western (*Almost Blue*, 1984) openly stole from Dylan through more than just his flagrant non sequiturs, image makeovers, and stylistic holidays. "Pump It Up" (from 1978's *This Year's Model*) is Costello's antimelody homage to "Subterranean Homesick Blues," and "Tokyo Storm Warning" (from 1986's *Blood and Chocolate*) is winding jet-set intrigue that's such a masterful Dylan parody it counts as plaudit. Perhaps the greatest of Costello's Dylan debts appeared on his *King of America* (1986), an artful anti-American country-and-western rebuke that became a Top 40 paradox, a Brit bemoaning the Yankee sacredness of Coca-Cola, and the best album of its decade.

Among Dylan's better interpreters, Richard Thompson of the Fairport Convention became one of the finest songwriters, guitarists and singers of the next pop generation. With Sandy Denny, Thompson helped arrange then-rare Dylan numbers like "I'll Keep It with Mine" and "Percy's Song." Like Dylan, Thompson understood how to update folk models without any loss of wit or character. With his wife, Linda, he produced a bona-fide classic with *Shoot Out the Lights* in 1984, which hooked up everyday imagery to new heights of fear, self-loathing and moral decay, and gutted romantic disappointment with a gravedigger's glee. His guitar playing made his stories seethe.

Since going solo, Thompson has persevered as one of those perennial cult and critic acts whose career is a lesson in how major labels falter with even the greatest pop talents. Guitar engines like "Nearly in Love" and "Valerie" on *Daring Adventures* were natural chart-busters, his tours were legion, but he never seemed to win enough marketing muscle to put him over (radio, as usual, confused marketing with gospel). His move to Capitol Records in the late 1980s signaled some hope (at least somebody cared about this titan), and *Amnesia* (1988) proved his fans worthy yet again. In concert, Thompson dedicated "Pharaoh" to George Bush, and songs like "Jerusalem on the Jukebox" and "Yankee Go Home" were tart, venomous songs about the cult of salesmanship and Anglophile ironies, respectively. Renowned on the folkie circuit with his numerous humorous solo acoustic appearances, Thompson made one of his best records as a producer, with 1990's *Hard Cash*, a collection of British labor songs from a television program of the same name that made Woody Guthrie sound like part of a larger international tradition of political troubadours. With *Rumor and Sigh* (1991), Thompson continued his folk-rock dialect: "1952 Vincent" turned a prized motorbike into a lover's reckless flaw and parting gift.

## temporary like achilles

So in the eighties, the musicians stumped the critics (again). And roots rock, far from telling us things we already knew, allowed a lot of newer fans some time to catch up on their history as rock contemplated middle age. Of course, this situation has only created a new climate of expectation. Roots records can't persist into the nineties except as something that's already been done to death, and the very nature of the back-to-basics mentality questions which roots bear the standard. Agitprop punkers the Minutemen covered Creedence's "Have You Ever Seen the Rain"; thrash-core gurus Hüsker Dü maced the Byrds' "Eight Miles High"; and even gloom duchess Siouxsie and her Banshees had a go at Dylan's "This Wheel's on Fire." (Dylan's gospel catalogue seems safe.)

Some sides of Dylan's influence lie dormant: the pop of the nineties, while still enjoying roots blasts from bands like Los Lobos, is careful in ways that Dylan never was. Accidents are akin to sins in this day and age, and the skill it takes for a popstar to play off mistakes and turn smudges of sound into expressive devices has all but vanished from contemporary rock. The number of high-profile acts who record live in the studio without overdubs is next to nil, and this streamlined ethic makes Dylan's records age with tattered ingenuity. And never does Dylan work against himself more than when he works up a studio finesse (as on "Tight-Connection to My Heart" on *Empire Burlesque*) with top-notch players (reggae masters Sly Dunbar and Robbie Shakespeare) and limps through a flawless mix with nothing to say. The things that made him great in his time make him sound even better today because he stands out even more.

When pop stars try to go socially relevant these days, it's more in terms of raising money for charitable causes than it is in drumming up good material that illuminates a democratic ideal. Live Aid would have a far more important legacy if it had produced some songs that cut through all the star competition. Of the charity songs in the eighties, only Miami Steve Van Zandt's "Sun City" rocks beyond its immediate context as a broadside against apartheid. (Even John Lennon and Yoko Ono's agitprop issue-fest *Some Time in New York City* has its lyrical aside, "Luck of the Irish.") U2 takes the Dylan tack with songs about Martin Luther King ("In the Name of Love") and the Irish troubles ("Sunday Bloody Sunday"), but easily inflates into self-serious messianic prattle. Peter Gabriel is among the few eighties superstars-with-a-conscience whose music still comes first (the soundtrack to *The Last Temptation of Christ*).

Looking back, you can see how Dylan's command as a socially conscious auteur had as much to do with the climate he became famous in as with his talent for articulating emergent political ideals. Now when he sings "Political World" (on *Oh Mercy*) he sounds just as stale and uninteresting as any of the demagogues he once railed against. (When did Dylan ever think the world wasn't political?) The rock market has gone not only factional but international: with MTV and the visual image simply another essential piece of any rocker's image, contemporary misfits have to sell themselves on television in ways Dylan never had to. (Although, to be fair, Dylan has yet to succumb to the soda-pop trend—none of his songs has been licensed to Madison Avenue for commercial jingles.) Still, when Dylan meanders into his video for "Political World" (directed by John Cougar Mellencamp), it's a study in obligation.

When you're done dissecting Dylan's accumulative relationship with his songs, players, listeners, and career, you're left with an unsatisfying sense of what makes him tick, and how he might restore himself to greatness. No other artist has been as prolific and yet so inscrutable. As Dylan points out to Anthony Scaduto in 1972, his songs may be peopled with characters, but on some level he's always singing about himself: "Before I wrote *John Wesley Harding* I discovered something. I discovered that when I used words like 'he' and 'it' and 'they' and putting down all sorts of people, I was really talking about no one but me. I went into *Harding* with that knowledge about all the stuff I was writing before then. You see, I didn't know that when I was writing those earlier songs . . ." (p. 332).

This seems to startle Scaduto—it's as if he can't imagine that anyone who could write a song like "Ballad of a Thin Man" might be talking about the arrogant stranger in all of us, who needs a dressing down every so often. On another level, it's a highly simplistic way of diverting attention from the questions you still come away with after listening to Dylan's records: What kind of personality can be so comfortable with such extremes? How can a musician be so powerful one night and so pathetic the next? Where does Dylan think his strengths lie? Returning to Dylan's records won't answer these questions, and it's doubtful anyone's music could. But his songs will give you a sense of how interesting those questions can be, and how much this singer's relationship with the music world can tell you about yourself. Now if only Dylan would act like he knows whom he's singing about when he's singing about himself.

# epilogue

**At his thirtieth anniversary** celebration in 1992, surrounded by friends such as Roger McGuinn, George Harrison, Tom Petty, Neil Young, and Lou Reed, Dylan played the fading rock icon as pale, puffy ghost, the burned-out shell of the voice-of-a-generation who had written the evening's pageant of classic songs. The marvel wasn't that so many stars had gathered on Madison Square Garden's stage to salute one man, but that everything being sung had come from *this* man—the ghost you saw before you. There was little that could cause this grand a tribute to go wrong: everybody besides Dylan seemed in good shape and in a pleasant mood, and, unlike a lot of rock spectacles, this event was both sincere and humble. (Of course, the hand of Columbia Records could be felt, especially behind appearances like Sophie B. Hawkins, whose roiling, literal take on "I Want You" was unbearable—and cut from the final recording.)

But when Irish singer-songwriter Sinead O'Connor came onstage, the audience stirred awkwardly. Seven days earlier she had appeared on *Saturday Night Live* and torn up a picture of the Pope. That protest had had several targets: the host that week was Andrew Dice Clay, and some female members of the *SNL* cast walked off the set to protest the cheap misogynist laughs that had made him famous. As she tore the Pope's photo up, Sinead's comment was "Fight the real enemy." She had considered refusing to appear on the same stage with Dice, but decided to use the opportunity to spotlight misogyny's higher sources.

## epilogue

At Dylan's tribute she was slated to sing "I Believe in You," but there was an awkward pause as she stepped to the mike. She took the measure of the audience in front of her, and decided to wait. That seemed provocative enough. The rumble began to grow, and soon it was clear that there were plenty of folks in the audience angered by O'Connor's presence. Apparently, the Pope is off-limits as a subject of protest to New York audiences. More likely, it was the specter of a woman refuting the male authority figure of a male-dominated religion that was reeling from widespread priest-pedophile scandals that it refused to acknowledge or take responsibility for. O'Connor's temerity in the face of such opposition continues to be a defining feature of her feminist persona.

But, standing on Dylan's stage, O'Connor must have felt a sense of *déjà vu*. Two years earlier, at a concert in New Jersey, she refused to sing "The Star-Spangled Banner" at a summer concert. In the following days, her protest became a tabloid item, with Frank Sinatra leading the charge as middle America lamented the disrespect shown its country. Nobody bothered to ask Frank Sinatra if he would sing the Irish national anthem when in Ireland.

But, as soon as the grumble at the Dylan anniversary concert began to grow, the mood turned cold, and it was apparent that Sinead would either have to acknowledge the sinister noises in the audience or let them shame her. She blustered, and then retorted with a sneering version of Bob Marley's "War"—sung as much in offense as in defense. Her gambit finished, she marched quickly offstage, only to receive a supercilious hug from Kris Kristofferson, who seemed to be trying to urge her to continue with her Dylan song. She dealt with his embrace like a pro running back disposing of a defensive end.

During the final weeks of that first Clinton campaign, when the right-wing era of Reagan and Bush was challenged successfully, to stand as a member of Dylan's audience and witness

# epilogue

O'Connor's dilemma up close was to feel extreme discomfiture. In the sixties, of course, this kind of cultural collision was not only conventional but *de rigeur*, especially at a Bob Dylan concert. Dylan himself sang at the March on Washington in 1963, and traveled to Greenville, Mississippi, during the Freedom Rides, to lend his support to voter registration drives during the civil rights movement. After he effectively renounced song protest with "My Back Pages," his adventuresome muse became a kind of protest in itself: against whatever kind of rock career anybody else might expect from him; against what ever kind of musical style was considered "hip" or "square"; and mostly against whatever "traditional" career expectations might be defied in the brave new context of rock'n'roll. At events like the Newport Folk Festival in 1965, Dylan was the rock star who had championed the very idea of singing to loud boos from a hostile audience.

But by the '80s and '90s, Dylan began to resemble someone more like Ray Charles, who had no compunctions about singing for Republican National Conventions even though The Republican Presidential candidates and platforms were explicitly racist. (Charles was part of the Republican delegations' less than 1% minority population during conventions of this era.) Dylan took many a gig in this period that could be considered neo-conservative at the very least: for the West Point Military Academy in 1990; or accepting a lifetime achievement award from the Grammys in 1991. By the spring of 1997, this political neutrality—or denial—had so much momentum that Dylan performed at the Vatican for the Pope himself a few short weeks after accepting the Congressional Medal of Honor from President Clinton without a hint of irony.

Can anyone imagine the Dylan of an earlier era allowing Sinead O'Connor to be booed offstage for defying the Pope—without so much as a retort? Alongside fiascos like his ambivalent 1985 LiveAid set and his indecipherable 1991 Grammy appearance (where he sang "Masters of War"), the thirtieth anniversary performance sealed the impression that Dylan was more a casualty of the '60s political legacy than a survivor. Who could have predicted that Dylan, the premiere symbol of '60s political activism, would someday make Frank Sinatra seem observant?

Apparently the Pope's untouchable status was second only to Dylan's, who proceeded to move the show forward as though nothing had happened. As the icons gathered to sing "My Back Pages" for the finale, it was clear they were singing more about aging than politics; and as touching as it was, it was hard not to notice a nervous Sinead O'Connor meandering in the midst of things, looking shell-shocked and out of place.

**At this writing**, in mid-1999, Dylan's "rehabilitation" in the public imagination is supposedly complete. *Time Out of Mind*, an album soaked in death and dejection, won overwhelming critical praise upon its late 1997 release, made Dylan a Grammy favorite, and joined many year-end critical lists. This came on the heels of Dylan's bout with a rare heart ailment in the spring of 1997, which hospitalized him and flooded his record label with phone calls. The publicity, and a *Newsweek* cover story, bulleted the album to a number ten debut on the charts, his highest ever.

The media reported Dylan's big year in tones of hushed reverence, as if his symbolic status held him above criticism. And yet if *Time Out of Mind* represented anything beyond Dylan's bloated self-pity, it spoke poorly of its audience. The CD opened with the words "I'm walking through streets that are dead," and descended from there. He bleated lines like "You took the silver, you took the gold/You left me standing out in the cold" with such sullen contempt it was hard to believe that this was the same guy whose imagination once intoxicated listeners into stupefaction.

Coasting on his reputation as the most original songwriter going, Dylan now copped his album titles from old Steely Dan songs. And his new numbers were anything but metaphoric: when he sang a lyric like "Trying to Get To Heaven /(Before they close the door)" he meant it only literally. In an era when many of the most interesting bands embraced the lo-fi conceit (Portishead, Pavement), Dylan went hi-fi. His recordings had sounded like crap long before it was cool, but now, producer Daniel Lanois (U2, Peter Gabriel) framed his gravelly mumble in gorgeously layered colors. Dylan wrote almost exclusively in the first-person in the humorless tone of a world-weary crank.

In his prime Dylan was the antithesis of the artist as static entity: you never knew what he would do next, but it was often the least likely move, hyper-counterintuitive, and it forced you to rethink your entire concept of rock and Dylan's place in it. This was the fount of sixties counterculture intellectualism, who dosed 1967's psychedelic Summer of Love with the subdued *John Wesley Harding*, and lobbed a relaxed C&W turn, *Nashville Skyline*, into Woodstock's hippie grandiosity.

Reports from many of Dylan's 1998 shows were glowing, which argued that Dylan still had greatness in him onstage. But his presence in popular culture is meager compared to the hype that still surrounds him. *Good as I Been to You* (1992) or *World Gone Wrong* (1994) are said to be the records that brought his muse back into focus. In rock, the oldies fallback recording has a tradition of being a place-holding career move, the kind that signals creative stagnation, when the performer can't figure out what to do next. With these records coming amidst a seven-year lull between original songs (1990's *Blood Red Sky* and 1997's *Time Out of Mind*), Dylan was lucky to dodge that charge. The material was well-chosen, but these performances lacked the cockeyed humor Dylan sang with as a younger man. His voice, long abused by nicotine and God knows what else, had less raspy charm than bedraggled cynicism, and he put these records over with what might be called the opposite of panache. Compared to the casual verve of the Band's *Moondog Matinee* (1973), these Dylan records sound exhausted, and not in particularly interesting ways.

## epilogue

*Time Out of Mind* scans like a poor Dylan parody. The sarcastic contempt Dylan smears across his eyeglasses is overbearing, and the ironies are few and frail. It culminates with a winding distention of a blues called "Highlands," which turns out to be yet another protracted narrative of longing for a woman, a lost love, a hope betrayed:

> She said you don't read women authors do you?
> I said you're wrong
> She said who've you read then
> I said I read Erica Jong

Unlike the waitress confrontation "Tangled Up in Blue," there's not much going on here. A woman accuses Dylan of not reading female authors. He disagrees, then offers up Erica Jong as evidence of his vast acquaintance with feminist fiction. Besides going for the sloppy, obvious rhyme, what are we to make of this? That Dylan reads Erica Jong as a way of rubbing feminists' noses in how mediocre their novelists can be? That Erica Jong counts as a woman novelist but only barely? The more cynical reading might be: Dylan reads women authors only when they're washed-up '70s post-celebrities who popularized the term "zipless fuck."

The overwhelmingly positive praise *Time Out of Mind* received points to a larger misperception surrounding fading rock idols, namely, the wish that even if their best work is behind them, that they remain vibrant icons despite the vast rut of commercialism rock culture now stands for. This is not meant to imply that all of Dylan's work in the last three decades is poor, but the overwhelming bulk of it lacks in comparison to his best years (1962-75). Indeed, the good work after *Rolling Thunder Revue* casts telling aspersions on his major releases. His singing with the Traveling Wilburys is shot through with humor and a sense of shared burdens with his fellow icons Tom Petty, George Harri-

son, and Roy Orbison. And he's participated in a number of tribute albums for the likes of Jimmie Rodgers and Doc Pomus that
have kept his voice at play in the ongoing rock dialogue about
sources and influences.

**Perhaps the most compelling** proof of Dylan's ir-
relevance came from moments notable for his absence. At the
MTV Video Awards in 1996, Jakob Dylan took the stage with his
band, the Wallflowers, to perform their hit "One Headlight."
Alongside him, Bruce Springsteen sang harmony as though this
youngster deserved it, and used his superstar status to do something besides boost his own stock. Jakob, perhaps the most bur-
dened of rock progeny, could use a big brother onstage, and
Springsteen coaxed some of the sweetest smiles out of the young
man his audience had ever seen. By contrast, his father, Bob Dylan, kept his distance from his son's career. And Dylan the elder
was not seen harmonizing on anybody else's son's stage.

And as Dylan was writing and recording *Time Out of Mind*,
another album was being made under the auspices of Nora
Guthrie, Woody Guthrie's daughter by Marjorie Mazia. Oversee-
ing the Guthrie papers at the Woody Guthrie Archives in New
York City, Nora had helped Dave Marsh put together a boister-
ous book of unpublished writings, *Pastures of Plenty*, in 1989. In
1995, she wrote the British songwriter Billy Bragg with an irresistible invitation: to compose music to some of the hundreds of
leftover song lyrics Woody had scribbled down and left behind.

Bragg, along with the roots-rock band Wilco, began collabo-
rating on a series of songs that became *Mermaid Avenue*, which
was finally released in 1998 to widespread critical praise. And it's
no wonder: *Mermaid Avenue* countered what Dylan had been
singing about with a zealous optimism that only rock could deliver. It made Dylan sound like a has-been as it elevated Bragg's
and Wilco's audience's best hopes regarding Guthrie's legacy.

By 1998, the Guthrie legend had been winnowed to a few
contradictory meanings. Guthrie was supposedly the American

## epilogue

Johnny Appleseed come to life, recalled mainly as a political troubador, the kind of writer who never found a socialist cliché he didn't like, whose sole purpose as a musician was to carry the leftist word. One of the most famous pictures of Guthrie features the logo writ large across his guitar: "This machine kills fascists."

But that stereotype of Guthrie has always been over-simplified, as anyone who reads Joe Klein's *Woody Guthrie: A Life* (Knopf, 1983) can attest. (Klein would find fame as Anonymous, the author of *Primary Colors*.) Guthrie's politics were only one aspect of his persona, and you could argue they were drawn directly from experience. The subtext of a lot of his songs was: If you didn't emerge from the Dust Bowl and the Depression as a radical progressive, you probably didn't have a brain, and your soul was up for grabs. But nobody can listen to Guthrie's songs for children without realizing he had a rakish sense of fun, and the romanticism behind songs like "Pastures of Plenty" and "Deportees" can't be explained by politics alone.

The contrast of Dylan's inward, psychological approach to Guthrie's outward, agitprop persona has always been a red herring. Dylan's greatness lies in just how ingeniously he straddles these two approaches, and keeps the listener guessing as to his ultimate intentions — and how much is pure accident. After all, his first public appearance after the *Basement Tapes* came at a Carnegie Hall Guthrie memorial in early 1968, where he offered up three Guthrie songs with the Band ("I Ain't Got No Home," "The Grand Coulee Dam," and "Dear Mrs. Roosevelt"). This set ranks with his Bangladesh appearance among the finest Dylan live sets ever recorded. Extending the folksy-ethereal mood of the *Basement Tapes* even as he brought these Guthrie songs some neurotic grit and emotional depth, Dylan embraces all the warmth and humor these songs have to offer, and the spontaneous communities that spring from homeless privation. The best Dylan may be even more complex — and inconsistent — than

## epilogue

authors like Greil Marcus (*Invisible Republic*) would have you believe.

At this point, it's impossible to imagine Dylan reimagining Guthrie the way Bragg and Jeff Tweedy of Wilco do on *Mermaid Avenue*. There's no "Ingrid Bergman" in Dylan the crusty, any more than there's a "California Stars" or an "The Unwelcome Guest," songs that revive Guthrie's humility as they approach his melodic naturalism. When Tweedy sings "We throw away enough to feed the hungry," he makes it truer in a way than perhaps Guthrie ever imagined.

Looking back, the least uncomfortable person at Madison Square Garden at that 1992 anniversary concert may have been Dylan himself, who, for all we know, was unaware of the Sinead O'Connor incident. Dylan may still have great records in him, but for a huge segment of his audience, his Nixonian jowls bespeak a narcissistic bitterness that has only intensified with age, and made his continued reliance on his '60s material all the more unseemly. If anything, he seems to know less of himself and his place in our era than he ever has.

# discography

## Part 1

The following section includes Dylan's entire Columbia and Asylum commercial catalogue covered in this book, as well as significant work he does on other people's records (like the 1971 Bangladesh benefit appearance). Catalogue numbers refer to CD issues (sometimes distinguished by a "-2"), which in many cases correspond to their vinyl counterparts. Where CD reissues update a vinyl catalogue number, both numbers are included where possible. Titles by Bob Dylan unless noted.

### Bob Dylan
(Columbia 8579, released March 1962)

You're No Good (J. Fuller) / Talkin' New York / In My Time of Dyin' (arr. Dylan) / Man of Constant Sorrow (trad.) / Fixin' to Die (B. White) / Pretty Peggy-o (trad.) / Highway 51 (C. Jones) / Gospel Plow (trad.) / Baby, Let Me Follow You Down (Rev. G. Davis) / House of the Risin' Sun (arr. Dylan) / Freight Train Blues (attrib. Acuff) / Song to Woody / See That My Grave Is Kept Clean (L. Jefferson)

### The Freewheelin' Bob Dylan
(Columbia 8786, released May 1963)

Blowin' in the Wind / Girl from the North Country / Masters of War / Down the Highway / Bob Dylan's Blues / A Hard Rain's A-Gonna Fall / Don't Think Twice, It's All Right / Bob Dylan's Dream / Oxford Town / Talkin' World War III Blues / Corrina, Corrina (arr. Dylan) / Honey, Just Allow Me One More Chance / I Shall Be Free

### The Times They Are A-Changin'
(Columbia 8905, released January 1964)

The Times They Are A-Changin' / Ballad of Hollis Brown / With God on Our Side / One Too Many Mornings / North Country Blues / Only

## discography

a Pawn in Their Game / Boots of Spanish Leather / When the Ship Comes In / The Lonesome Death of Hattie Carroll / Restless Farewell

### Another Side of Bob Dylan
(Columbia 8993, released August 1964)

All I Really Want to Do / Black Crow Blues / Spanish Harlem Incident / Chimes of Freedom / I Shall Be Free No. 10 / To Ramona / Motorpsycho Nitemare / My Back Pages / I Don't Believe You / Ballad in Plain D / It Ain't Me, Babe

### Bringing It All Back Home
(Columbia 9128, released March 1965)

Subterranean Homesick Blues / She Belongs to Me / Maggie's Farm / Love Minus Zero—No Limit / Outlaw Blues / On the Road Again / Bob Dylan's 115th Dream / Mr. Tambourine Man / Gates of Eden / It's Alright, Ma (I'm Only Bleeding) / It's All Over Now, Baby Blue

### Highway 61 Revisited
(Columbia 9189, released September 1965)

Like a Rolling Stone / Tombstone Blues / It Takes a Lot to Laugh, It Takes a Train to Cry / From a Buick 6 / Ballad of a Thin Man / Queen Jane Approximately / Highway 61 Revisited / Just Like Tom Thumb's Blues / Desolation Row

### Blonde on Blonde
(Columbia 841, released June 1966)

Rainy Day Women #12 & 35 / Pledging My Time / Visions of Johanna / One of Us Must Know (Sooner or Later) / I Want You / Stuck Inside of Mobile with Memphis Blues Again / Leopard-Skin Pill-Box Hat / Just Like a Woman / Most Likely You Go Your Way and I'll Go Mine / Temporary Like Achilles / Absolutely Sweet Marie / 4th Time Around / Obviously 5 Believers / Sad-Eyed Lady of the Lowlands

### John Wesley Harding
(Columbia 9604, released December 1967)

John Wesley Harding / As I Went Out One Morning / I Dreamed I Saw St. Augustine / All Along the Watchtower / The Ballad of Frankie

# discography

Lee and Judas Priest / Drifter's Escape / Dear Landlord / I Am a Lonesome Hobo / I Pity the Poor Immigrant / The Wicked Messenger / Down Along the Cove / I'll Be Your Baby Tonight


### Nashville Skyline
(Columbia 9825, released May 1969)

Girl from the North Country / Nashville Skyline Rag / To Be Alone with You / I Threw It All Away / Peggy Day / Lay, Lady, Lay / One More Night / Tell Me That It Isn't True / Country Pie / Tonight I'll Be Staying Here with You


### Self-Portrait
(Columbia 30050, released June 1970)

All the Tired Horses / Alberta #1 / I've Forgotten More Than You'll Ever Know / Days of '49 / Early Morning Rain / In Search of Little Sadie / Let It Be Me / Little Sadie / Woogie Boogie / Belle Isle / Living the Blues / Like a Rolling Stone / Copper Kettle / Gotta Travel On / Blue Moon / The Boxer / Quinn the Eskimo (The Mighty Quinn) / Take Me as I Am / Take a Message to Mary / It Hurts Me Too / Minstrel Boy / She Belongs to Me / Wigwam / Alberta #2


### New Morning
(Columbia 30290, released October 1970)

If Not for You / Day of the Locusts / Time Passes Slowly / Went to See the Gypsy / Winterlude / If Dogs Run Free / New Morning / Sign on the Window / One More Weekend / The Man in Me / Three Angels / Father of Night


### Bob Dylan's Greatest Hits, Volume 2
(Columbia 31120, released November 1971)

Watching the River Flow / Don't Think Twice, It's All Right / Lay, Lady, Lay / Stuck Inside of Mobile with the Memphis Blues Again / I'll Be Your Baby Tonight / All I Really Want to Do / My Back Pages / Maggie's Farm / Tonight I'll Be Staying Here with You / Positively 4th Street / All Along the Watchtower / Quinn the Eskimo (The Mighty Quinn) / Just Like Tom Thumb's Blues / A Hard Rain's A-Gonna

Fall / If Not for You / New Morning / Tomorrow Is a Long Time /
When I Paint My Masterpiece / I Shall Be Released / You Ain't Goin'
Nowhere / Down in the Flood

### *The Concert for Bangla Desh*
(Apple 3385, released December 1971)

Dylan's set (evening show): A Hard Rain's A-Gonna Fall / It Takes a Lot
to Laugh, It Takes a Train to Cry / Blowin' in the Wind / Mr. Tambourine Man / Just Like a Woman

### *Pat Garrett and Billy the Kid* (soundtrack)
(Columbia 32460, released May 1973)

Main Title Theme (Billy) / Cantina Theme (Workin' for the Law) / Billy
1 / Bunkhouse Theme / River Theme / Turkey Chase / Knockin' on
Heaven's Door / Final Theme / Billy 4 / Billy 7

### *Dylan*
(Columbia 32747, released December 1973)

Lily of the West (E. Davies, J. Peterson) / Can't Help Falling in Love
(G. Weiss, H. Peretti, L. Creatore) / Sarah Jane (trad.) / The Ballad of
Ira Hayes (P. La Farge) / Mr. Bojangles (J. J. Walker) / Mary Ann
(trad.) / Big Yellow Taxi (J. Mitchell) / A Fool Such As I (B. Trader) /
Spanish Is the Loving Tongue (trad.)

### *Planet Waves*
(Asylum 1003, released January 1974; reissued as Columbia 37637,
1989)

On a Night Like This / Going, Going, Gone / Tough Mama / Hazel /
Something There Is About You / Forever Young (2 versions) / Dirge /
You Angel You / Never Say Goodbye / Wedding Song

### *Before the Flood*
(Asylum 201, released June 1974; reissued as Columbia 37661, 1989)

Most Likely You Go Your Way and I'll Go Mine / Lay, Lady, Lay /
Rainy Day Women #12 & 35 / Knockin' on Heaven's Door / It Ain't

## discography

Me, Babe / Ballad of a Thin Man / Up on Cripple Creek (R. Robertson) / I Shall Be Released / Endless Highway (R. Robertson) / The Night They Drove Old Dixie Down (R. Robertson) / Stage Fright (R. Robertson) / Don't Think Twice, It's All Right / Just Like a Woman / It's Alright, Ma (I'm Only Bleeding) / The Shape I'm In (R. Robertson) / When You Awake (R. Robertson, R. Manuel) / The Weight (R. Robertson) / All Along the Watchtower / Highway 61 Revisited / Like a Rolling Stone / Blowin' in the Wind

### Blood on the Tracks
(Columbia 33235, released January 1975)

Tangled Up in Blue / Simple Twist of Fate / You're a Big Girl Now / Idiot Wind / You're Gonna Make Me Lonesome When You Go / Meet Me in the Morning / Lily, Rosemary and the Jack of Hearts / If You See Her, Say Hello / Shelter from the Storm / Buckets of Rain

### The Basement Tapes (with the Band)
(Columbia 33682, released July 1975)

Odds and Ends / Orange Juice Blues (Blues for Breakfast) (R. Manuel) / Million Dollar Bash / Yazoo Street Scandal (R. Robertson) / Going to Acapulco / Katie's Been Gone (R. Robertson, R. Manuel) / Lo and Behold / Bessie Smith (R. Danko, R. Robertson) / Clothes Line Saga / Apple Suckling Tree / Please, Mrs. Henry / Tears of Rage (with R. Manuel) / Too Much of Nothing / Yea! Heavy and a Bottle of Bread / Ain't No More Cane (trad., arr. the Band) / Crash on the Levee (Down in the Flood) / Ruben Remus (R. Robertson, R. Manuel) / Tiny Montgomery / You Ain't Goin' Nowhere / Don't Ya Tell Henry / Nothing Was Delivered / Open the Door, Homer / Long Distance Operator / This Wheel's on Fire (with R. Danko)

### Desire
(Columbia 33893, released January 1976)
All songs by Bob Dylan and Jacques Levy except as indicated.

Hurricane / Isis / Mozambique / One More Cup of Coffee (Valley Below) (Dylan) / Oh, Sister / Joey / Romance in Durango / Black Diamond Bay / Sara (Dylan)

# discography

### Hard Rain
(Columbia 34349, released September 1976)

Maggie's Farm / One Too Many Mornings / Stuck Inside of Mobile with the Memphis Blues Again / Oh, Sister (with J. Levy) / Lay, Lady, Lay / Shelter from the Storm / You're a Big Girl Now / I Threw It All Away / Idiot Wind

### The Last Waltz
(Warner Bros. 3146, released April 1978)

Dylan sings: Baby, Let Me Follow You Down (2 versions) / Forever Young / I Shall Be Released

### Street Legal
(Columbia 35453, released June 1978)

Changing of the Guards / New Pony / No Time to Think / Baby Stop Crying / Is Your Love in Vain? / Señor (Tales of Yankee Power) / True Love Tends to Forget / We Better Talk This Over / Where Are You Tonight? (Journey Through Dark Heat)

### Bob Dylan at Budokan
(Columbia 36067, released May 1979)

Mr. Tambourine Man / Shelter from the Storm / Love Minus Zero—No Limit / Ballad of a Thin Man / Don't Think Twice, It's All Right / Maggie's Farm / One More Cup of Coffee (Valley Below) / Like a Rolling Stone / I Shall Be Released / Is Your Love in Vain? / Going, Going, Gone / Blowin' in the Wind / Just Like a Woman / Oh, Sister (with J. Levy) / Simple Twist of Fate / All Along the Watchtower / I Want You / All I Really Want to Do / Knockin' on Heaven's Door / It's Alright, Ma (I'm Only Bleeding) / Forever Young / The Times They Are A-Changin'

### Slow Train Coming
(Columbia 36120, released August 1979)

Gotta Serve Somebody / Precious Angel / I Believe in You / Slow Train / Gonna Change My Way of Thinking / Do Right to Me Baby (Do

## discography

Unto Others) / When You Gonna Wake Up? / Man Gave Names to All the Animals / When He Returns

### Saved
(Columbia 36553, released June 1980)

A Satisfied Mind (R. Hayes, J. Rhodes) / Saved (with T. Drummond) / Covenant Woman / What Can I Do For You? / Solid Rock / Pressing On / In the Garden / Saving Grace / Are You Ready?

### Shot of Love
(Columbia 37496, released August 1981)

Shot of Love / Heart of Mine / Property of Jesus / Lenny Bruce / Watered-Down Love / The Groom's Still Waiting at the Altar / Dead Man, Dead Man / In the Summertime / Trouble / Every Grain of Sand

### Infidels
(Columbia 38819, released November 1983)

Jokerman / Sweetheart Like You / Neighborhood Bully / License to Kill / Man of Peace / Union Sundown / I and I / Don't Fall Apart on Me Tonight

### Real Live
Columbia 39944, released December 1984)

Highway 61 Revisited / Maggie's Farm / I and I / License to Kill / It Ain't Me, Babe / Tangled Up in Blue / Masters of War / Ballad of a Thin Man / Girl from the North Country / Tombstone Blues

### Empire Burlesque
(Columbia 40110, released June 1985)

Tight Connection to My Heart (Has Anybody Seen My Love) / Seeing the Real You at Last / I'll Remember You / Clean Cut Kid / Never Gonna Be the Same Again / Trust Yourself / Emotionally Yours / When the Night Comes Falling from the Sky / Something's Burning, Baby / Dark Eyes

# discography

**We Are the World**
(Columbia 40043, 1985)

**Sun City**
(Manhattan / Capitol 53019, 1985)

**Biograph**
(Columbia 38830, released November 1985)

Lay, Lady, Lay / Baby, Let Me Follow You Down / If Not for You / I'll Be Your Baby Tonight / I'll Keep It with Mine / The Times They Are A-Changin' / Blowin' in the Wind / Masters of War / Lonesome Death of Hattie Carroll / Percy's Song / Mixed Up Confusion / Tombstome Blues / The Groom's Still Waiting at the Altar / Most Likely You Go Your Way and I'll Go Mine / Like a Rolling Stone / Jet Pilot / Lay Down Your Weary Tune / Subterranean Homesick Blues / I Don't Believe You (She Acts Like We Never Have Met) (live) / Visions of Johanna (live) / Every Grain of Sand / Quinn the Eskimo (The Mighty Quinn) / Mr. Tambourine Man / Dear Landlord / It Ain't Me, Babe / You Angel You / Million Dollar Bash / To Ramona / You're a Big Girl Now / Abandoned Love / Tangled Up in Blue / It's All Over Now, Baby Blue (live) / Can You Please Crawl Out Your Window? / Positively 4th Street / Isis (live) (with J. Levy) / Caribbean Wind / Up to Me / Baby, I'm in the Mood for You / I Wanna Be Your Lover / I Want You / Heart of Mine (live) / On a Night Like This / Just Like a Woman / Romance in Durango (live) (with J. Levy) / Señor (Tales of Yankee Power) / Gotta Serve Somebody / I Believe in You / Time Passes Slowly / I Shall Be Released / Knockin' on Heaven's Door / All Along the Watchtower / Solid Rock / Forever Young

**Knocked Out Loaded**
(Columbia 40439, released August 1986)

You Wanna Ramble (H. Parker, Jr.) / They Killed Him (K. Kristofferson) / Driftin' Too Far from Shore / Precious Memories (trad.) / Maybe Someday / Brownsville Girl (with S. Shepard) / Got My Mind Made Up (with T. Petty) / Under Your Spell (with C. B. Sager)

**Hearts of Fire (soundtrack)**
(Columbia 40870, released October 1986)

The Usual (J. Hiatt) / Night After Night / I Had a Dream About You, Baby

# discography

## *A Vision Shared: A Tribute to Woody Guthrie and Leadbelly*
(Columbia 44034, 1988)

Bob Dylan solo acoustic: Pretty Boy Floyd (W. Guthrie)

## *Down in the Groove*
(Columbia 40957, released June 1988)

Let's Stick Together (W. Harrison) / When Did You Leave Heaven? (W. Bullock, R. Whiting) / Sally Sue Brown (J. Alexander, E. Montgomery, T. Stafford) / Death Is Not the End / Had a Dream About You, Baby / Ugliest Girl in the World (with R. Hunter) / Silvio (with R. Hunter) / Ninety Miles an Hour (Down a Dead End Street) (H. Blair, D. Robertson) / Shenandoah (trad.) / Rank Strangers to Me (A. Brumley)

## *Oh Mercy*
(Columbia 45281, released September 1989)

Political World / Where Teardrops Fall / Everything Is Broken / Ring Them Bells / Man in the Long Black Coat / Most of the Time / What Good Am I? / Disease of Conceit / What Was It You Wanted / Shooting Star

## *Dylan and the Dead*
(Columbia 45056, released June 1989)

Slow Train / I Want You / Gotta Serve Somebody / Queen Jane Approximately / Joey / All Along the Watchtower / Knockin' on Heaven's Door

## *A Tribute to Woody Guthrie*
(Columbia 31171, 1989) Dylan with the Band, January 20, 1968:

I Ain't Got No Home / Dear Mrs. Roosevelt / Grand Coulee Dam (all by W. Guthrie)

## *Traveling Wilburys, Volume 1*
(Wilbury Records / Warner Bros. 9 25796-2, released October 1988)
All songs written by the Traveling Wilburys

Handle with Care / Dirty World / Last Night / Not Alone Any More / Congratulations / Heading for the Light / Margarita / Tweeter and the Monkey Man / End of the Line

# discography

### Nobody's Child
(Warner 26280-2, 1990)


### Under the Red Sky
(Columbia 46794, released November 1990)

Wiggle Wiggle / Under the Red Sky / Unbelievable / Born in Time /
T.V. Talkin' Song / 10,000 Men / 2 × 2 / God Knows / Handy Dandy /
Cat's in the Well


### Traveling Wilburys, Volume 3
(Wilbury Records / Warner Bros. 9 26324-2, released September
1990)
All songs written by the Traveling Wilburys

She's My Baby / Inside Out / If You Belonged to Me / The Devil's Been
Busy / 7 Deadly Sins / Poor House / Where Were You Last Night? /
Cool Dry Place / New Blue Moon / You Took My Breath Away /
Wilbury Twist


### Bob Dylan: The Bootleg Series, Volumes 1–3 (Rare & Unreleased), 1961–1991
(Columbia 47382, released March 1991)

Hard Times in New York Town (adapted from P. Seeger) / He Was a
Friend of Mine (trad.) / Man on the Street / No More Auction Block
(trad.) / House Carpenter / Talkin' Bear Mountain Picnic Massacre
Blues / Let Me Die in My Footsteps / Rambling, Gambling Willie /
Talkin' Hava Negeilah Blues / Quit Your Low Down Ways / Worried
Blues (Wood) / Kingsport Town / Walkin' Down the Line / Walls of
Red Wing / Paths of Victory / Talkin' John Birch Paranoid Blues / Who
Killed Davey Moore? / Only a Hobo / Moonshiner / When the Ship
Comes In / The Times They Are A-Changin' / Last Thoughts on Woody
Guthrie / Seven Curses / Eternal Circle / Suze (The Cough Song) /
Mama, You Been on My Mind / Farewell, Angelina / Subterranean
Homesick Blues / If You Gotta Go, Go Now / Sitting on a Barbed
Wire Fence / Like a Rolling Stone / It Takes a Lot to Laugh, It Takes
a Train to Cry / I'll Keep It with Mine / She's Your Lover Now / I Shall
Be Released / Santa Fe / If Not For You / Wallflower / Nobody 'Cept
You / Tangled Up in Blue / Call Letter Blues / Idiot Wind / If You See
Her, Say Hello / Golden Loom / Catfish / Seven Days / Ye Shall Be

# discography

Changed / Every Grain of Sand / You Changed My Life / Need a Woman / Angelina / Someone's Got a Hold of My Heart / Tell Me / Lord Protect My Child / Foot Of Pride / Blind Willie McTell / When the Night Comes Falling from the Sky / Series of Dreams

## Part 2

Primary source Bob Dylan bootlegs and miscellaneous recordings. (For a thorough listing of noncommercial Dylan titles until 1978, see Paul Cable's exhaustive *Bob Dylan: His Unreleased Recordings*.)

### Bob Dylan, Zimmerman: Ten of Swords, 1961–1966

(Tarantula 16319, 1985, 10 LPs)

Candy-Man (trad., arr. Rev. G. Davis) / Baby, Please Don't Go (Big Joe Williams) / Hard Times in New York (adapted from P. Seeger) / Stealin' (trad.) / Poor Lazarus (trad.) / I Ain't Got No Home (W. Guthrie) / It's Hard to Be Blind (trad., arr. Rev. G. Davis) / Dink's Song (trad., arr. Lomax) / Wade in the Water (trad.) / In the Evening (B. McGhee) / Baby, Let Me Follow You Down (Rev. G. Davis) / Sally Gal (two versions, adapted from W. Guthrie's "Sally, Don't You Grieve") / Man of Constant Sorrow (trad.) / Omie Wise (trad.) / I Was Young When I Left Home (adapted from trad. "Nine Hundred Miles") / Cocaine (trad. arr. Rev. G. Davis) / V.D. Blues (W. Guthrie) / V.D. Waltz (Guthrie) / V.D. City (W. Guthrie) / V.D. Gunner's Blues (W. Guthrie) / Hezikiah Jones (Buckley) / East Orange Monologue / Baby Please Don't Go (Williams) / Milk Cow's Calf Blues (trad., arr. R. Johnson) / Talking Bear Mountain Picnic Massacre Blues / I Heard That Lonesome Whistle (Williams / Davis) / Talkin Hava Negeilah Blues / Worried Blues (Wood) / Wichita (Going to Louisiana) (trad.) (two versions) / Quit Your Lowdown Ways / He Was a Friend of Mine (trad., arr. Dylan) / Man on the Street / Hard Times in New York City / Talking Bear Mountain Massacre Blues / Standing on the Highway / Poor Boy Blues / Ballad for a Friend / Man on the Street / Ramblin' Gamblin' Willie (two versions) / Mixed Up Confusion / Corrina, Corrina (trad.) / Talkin' John Birch Paranoid Blues / Let Me Die in My Footsteps / Baby, I'm in the Mood for You / The Death of Emmett Till / Ain't Gonna Grieve / Long Time Gone / Long Ago, Far Away / Hero Blues / Watcha Gonna Do? (2 versions) / Gypsy Lou / Guess I'm Doin' Fine / Walkin' Down the Line / All Over You / Bound to Lose,

# discography

Bound to Win / Barbara Allen (trad.) / Moonshine Blues (trad.) / Motherless Children (trad.) / Handsome Molly (trad.) / John Brown / Don't Think Twice, It's All Right / Ain't No More Cane (Ledbetter) / Cocaine (trad., arr. Rev. G. Davis) / The Cuckoo Is a Pretty Bird (trad.) / West Texas (trad.) / A Hard Rain's A-Gonna Fall / I Shall Be Free / I'd Hate to Be You on That Dreadful Day / When the Ship Comes In / The Times They Are A-Changin' / Tomorrow Is a Long Time / Farewell / Ballad of Hollis Brown / Kind-Hearted Woman Blues (Johnson) / See That My Grave Is Kept Clean (Jefferson) / Black Cross / No More Auction Block (trad.) / Rocks and Gravel (McGhee) / A Hard Rain's A-Gonna Fall / Ramblin' Down Through the World (adapted from W. Guthrie) / Who Killed Davey Moore? / Her Blues / Dusty Old Fairgrounds / Last Thought on Woody Guthrie / Mr. Tambourine Man / Rocks and Gravel / Moonshine Blues / The Cough Song / Mama, You Been on My Mind (two versions) / Walls of Redwing / Only a Hobo / Paths of Victory / Percy's Song / Farewell / Everytime Somebody Comes to Town (with G. Harrison) / I'd Have You Anytime (with G. Harrison) / It Takes a Lot to Laugh, It Takes a Train to Cry / From a Buick 6 / Barbed Wire Fence / Desolation Row / You're Her Lover Now / Can You Please Crawl Out Your Window (2 versions) / I Wanna Be Your Lover / Visions of Johanna / Lay Down Your Weary Tune / Bob Dylan's New Orleans Rag / I'll Keep It with Mine / Denise / That's Alright, Mama—Sally Free and Easy (Crudup / Tawney) / East Laredo Blues / Bob Dylan's New Orleans Rag / California / If You Gotta Go, Go Now / Love Minus Zero—No Limit / She Belongs to Me / It's All Over Now, Baby Blue / She's Your Lover Now / Instrumental / Tell Me, Momma / I Don't Believe You / Baby, Let Me Follow You Down (Rev. G. Davis) / Just Like Tom Thumb's Blues / Leopard-Skin Pill-Box Hat / One Too Many Mornings / Ballad of a Thin Man / Like a Rolling Stone

### Broadside Reunion, Volume 6
(Broadside-Folkways BR-5315)

Dylan as Blind Boy Grunt: Train A-Travelin' / The Death of Emmett Till / Donald White / Dreadful Day

### Bob Dylan, On the Road 1974–1975
(Zap 7877)

I Don't Believe You / She Belongs to Me / It's All Over Now, Baby Blue / Except You / Love Minus Zero—No Limit / Simple Twist of

## discography

Fate / A Hard Rain's A-Gonna Fall / Desolation Row / Wedding Song / Visions of Johanna

### Bob Dylan, *The Great White Wonder*
(blank label, double album, c. 1970)

Baby, Please Don't Go (Big Joe Williams) / Dylan and Seeger talking / Dink's Song / See That My Grave Is Kept Clean (L. Jefferson) / East Orange N.J. / Man of Constant Sorrow / New Orleans Rag / If You Gotta Go, Go Now / Only a Hobo / Killing Me Alive (with the Band) / Quinn the Eskimo (The Mighty Quinn) / This Wheel's on Fire / Candy Man / Ramblin' Around / Hezikiah Jones (Black Cross) / I Ain't Got No Home / The Death of Emmett Till / Poor Lazarus / I Shall Be Released / Open the Door, Rachel / Too Much of Nothing / Nothing Is Better / Tears of Rage / Living the Blues

### Bob Dylan, *Live in England, May 1966*
(Back Trax CD 04-88002, 1988)

4th Time Around / Desolation Row / Just Like a Woman / Mr. Tambourine Man / Tell Me, Momma / Baby, Let Me Follow You Down / Just Like Tom Thumbs Blues / Leopard-Skin Pill-Box Hat / One Too Many Mornings / Ballad of a Thin Man / Like a Rolling Stone

### Bob Dylan, *Blind Boy Grunt and the Hawks*
(Surprise, double album, 1986)

All You Have to Do Is Dream / I Can't Make It Alone / I'm Not There / Get Your Rocks Off / Down On Me / Bonnie Ship the Diamond / He's Young But He's Daily Growing (trad.) / Open the Door, Homer / Instrumental / One Man's Loss / The Hills of Mexico / One for the Road / I'm Alright / One Single River / I Shall Be Released / Prelude / Try Me, Little Girl / I Don't Hurt Anymore (H. Snow) / People Get Ready (C. Mayfield) / Too Much of Nothing / Instrumental / Baby Ain't That Fine / A Night Without Sleep / A Fool Such As I (B. Trader) / Gonna Get You Now / Apple Suckling Tree / Stones That You Throw / Sign on the Cross / Lock Your Door / Baby, Won't You Let Me Be Your Baby / Don't You Try Me Now / All You Have to Do Is Dream

The Band: Instrumental / You Say You Love Me / Untitled (Garth—piano) / Ferdinand Instrumental / You Say You Love Me / Guitars

## discography

The Band with Herbert Khaury a.k.a. Tiny Tim: Be My Baby / I Got You Babe / Memphis / Sonny Boy

### Bob Dylan, *Love Songs for America*
(Swinging Pig CD 055-2, 1990)
Recorded at the Boston Garden on January 14, 1974 (afternoon show)

Rainy Day Women #12 & 35 / Lay, Lady, Lay / Just Like Tom Thumb's Blues / It Ain't Me, Babe / I Don't Believe You / Ballad of a Thin Man / All Along the Watchtower / Ballad of Hollis Brown / Knockin' on Heaven's Door / The Times They Are A-Changin' / Don't Think Twice, It's All Right / Gates of Eden

The Band: Stage Fright / The Night They Drove Old Dixie Down / King Harvest (Has Surely Come) / This Wheel's on Fire / I Shall Be Released / Up on Cripple Creek

### Bob Dylan, *Masterpieces*
(CBS / Sony 57AP-875 / 6 / 7, released March 1978 in Japan, Australia, New Zealand) An early import version of *Biograph*

Knockin' on Heaven's Door / Mr. Tambourine Man / Just Like a Woman / I Shall Be Released / Tears of Rage / All Along the Watchtower / One More Cup of Coffee / Like a Rolling Stone / The Mighty Quinn (Quinn the Eskimo) / Tomorrow Is a Long Time / Lay, Lady, Lay / Idiot Wind / Mixed Up Confusion / Positively 4th Street / Can *You* Please Crawl Out Your Window? / Just Like Tom Thumb's Blues (live with the Band, 1966) / Spanish Is the Loving Tongue / George Jackson (Big Band Version) / Rita May / Blowin' in the Wind / Hard Rain's A-Gonna Fall / The Times They Are A-Changin' / Masters of War / Hurricane / Maggie's Farm / Subterranean Homesick Blues / Ballad of a Thin Man / Mozambique / This Wheel's on Fire / I Want You / Rainy Day Women #12 & 35 / Don't Think Twice, It's All Right / Song to Woody / It Ain't Me Babe / Love Minus Zero—No Limit / I'll Be Your Baby Tonight / If Not for You / If You See Her, Say Hello / Sara

### Part 3
The following records by other artists are referred to in the text. Again, CD numbers prevail, except where rare, out-of-print vinyl is the only

## discography

available listing; N.A. denotes sketchy index information (a good amount of material circulates on cassette). Dylan songs listed where applicable.

**The Alpha Band, *The Alpha Band***
(Arista 4102, 1976)

**The Alpha Band, *Spark in the Dark***
(Arista 4145, 1977)

**The Alpha Band, *Statue Makers of Hollywood***

**Dave Alvin, *Romeo's Escape***
(Epic 40921, 1987)

**Joan Baez, *Farewell, Angelina***
(Vanguard 9200, 1965)

Farewell, Angelina / Daddy, You Been on My Mind / It's All Over Now, Baby Blue / A Hard Rain's A-Gonna Fall

**Joan Baez, *Any Day Now***
(Vanguard 79306, 1968)

Love Minus Zero—No Limit / North Country Blues / You Ain't Goin' Nowhere / Drifter's Escape / I Pity the Poor Immigrant / Tears of Rage / Sad-Eyed Lady of the Lowlands / Love Is Just a Four-Letter Word / I Dreamed I Saw St. Augustine / The Walls of Redwing / Dear Landlord / One Too Many Mornings / I Shall Be Released / Boots of Spanish Leather / Walkin' Down the Line / Restless Farewell

**The Band, *Music from Big Pink***
(Capitol 2955, 1968)

This Wheel's on Fire

**The Band, *Cahoots***
(Capitol 651, 1971)

When I Paint My Masterpiece

# discography

**The Band, *To Kingdom Come***
(Capitol 921701 / 2, 1989)

Tears of Rage (with R. Manuel) / I Shall Be Released / When I Paint My Masterpiece

**The Band, *The Band***
(Capitol 132, 1969)

**The Band, *Rock of Ages***
(Capitol 11045-2, 1972)

**The Band, *Moondog Matinee***
(Capitol 11214, 1973)

**The Beatles, *Sgt. Pepper's Lonely Hearts Club Band***
(Capitol 2653, 1967)

**The Beatles, *Let It Be***
(Apple 34001, 1970)

**Harry Belafonte, *Midnight Special***
(RCA 2449, 1962)

Dylan on harmonica

**David Bowie, *Pin-Ups***
(RCA 0291, 1973)

**T-Bone Burnett, *Truth Decay***
(Takoma 72780, 1980)

**T-Bone Burnett, *Trap Door***
(Warner Bros. 23691, 1982)

**T-Bone Burnette, *T-Bone Burnett***
(Dot 5809, 1986)

**The Byrds, *Sweetheart of the Rodeo***
(Columbia 9670, 1968)

You Ain't Goin' Nowhere / Nothing Was Delivered

## discography

**The Byrds, *The Byrds***
(Columbia / Legacy 46773, 1990)

Mr. Tambourine Man / Chimes of Freedom / All I Really Want to Do /
Spanish Harlem Incident / It's All Over Now, Baby Blue / Lay Down
Your Weary Tune / He Was a Friend of Mine / The Times They Are
A-Changin' / My Back Pages / You Ain't Goin' Nowhere / Nothing Was
Delivered / This Wheel's on Fire (with R. Danko) / Lay, Lady, Lay /
Positively 4th Street / Just Like a Woman / Paths of Victory

**Judy Collins, *In My Life***
(Elektra 74027, 1967)

Just Like Tom Thumb's Blues

**Elvis Costello, *My Aim Is True***
(Columbia 35037, 1977)

**Elvis Costello, *This Year's Model***
(Columbia 35331, 1978)

**Elvis Costello, *Get Happy***
(Columbia 36347, 1981)

**Elvis Costello, *Trust***
(Columbia 37051, 1981)

**Elvis Costello, *Almost Blue***
(Columbia 37562, 1984)

**Elvis Costello, *King of America***
(Columbia 40173, 1986)

**Elvis Costello, *Blood and Chocolate***
(Columbia 40518, 1986)

**Coulson, Dean, McGuiness and Flint** (also known as **McGuiness-Flint**) ***Lo &
Behold***
(Sire 7405, 1973)

Eternal Circle / Lo and Behold / Let Me Die in My Footsteps / Open
the Door, Homer / Lay Down Your Weary Tune / Don't You Tell

# discography

Henry / Get Your Rocks Off / The Death of Emmett Till / Odds and Ends / Sign on the Cross

**Sandy Denny, *The North Star Grassman and the Ravens***
(N.A., 1971)

Down in the Flood

**Fairport Convention, *What We Did On Our Holidays***
(1968, reissued as Carthage 4430, 1987)

I'll Keep It with Mine

**Fairport Convention, *Unhalfbricking***
(1969, reissued as Carthage 4418, 1985)

Million Dollar Bash / If You Gotta Go, Go Now

**Bryan Ferry, *These Foolish Things***
(1973; reissued as Reprise CD 26082-2, 1990)

A Hard Rain's A-Gonna Fall (also available in Bryan Ferry–Roxy Music collection *Street Life: 20 Greatest Hits*, Reprise 1-25857, 1989)

**Flying Burrito Brothers, *Gilded Palace of Sin***
(A&M 4175, 1969)

**Peter Gabriel, *Passion* (soundtrack to *The Last Temptation of Christ*)**
(Geffen 24206-2, 1989)

**Alen Ginsberg, *First Blues—Rags, Ballads & Harmonium Songs 1971–74***
(N.A.)

**Allen Ginsberg, *Holy Soul / Jelly Roll***
(N.A.)

**Barry Goldberg, *Barry Goldberg***
(Atco 7040, 1973 )
Bob Dylan, producer

# discography

**Woody Guthrie, *Columbia River Collection***
(Rounder 1036, 1987)


**Woody Guthrie, *Dust Bowl Ballads***
(Rounder 1040, 1988)


**John Hammond, Jr., *So Many Roads***
(Columbia, N.A., 1966)


**George Harrison, *All Things Must Pass***
(Apple 639, 1970)

If Not for You / I'd Have You Anytime (Harrison-Dylan)


**Richie Havens, *Mixed Bag***
(Verve 3006, 1968)

Just Like a Woman


**The Jimi Hendrix Experience, *Electric Ladyland***
(Reprise 6307, 1968)

All Along the Watchtower


**Jimi Hendrix, *Jimi Plays Monterey***
(Reprise 25358-2, 1986)

Like a Rolling Stone


**Roscoe Holcomb, *Close to Home***
(Folkways 2374, 1975)


**Ian and Sylvia, *Nashville***
(Vanguard 79284, 1968)

This Wheel's on Fire

## discography

**Ian and Sylvia, *Play One More***
(Vanguard, N.A., 1966)

**Jason and the Scorchers, *Fervor***
(EMI 19008, 1983)

Absolutely Sweet Marie

**Jefferson Airplane, *After Bathing at Baxter's***
(RCA 1511, 1967; reissued as RCA 4545)

**John Lennon, *John Lennon / Plastic Ono Band***
(Apple 3372, 1970)

**John Lennon, *Some Time in New York City*** (with Yoko Ono and Elephant's
Memory)
(Apple 3392, 1972)

**John Lennon, *Rock 'n' Roll***
(Apple 3419, 1975)

**Jerry Lee Lewis, *Jerry Lee Lewis***
(Elektra 6E-184, 1979)

Rita Mae

**Roger McGuinn, *Cardiff Rose***
(Columbia 34154, 1976)

Up to Me

**Roger McGuinn, *Will the Circle Be Unbroken / Volume 2***
(Universal 12500, 1989)

You Ain't Goin' Nowhere

**Manfred Mann, *The Very Best of Manfred Mann***
(MFP / EMI 4156511, 1985)

Quinn the Eskimo (The Mighty Quinn)

# discography

**Van Morrison, *Astral Weeks***
(Warner Bros. 1768-2, 1968)

**Van Morrison, *Moondance***
(Warner Bros. 1835, 1970)

**Van Morrison, *His Band and the Street Choir***
(Warner Bros. 1884, 1970)

**Van Morrison, *Tupelo Honey***
(Warner Bros. 1950, 1971)

**Van Morrison, *St. Dominic's Preview***
(Warner Bros. 2633, 1972)

**Van Morrison, *It's Too Late to Stop Now***
(Warner Bros. 2760-2, 1974)

**Van Morrison, *Into the Music***
(Warner Bros. 3390, 1979)

**Van Morrison, *Irish Heartbeat***
(Mercury 834 496-2, 1988)

**Van Morrison, *Avalon Sunset***
(Mercury 389 262-2, 1989)

**Van Morrison, *Enlightenment***
(Mercury 847 100-2, 1990)

**Van Morrison, *Hymns to the Silence***
(Polydor 314 511 546-2, 1991)

**National Lampoon's Radio Dinner**
(Banana 38, 1972)

**Neville Brothers, *Yellow Moon***
(A&M 5240, 1989)

With God on Our Side / The Ballad of Hollis Brown

## discography

**Randy Newman, *Sail Away***
(Reprise 1064, 1972)

**Nico, *Chelsea Girl***
(Polydor 835 209-2, 1967)

I'll Keep It with Mine

**Roy Orbison, *Mystery Girl***
(Virgin 91058-2, 1989)

**Gram Parsons, *GP* (1973) and *Grievous Angel***
(1974) (reissued on one CD, Reprise 26108-2, 1990)

**Tom Petty and the Heartbreakers, *"Let Me Up (I've Had Enough)"***
(MCA 5836, 1987)

**Tom Petty and the Heartbreakers, *Full Moon Fever***
(MCA 6253, 1989)

**Tom Petty and the Heatbreakers, *Southern Accents***
(MCA 4586, 1985)

**Elvis Presley, *Spinout***
(soundtrack, RCA 3702, 1966)

Tomorrow Is a Long Time

**Prince, *Sign O' the Times***
(Paisley Park 25577-2, 1987)

**R.E.M., *Document***
(IRS 42059, 1987)

***The Replacements, Let It Be***
(Twin Tone 8441, 1984)

**The Replacements, *Tim***
(Sire 25330-2, 1985)

**The Replacements, *Pleased to Meet Me***
(Sire 25557-2, 1987)

**The Replacements, *Don't Tell a Soul***
(Sire 25831-2, 1989)

## discography

**The Replacements, *All Shook Down***
(Sire 26298-2, 1990)


**The Replacements, *Don't Buy or Sell, It's Crap***
(Pro-CD 4632, 1991)

Like a Rolling Pin


**The Rolling Stones, *Their Satanic Majesties Request***
(London 2, 1967; reissued Aiskco 80022, 1986)


**The Rolling Stones, *Beggars Banquet***
(London 539, 1968; Aiskco 75392, 1986)


**The Rolling Stones, *Let It Bleed***
(London 4, 1969; Aiskco 80042, 1986)


**The Rolling Stones, *Sticky Fingers***
(Rolling Stones 59100, 1971; Rolling Stones, 40488, 1986)


**The Rolling Stones, *Exile on Main Street***
(Rolling Stones 2900, 1972; reissued Rolling Stones 40489, 1986)


**The Rolling Stones, *Steel Wheels***
(Rolling Stones Columbia 45333, 1989)


**Leon Russell, *Leon Russell and the Shelter People***
(1971; reissued as DDC 8005, 1989)

A Hard Rain's A-Gonna Fall / It's All Over Now, Baby Blue / Love Minus Zero—No Limit / She Belongs to Me


**Pete Seeger, *We Shall Overcome***
(Columbia 45312, 1989)

A Hard Rain's A-Gonna Fall

# discography

**Paul Simon, *There Goes Rhymin' Simon***
(Columbia 32280, 1973)

**Paul Simon, *Graceland***
(Warner Bros. 25447-2, 1986)

**Bruce Springsteen, *Born to Run***
(Columbia 33795, 1975)

**Bruce Springsteen, *Darkness on the Edge of Town***
(Columbia 35318, 1978)

**Bruce Springsteen, *The River***
(Columbia 36854-2, 1980)

**Bruce Springsteen, *Nebraska***
(Columbia 38358, 1982)

**Bruce Springsteen, *Born in the U.S.A.***
(Columbia 38653, 1984)

**Bruce Springsteen, *Bruce Springsteen and The E Street Band,
Live / 1975–1985***
(Columbia 40588, 1986)

**Bruce Springsteen, *Tunnel of Love***
(Columbia 40999, 1987)

**Rod Stewart, *Gasoline Alley***
(Mercury 61264, 1970)

Only a Hobo

**Rod Stewart, *Every Picture Tells a Story***
(Mercury 609, 1971)

Tomorrow Is a Long Time

## discography

**Talking Heads,** *Stop Making Sense*
(Sire 25121, 1984)

**Various artists,** *Anthology of American Music*
(Folkways 2951-3, 1952)

**Various artists,** *Newport Broadside* (topical songs)
(Vanguard 79144, 1963)

**Various artists,** *Old Time Music at Newport*
(Vanguard 9147, 1964)

**Various artists,** *Will the Circle Be Unbroken*
(United Artists 9801, 1972)

**Various artists,** *I Shall Be Unreleased: The Songs of Bob Dylan*
(Rhino/Sony Music R2 70518, 1991)

Only a Hobo (Rod Stewart) / Love Is Just a Four-Letter Word (Joan Baez) / If You Gotta Go, Go Now (Manfred Mann) / Walk Out in the Rain (Eric Clapton) / Seven Days (Ron Wood) / Wanted Man (Johnny Cash with Carl Perkins and the Tennessee Three) / Farewell Angelina (New Riders of the Purple Sage) / Walkin' Down the Line (Rick Nelson) / Wallflower (Doug Sahm) / (If I Had to Do It All Over Again, I'd Do It) All Over You (Raiders) / Dusty Old Fairgrounds (Blue Ash) / Ain't No Man Righteous, No Not One (Jah Malla) / Quit Your Lowdown Ways (the Hollies) / Golden Loom (Roger McGuinn) / John Brown (the Staple Singers) / Farewell (Dion and the Wanderers) / Paths of Victory (Pete Seeger) / Blind Willie McTell (Dream Syndicate)

**Hank Williams,** *Just Me and My Guitar*
(Country Music Foundation 006, 1985)

**Big Joe Williams, Lonnie Johnson, and Victoria Spivey,** *Three Kings and a Queen*
(Spivey LP 1004, 1964)

Dylan on harmonica

# discography

**Yo La Tengo, *President Yo La Tengo***
(1989; reissued with *New Wave Hot Dog*, Coyote CD 89153-2, 1989)

I Threw It All Away

**Neil Young, *Everybody Knows This Is Nowhere***
(Reprise 6349, 1969)

**Neil Young, *Time Fades Away***
(Reprise 2151, 1973)

**Neil Young, *Tonight's the Night***
(Reprise 2221, 1975)

**Neil Young, *Rust Never Sleeps***
(Reprise 2295, 1979)

**Neil Young, *Re-ac-tor***
(Reprise 2304, 1981)

**Neil Young, *Life***
(Geffen 25154, 1986)

**Neil Young, *Old Ways***
(Geffen 24068, 1985)

**Neil Young, *Freedom***
(Reprise 25899, 1989)

**Neil Young, *Ragged Glory***
(Reprise 26315, 1990)

**Neil Young, *Weld***
(Reprise Z6746, 1991)

Blowin' in the Wind

## discography

**X, Wild Gift**

(1981; reissued with *Los Angeles* as Slash 25771-2, 1988)

**X, More Fun in the New World**

(Elektra 60283-1, 1983)

**X, "4th of July"**

(D. Alvin)

**X, "Positively 4th Street"**

(Elektra single 7-69462, 1987)

# update to discography

**Good as I Been to You**

(1992)

Frankie & Albert / Jim Jones / Blackjack Davey / Canadee-i-o / Sittin' on Top of the World / Little Maggie / Hard Times / Step It Up And Go / Tomorrow Night / Arthur McBride / You're Gonna Quit Me / Diamond Joe / Froggie Went a Courtin' (all traditional/arranged by Bob Dylan)

**Various Artists: The 30th Anniversary Concert Celebration**

(1993)

Like a Rolling Stone / Leopard-Skin Pill-Box Hat / Introduction by Kris Kristofferson / Blowin' in the Wind / Foot of Pride / Masters of War / The Times They Are A-Changin' / It Ain't Me, Babe / What Was It You Wanted? / I'll Be Your Baby Tonight / Highway 61 Revisited / Seven Days / Just Like a Woman / When the Ship Comes In / You Ain't Goin' Nowhere / Just Like Tom Thumb's Blues / All Along the Watchtower / I Shall Be Released / Don't Think Twice, It's All Right / Emotionally Yours / When I Paint My Masterpiece / Absolutely Sweet Marie / License to Kill / Rainy Day Women #12 & 35 / Mr. Tambourine Man / It's Alright, Ma (I'm Only Bleeding) / My Back Pages / Knockin' on Heaven's Door / Girl of the North Country

# discography

### World Gone Wrong
(1993)

World Gone Wrong / Love Henry / Ragged & Dirty / Blood in My Eyes / Broke Down Engine / Delia / Stack-A-Lee / Two Soldiers / Jack-A-Roe / Lone Pilgrim (B.F. White and Adger M. Pace)

### Bob Dylan's Greatest Hits, Vol. 3
(1994)

Tangled Up in Blue / Changing of the Guards / The Groom's Still Waiting at the Altar / Hurricane / Forever Young / Jokerman / Dignity / Silvio / Ring Them Bells / Gotta Serve Somebody / Series of Dreams / Brownsville Girl / Under the Red Sky / Knockin' on Heaven's Door

### MTV Uplugged
(1995)

Tombstone Blues / Shooting Star / All Along the Watchtower / The Times They Are A-Changin' / John Brown / Rainy Day Women #12 & 35 / Desolation Row / Dignity / Knockin' on Heaven's Door / Like a Rolling Stone / With God on Our Side

### Time Out Of Mind
(1997)

Love Sick / Dirt Road Blues / Standing In The Doorway / Million Miles / Tryin' To Get To Heaven / Til I Fell In Love With You / Not Dark Yet / Cold Irons Bound / Make You Feel My Love / Can't Wait / Highlands

### Live 1966–The Bootleg Series Vol. 4
(1998)

She Belongs To Me / 4th Time Around / Visions of Johanna / It's All Over Now, Baby Blue / Desolation Row / Just Like a Woman / Mr. Tambourine Man / Tell Me, Momma / I Don't Believe You (She Acts Like We Never Have Met) / Baby, Let Me Follow You Down / Just Like Tom Thumb's Blues / Leopard-Skin Pill-Box Hat / One Too Many Mornings / Ballad Of A Thin Man / Like A Rolling Stone

# selected bibliography

Bangs, Lester. *Psychotic Reactions and Carburetor Dung*, ed. Greil Marcus (Alfred A. Knopf, 1987).

Bauldie, John, ed. *Wanted Man: In Search of Bob Dylan* (Citadel Underground, 1991).

Bowden, Betsy. *Performed Literature* (University of Indiana Press, 1982).

Cable, Paul. *Bob Dylan: His Unreleased Recordings* (Schirmer Books, 1978).

Christgau, Robert. *Christgau's Record Guide of the '80s* (Pantheon, 1990).

———. *Christgau's Record Guide of the '70s* (Ticknor & Fields, 1981).

Cott, Jonathan. *Dylan* (Rolling Stone/Doubleday, 1984).

Crowe, Cameron. Liner notes to *Biograph* (Columbia C5X 38830, 1985).

Curtis, Jim. *Rock Eras: Interpretations of Music and Society* (Bowling Green State University Popular Press, 1987).

Dalton, David. *James Dean: Mutant King* (St. Martin's Press, 1983).

Day, Aidan. *Jokerman: Reading the Lyrics of Bob Dylan* (Basil Blackwell, 1988).

Dickstein, Morris. *Gates of Eden: American Culture in the Sixties* (Basic Books, 1977).

Dylan, Bob. *Lyrics: 1962–1985.* 2d ed. (Alfred A. Knopf, 1985).

———. *The Songs of Bob Dylan: From 1966 Through 1975* (Alfred A. Knopf, 1976).

———. *Tarantula* (Macmillan, 1971).

Eisen, Jonathan, ed. *The Age of Rock* (Random House, 1969). Includes Richard Fariña's "Baez and Dylan: A Generation Singing Out"; Lawrence Goldman's "Bobby Dylan—Folk-Rock Hero," and Jon Landau's review of *John Wesley Harding*.

# selected bibliography

Eliot, Marc. *Death of a Rebel, Starring Phil Ochs and a Small Circle of Friends* (Anchor Books, 1979).

Flanagan, Bill. *Written in My Soul: Rock's Great Songwriters Talk About Creating Their Music* (Contemporary, 1986).

Confronts the theory that songwriters are usually the least interesting people to talk to about their work, but argues that it's more interesting than hearing them talk about their lives.

Gitlin, Todd. *The Sixties: Years of Hope, Days of Rage* (Bantam Books, 1987).

Gray, Michael. *Song and Dance Man: The Art of Bob Dylan* (Dutton, 1972).

For a long time, Gray had the monopoly on Dylan commentary with this thoughtful and often humorous account of early Dylanology. Perhaps because the British have always been more conscious of Dylan's debts to Blake and Rimbaud, this is still an excellent guide to Dylan's use of language.

Gross, Michael. *Bob Dylan: An Illustrated History* (Grosset & Dunlap, 1978).

Guthrie, Woody. *Bound for Glory* (Dutton, 1943).

The book that jump-charged Dylan from Minneapolis to the Graystone Park State Hospital, and still one of the best road books ever. Even though Guthrie's editors were forced to tidy up plenty of his rambling, unstoppable prose, there are still lengthy, evocative passages here that go a long way toward bringing Guthrie's voice home to the page, and give the reader a sense of how drifting was akin to religion during the dust-bowl era. Read it before (or instead of) watching the movie.

Harris, David. *Dreams Die Hard: Three Men's Journey Through the Sixties* (St. Martin's Press, 1982).

Joan Baez's first husband was more than just America's best-known draft resister and leader of hunger strikes: his story is emblematic in ways that blast the myth of the 1960s wide open. He was ridiculed by his college friends as having a martyr complex. Stanford's student-body president, and leader of the Students for a Democratic Society, he fell under the idealistic spell of Allard Lowenstein and traveled to Mississippi in 1963. Harris's celebrity marriage unraveled, and he turned into, of all things, a writer for the *New York Times Magazine*, as he watched Berkeley foes like Ed Meese and Governor Ronald Reagan ascend to the White House. In the grip of a schizophrenic seizure, guided by voices in his teeth, his friend Dennis Sweeney murders Lowenstein in his Manhattan law office in 1980.

Herdman, John. *Voice Without Restraint: Bob Dylan's Lyrics and Their Background* (Delilah Press, 1982).

Heylin, Clinton. *Bob Dylan Behind the Shades: A Biography* (New York: Summit Books, 1991).

Humphries, Patrick, and John Bauldie. *Absolutely Dylan: An Illustrated Biography* (Viking Studio Books, 1991).

Klein, Joe. *Woody Guthrie: A Life* (Alfred A. Knopf, 1980).

Klein's a political reporter with a nose for class tensions, and this biography written during an era when anticommunism was again on the rise bests any yet written about Dylan, drawing Guthrie in terms that are as sympathetic as they are realistic. The detailed accounts of Guthrie's California days make him a character too big for Steinbeck. A source book for song dates, themes, biographical references, and everything *Bound for Glory* can't be bothered to explain.

Kooper, Al. *Backstage Passes: Rock 'n' Roll Life in the Sixties* (Stein & Day, 1977).

Kramer, Daniel. *Bob Dylan* (Castle Books, 1967).

Marcus, Greil. *Mystery Train*, 3d ed. (Dutton, 1990).

Includes some of the best descriptions of the Band and its post-Dylan mission.

Marsh, Dave. *The Heart of Rock and Soul* (Plume, 1989).

Marsh argues that with "Like a Rolling Stone," "I Want You," the Byrds' "Mr. Tambourine Man," "One of Us Must Know (Sooner or Later)," "Just Like Tom Thumb's Blues" (live with the Band), and "Positively 4th Street," Dylan, despite his resistance and untidy style, may have counted as one of his era's best avant jinglesmiths. Still, to buy Marsh's view, you'd have to also believe that "Can You Please Crawl Out Your Window" is "overrated ephemera" (??!) and that "Rainy Day Women #12 and 35" is "godawful." And what about "Mixed Up Confusion," his very first 45; "Subterranean Homesick Blues," his first Top 40; "Just

## selected bibliography

Like a Woman," his first hit ballad; "Leopard-Skin Pill-Box Hat," "I Threw It All Away," and "Lay, Lady, Lay"—and where, oh where is "The Groom's Still Waiting at the Altar"?

Marsh, Dave, and Harold Leventhal, eds. *Pastures of Plenty: The Writings of Woody Guthrie* (New York: Harper Collins, 1990).

McGregor, Craig, ed. *Bob Dylan: A Retrospective* (Morrow, 1972).

Mellers, Wilfrid. *A Darker Shade of Pale* (Oxford University Press, 1985).

Meltzer, R. *Gulcher* (Straight Arrow Books, 1972).

Postcards from a disaffected boho, who mentions Dylan with such reverence that he hints at a subtextual book all its own, with winding passageways and random darts of invective that resemble his hero's.

Miles [*sic*]. *Bob Dylan in His Own Words* (Quick Fox, 1978).

The best bathroom reading around.

Miller, Jim. *Democracy Is in the Streets* (Simon & Schuster, 1987).

Stiff but essential, this account of Tom Hayden's masterpiece (The Port Huron Statement) cuts through all the brouhaha for an idea-driven history of what the revolution was supposed to be about.

Murray, Albert. *Stomping the Blues* (Da Capo, 1976).

Ricks, Christopher. *The Force of Poetry* (Oxford University Press, 1987).

Rick understands Dylan better than Mellers does—if only he'd write more about him.

Rinzler, Alan. *Bob Dylan: The Illustrated Record* (Harmony Books, 1978).

*Rolling Stone* editors. *Knockin' on Dylan's Door: On the Road in 1974* (Straight Arrow/Pocket Books, 1974).

Scaduto, Anthony. *Bob Dylan: The Authorized Biography* (Grosset & Dunlap, 1971).

The earliest and best biography. Scaduto doesn't assume Dylan is any smarter than he is, and this makes for unpretentious reading. Its blurb came from Dylan himself: "I like your book. That's the weird thing about it."

Shelton, Robert. *No Direction Home: The Life and Music of Bob Dylan* (Beech Tree/Morrow, 1986).

## selected bibliography

Written by the byline that brought Dylan's young act to the pages of the *New York Times*, Shelton's long-awaited biography is an ocean of detail and telling quotes that hangs together only for the most ardent of fans. Larger themes are plowed under beneath thickets of self-congratulation and offhanded dismissals—his treatment of Dylan's divorce story rings of protest-too-much dismissal.

Shepard, Sam. *Rolling Thunder Logbook* (Viking, 1977).

The playwright joins the mysterious tour and takes as good a shot at explaining life on the road with Dylan as seems possible (he makes Larry Sloman read like a self-obsessed ninny). A small crush on Baez doesn't get in the way of his jokes; the book conveys all the serendipity and gentle ennui that *Renaldo and Clara* botched.

Sloman, Larry. *On the Road with Bob Dylan: Rolling with the Thunder* (Bantam, 1978).

Spitz, Bob. *Dylan: A Biography* (McGraw-Hill, 1989).

He thanks Albert Goldman in the acknowledgments, but that's almost redundant. He fictionalizes quotes from Dylan's father, Abe, and that's routine. For all intents and purposes, except perhaps his professed sympathy towards his subject, Spitz is Goldman, Jr., relying on Dylan (his ex-wife is notably absent from all biographies), and arguing on about a myth that the book never details.

Thomson, Elizabeth, and David Gutman, eds. *The Dylan Companion* (New York: Delta, 1991).

Thompson, Toby. *Positively Main Street: An Unorthodox View of Bob Dylan* (Coward-McCann, 1971).

Acting at the behest of *The Village Voice*, Thompson went to Hibbing, sniffed around the Zimmerman hardware store, dug up some old girlfriends, and turned in the first stab at Dylan's roots. Immediately trumped by Scaduto.

Tosches, Nick. *Country: Living Legends and Dying Metaphors in America's Biggest Music* (Scribners, 1977).

Like his biography of Jerry Lee Lewis (*Hellfire*), this delving into country-and-western music is more myth than fact, long on stories and short on restraint, rife with dead ends, wisecracks, blanks, and empties—and as readable as the music is listenable.

Williams, Paul. *Performing Artist: The Music of Bob Dylan, Vol. 1, 1960–1973* (Underwood/Miller, 1990).


The following fanzines and clearing houses for Dylan material were most useful:

*The Telegraph*, Wanted Man Publications, P.O. Box 22, Rumbford, Essex, RM1, 2RF, England.

*Look Back,* P.O. Box 857, Chardon, Ohio 44024.

*Isis* newsletter, c/o *Rolling Tomes*, P.O. Box 1943, Grand Junction, Colorado 81502.

*My Back Pages*, "The Bob Dylan Bookshelf," P.O. Box 2 (North P.D.O.), Manchester, M8 7BL, England.

# acknowledgments

Among friends, Phil Lipman, Matt Liebendorfer, Chris and Leslie Brokaw, Karen Leipzigger, Andrew Caffrey, Anthony Brooks, Eugene Carr, Eric Zakim, and Steve Vineberg are among the people I count as valuable conversationalists on rock, which means on just about anything. Milo Miles was an editor whose influence is on every page.

Charlie Taylor, Jimmy Guterman, Sarah Wright, and Clint Conley read early versions of the manuscript, made useful comments, and delicately pointed out omissions, fictions, and grand delusions. Guterman deserves special mention: his advice and generous idea-sharing made the idea of getting lost inside Dylan less isolating. He won't admit it, but his palatial office bears a statuesque Sy Sperling award for most selfless trend-setter.

Steve Schechter, Gil Asakawa, and Leland Rucker helped out with some invaluable source material, including videotapes, forgotten folkie records, and the kinds of artifacts and companionship only collectors can appreciate.

Marty Asher is a patient and forgiving editor. Seeing Dylan for the first time at Radio City Music Hall in 1988, he took a look around at the crowd we were in and said, "It's like going to see the Statue of Liberty." Patrick Dillon was once again a copious copy editor and then some. Edward Kastenmeier shuttled the manuscript about and returned phone calls (!). Robert Cornfield crunched numbers and promised my Ozzy Osbourne cookbook was a sure sell.

And Sara Laschever—words escape me. Everything must go.

# index

# index

# index

# index

# index

# index

# index

# index

# index

# index

# index

# index

# index

# index

# index

# index

# index

# index

# index

# index

# index

# permissions acknowledgments

Grateful acknowledgment is made to the following for permission to reprint previously published material:

*Acuff-Rose Music, Inc.:* Excerpt from "Be Careful of Stones That You Throw" by Bonnie Dodd. Copyright 1949, copyright renewed 1977 by Acuff-Rose Music, Inc. (BMI). Used by permission. International copyright secured. All rights reserved.

*Fall River Music Inc. / Sanga Music Inc.:* Excerpt from "Pretty Boy Floyd" by Woody Guthrie. Copyright © 1958 (renewed) by Fall River Music Inc.; excerpt from "1913 Massacre" by Woody Guthrie. Copyright © 1961 (renewed) by Sanga Music Inc. All rights reserved. Used by permission.

*Alfred A. Knopf, Inc.:* Excerpt from "The Clash" from *Psychotic Reactions and Carburetor Dung* by Lester Bangs. Copyright © 1987 by The Estate of Lester Bangs. Reprinted by permission.

*William Morris Agency, Inc.:* Excerpts from quotes by Eric Von Schmidt, Joan Baez, and Bob Dylan from *Bob Dylan: An Intimate Biography* by Anthony Scaduto (Grosset & Dunlap, New York). Copyright © 1971 by Anthony Scaduto. Reprinted by permission of William Morris Agency, Inc., on behalf of the author.

*William Morrow & Company, Inc., and Robert Shelton:* Excerpts from *No Direction Home* by Robert Shelton. Copyright © 1986 by Robert Shelton. Reprinted by permission of William Morrow & Company, Inc., and Robert Shelton.

*The New Yorker:* Excerpts from "The Crackin', Breakin', Shakin' Sounds" by Nat Hentoff (*The New Yorker*, Oct. 24, 1964). Copyright © 1964 by The New Yorker Magazine, Inc. Reprinted by permission.

*Omnibus Press:* Excerpts from "Bob Dylan in His Own Words" compiled by Miles. Reprinted by permission of Omnibus Press, 8/9 Frith Street, London W1V 5TZ.

*Raines & Raines:* Excerpt from "Joey Gallo Was No Hero" by Lester Bangs (*The Village Voice*, March 8, 1976). Copyright © 1976 by Lester Bangs. Reprinted by permission of The Estate of Lester Bangs